Derek Walcott

Updated Edition

Twayne's World Authors Series

Caribbean Literature

TWAS 600

DEREK WALCOTT
Photograph by Jerry Bauer

Derek Walcott

Updated Edition

Robert D. Hamner

Hardin-Simmons University

Twayne Publishers • New York
Maxwell Macmillan Canada • Toronto
Maxwell Macmillan International • New York Oxford Singapore Sydney

Twayne's World Authors Series No. 600

Derek Walcott, Updated Edition
Robert D. Hamner

Twayne Publishers
Macmillan Publishing Company
866 Third Avenue
New York, New York 10022

Maxwell Macmillan Canada, Inc.
1200 Eglinton Avenue East
Suite 200
Don Mills, Ontario M3C 3N1

Library of Congress Cataloging-in-Publication Data

Hamner, Robert D.
  Derek Walcott / Robert D. Hamner.—Updated ed.
    p.   cm.—(Twayne's world authors series; 600. Caribbean)
  Includes bibliographical references (p.   ) and index.
  ISBN 0-8057-4301-4 (alk. paper)
    1. Walcott, Derek—Criticism and interpretation. 2. West Indies in literature. I. Title. II. Series.
PR9272.9.W3Z69   1993   93-16907
811—dc20   CIP

10 9 8 7 6 5 4 3 2 1

Printed in the United States of America

With love to Carol

Contents

Preface

British West Indian literature has established its well-deserved reputation on the quality of its fiction. V. S. Naipaul (Trinidad) and Wilson Harris (Guyana) are but two leaders of a growing number of prose writers who have captured the imagination of discerning readers throughout the world. For many years, however, poets in the English-speaking Caribbean have lagged far behind the accomplishments of its novelists.

Francophone artists Saint-John Perse (1887–1975, Guadeloupe) and Aimé Césaire (born 1913, Martinique) showed early in the twentieth century how the Caribbean's vast poetic resources could be developed to a level that transcended regional labels. But it was not until the 1960s that poets close to their stature emerged in the former British islands. The breakthrough came in 1962 with the publication of Derek Walcott's first major collection, *In a Green Night.* Five years later another landmark was reached with the appearance of Edward Brathwaite's *Rights of Passage* (1967).

Brathwaite's major contribution has been his exploration of the African heritage in West Indian culture. Walcott's interests have been broader, for he has pursued the roots of his ancestry in all directions. As a result, he displays a wide range of expression, from classical high seriousness to the earthiest vernacular. At a time when poets are frequently evaluated in terms of the social and political causes they espouse, Brathwaite is usually praised by those who wish to seek their identity in Africa, and Walcott is often distrusted because of his "mulatto" ambivalence toward racial and political allegiances.

Yet it is Walcott's ambivalence (or at least his acute consciousness of the complexities of his situation) that makes his work all the more valuable. From the standpoints of sociology and psychology, he has much to say. More important, he has also established an aesthetically pleasing style of expression. If he has been criticized for sounding too much like some of the masters of Western literature, he is willing to admit that he has profited greatly from his predecessors. He has never been too proud to learn; he has no inordinate fear of the charge of imitation; in fact, the echoes of past and contemporary artists in his work increase the resonance of his own authentic voice. Since for many years critics and second-rate poets have overpraised experimentalism simply for the sake of originality, it is refreshing to come upon an artist who is not afraid to build where others have surveyed and laid foundations—and one who is at the same time capable of maintaining his individual integrity.

Walcott is not only the preeminent poet of the West Indies, he is also the area's leading dramatist. His role as dramatist is especially crucial in that the stage affords a more immediate means of communication with groups of people than poetry does. In addition to writing plays (one of which won an Obie in New York in 1971), he founded the Trinidad Theatre Workshop in 1959, and he has provided inspiration and advice for many other theatrical groups that have sprung up throughout the Caribbean.

As a poet and a dramatist Walcott has become a viable standard by which not only West Indian but all contemporary English verse and theater may be judged. Since my *Derek Walcott* was first published by Twayne in 1981, Walcott's work has gained worldwide recognition and earned him the 1992 Nobel Prize for Literature. Given the fact that between 1981 and his receipt of the Nobel Prize Walcott has published five more poetry volumes and another collection of plays, the time has come to update my earlier study of his career.

Chapter 1 offers a general survey of the literary situation in the West Indies out of which Walcott emerged. It also outlines briefly the various phases of his development and attempts to define the cohesive forces that run through his major works. Chapter 2 deals with his apprenticeship years, 1948–1958, primarily examining poems and plays that have not been published outside the region. Chapter 3 covers Walcott's highly enriching stay in New York City in 1958, thanks to a Rockefeller Fellowship, and examines his association with the Trinidad Theatre Workshop until 1967, when his company made its first international tours.

Chapter 4 partially overlaps 1967 and continues through 1973, devoting particular attention to Walcott's *Dream on Monkey Mountain,* three of his lesser known plays from the period including *In a Fine Castle* (later published as *The Last Carnival*), and his highly revealing autobiographical poem *Another Life.* Chapter 5 analyzes such plays as *The Joker of Seville* (an adaptation of the Spanish classic *El Burlador de Sevilla*), *O Babylon!* (on Jamaica's Rastafarian culture), and *Pantomime* (a tour de force on the Crusoe and Friday theme). After considering the two verse collections, *Sea Grapes* and *The Star-Apple Kingdom,* the chapter closes at a significant turning point in Walcott's career—his decision to resign from the Trinidad Theatre Workshop and to take up residence in the United States.

Beginning with *The Fortunate Traveller* (1981), chapter 6 examines Walcott's five collections of poetry and the *Three Plays* that have been published into the 1990s. During this period Walcott personifies the "fortunate traveller" himself, gradually shifting emphasis from Crusoe to Odysseus as his central figure. Each of his books has added to his stature, none perhaps as significantly as the epic *Omeros* (1990).

Chapter 7 rounds out this study of Walcott's career by focusing on his many expository articles, essays, and interviews, all of which complement the creative writing. The discursive prose reinforces insights into his poems and plays that otherwise might only be surmised.

I first met Derek Walcott in 1975, when I already had high regard for his poetry and plays. When I asked what he considered to be his best work, he was quick to answer that he hoped he had not yet written it. He had not, and the world continues to be enriched by his genius. It was a privilege to write the first book-length study of Walcott's career in 1981. Now, with even deeper appreciation, I have the opportunity to update that text. Taken together, the weight of evidence is sufficient to establish Walcott as provocative, stimulating, and one of the most complete poets now writing in the English language.

Acknowledgments

Professors Joseph Jones of the University of Texas at Austin and Robert McDowell of the University of Texas at Arlington rendered invaluable assistance to me while I was writing the original version of Twayne's *Derek Walcott* in 1981. A Fulbright grant to teach and travel in the Caribbean area in 1975–1976 and financial aid from Hardin-Simmons University and the Hugh Roy Cullen Fund for Faculty Enrichment provided support that enabled me to complete the research for the earlier book as well as this present edition. Librarians too numerous to name have rendered assistance over the years, and I will never be able to repay their kindness.

I would be remiss were I to overlook Derek Walcott's generosity in inviting me to attend rehearsals of the Trinidad Theatre Workshop and permitting access to rare manuscripts and data. Carol Chin of Twayne Publishers has been very helpful in preparing this revised 1993 text.

My wife Carol and my sons Jared and Ryan have borne patiently with me over the years as I have traveled and secluded myself with a labor that sometimes seems all-consuming.

I acknowledge with pleasure the following publishers for granting permission to quote copyrighted material from works by Derek Walcott:

Reprinted with the permission of Farrar, Straus, and Giroux, Inc., under the copyright of Derek Walcott: excerpts from *In a Green Night*, Copyright © 1962; from *Another Life,* Copyright © 1973; from *The Gulf,* Copyright © 1969, 1970; from *Selected Poems,* Copyright © 1964; from *The Castaway*, Copyright © 1965; from *The Star-Apple Kingdom,* Copyright © 1979; from *Dream on Monkey Mountain,* Copyright © 1970; from Sea Grapes, Copyright © 1976; from *The Joker of Seville and O Babylon!,* Copyright © 1978; from *Remembrance and Pantomime,* Copyright © 1980; from *The Fortunate Traveller,* Copyright © 1981; from *Midsummer,* Copyright © 1984; from *Three Plays,* Copyright © 1986; from *The Arkansas Testament,* Copyright © 1987; from *Omeros,* Copyright © 1990.

Reprinted with the permission of Jonathan Cape Ltd., of the Random Century Group, under the copyright of Derek Walcott: selections from *The Castaway and Other Poems,* © 1963, 1964, 1965; from *The Gulf,* © 1963, 1964, 1965, 1969, 1970; from *Sea Grapes,* © 1976; and from *The*

Joker of Seville and O Babylon!, © 1978, for the British Commonwealth and Empire including Canada; selections from from *The Star-Apple Kingdom*, © 1977, 1978, 1979, for the British Commonwealth and Empire excluding Canada.

Reprinted by permission of Faber and Faber, Ltd., for the British Commonwealth, excluding Canada, from *The Arkansas Testament, Collected Poems, The Fortunate Traveller, Midsummer* and *Omeros* by Derek Walcott.

Chronology

1930   Derek Walcott and his twin brother, Roderick, are born in Castries, St. Lucia, 23 January.

1948   *25 Poems* privately printed.

1949   *Epitaph for the Young* privately printed.

1950   Founded St. Lucia Arts Guild. *Henri Christophe* performed.

1953   Receives baccalaureate, University of the West Indies, Jamaica.

1954   *The Sea at Dauphin* performed. Marries Faye Moyston.

1958   Rockefeller Fellowship in New York. Writes *Ti-Jean and His Brothers*. *Drums and Colours* performed.

1959   Founds theatrical group later known as the Trinidad Theatre Workshop. *Malcochon* performed.

1961   Receives Guinness Award for Poetry.

1962   *In a Green Night*. Marries Margaret Maillard.

1964   *Selected Poems*.

1965   *The Castaway* (Royal Society of Literature Award).

1966   Trinidad Theatre Workshop opens at Basement Theatre.

1967   *Dream on Monkey Mountain* premiers in Toronto (Obie Award in New York, 1971).

1969   *The Gulf* (Cholmondeley Award).

1970   *Dream on Monkey Mountain and Other Plays*. *In a Fine Castle* performed.

1973   *Another Life* (Jock Campbell New Statesman Award, 1974). *Franklin* and *The Charlatan* performed.

1974   *The Joker of Seville* commissioned by Royal Shakespeare Company.

1976   *Sea Grapes*. *O Babylon!* performed. Resigns from Trinidad Theatre Workshop.

1977   *Remembrance* performed. Receives Guggenheim Fellowship.

1978   *The Joker of Seville and O Babylon! Pantomime* performed.

1979   *The Star-Apple Kingdom.* Elected to the American Academy and Institute of Arts.

1980   *Remembrance and Pantomime.* Receives Welsh Arts Council's International Writers Prize.

1981   *The Fortunate Traveller. Beef, No Chicken* performed. Begins teaching at Boston University. Receives Royal Society of Literature's Heinemann Award and John D. and Catherine MacArthur Foundation Award.

1982   *The Last Carnival* (revision of *In a Fine Castle*) and *The Isle Is Full of Noises* performed. Marries Norline Metivier.

1983   *A Branch of the Blue Nile* performed. *The Rig* filmed.

1984   *Midsummer. The Haitian Earth* performed.

1986   *Three Plays. Collected Poems 1948–1984. To Die for Grenada* performed.

1987   *The Arkansas Testament.*

1989   *The Ghost Dance* performed.

1990   *Omeros* (W. H. Smith Prize, 1991). *Viva Detroit* performed.

1991   *Steel* performed.

1992   Receives Nobel Prize for Literature. *The Odyssey* performed.

Chapter One

Centaurs under the Sun: The Climate for Poetry

V. S. Naipaul argues in *The Middle Passage* that "[h]istory is built around achievement and creation; and nothing was created in the West Indies."[1] Naipaul gives frank utterance to a generally accepted concept. As for achievement, the past belongs to conquistadors, empire builders, and plantation owners; as for creativity, West Indian societies derive so much from foreign cultures that they seem to have generated nothing that is wholly their own. Nevertheless, the West Indies do not exist in a void. The record is long and brutal, marked with the names and deeds of famous men such as Columbus, Raleigh, Toussaint, Martí, and Garvey. Discoverers and conquerors gave way to the rebellious Haitian slave Toussaint (1743–1803), who could withstand the armed forces of Napoleon, and to the Jamaican social reformer Garvey (1887–1940), who is as responsible as any other single individual for awakening the downtrodden black man to his own inner worth.

Colonial Background: An Emerging Literature

Literature followed the pattern of history as the islands progressed toward independence and greater self-realization. The colonizing countries Spain, England, France, and the Netherlands imposed their languages and dominated the writing of their colonies deep into the twentieth century. Writing *about* the West Indies began with European discovery of the New World; writing *in* the West Indies followed immediately upon settlement by Europeans; writing *by* West Indians—that is, by slaves and colonists whose home was in the islands and not in Europe—emerged in the eighteenth century. The problem is that all of this literature from the past and much of what has been written up to the present is derivative, subservient in form or style if not in content to foreign European and American traditions. This is a major concern for sensitive nationalists of newly emerged nations and for sociologically oriented critics. It should be noted, however, that in spite of the history of

1

enslavement and of colonial domination, individual writers have risen
through the West Indian milieu to establish themselves as highly competent, even outstanding, artists. The French have Aimé Césaire and
Frantz Fanon of Martinique; the Spanish have Alejo Carpentier and
Nicolás Guillén of Cuba; and this is to name only a few non-English
writers in the Caribbean.

Since the 1950s the British West Indies have been experiencing a
remarkable literary renaissance. Louis James was moved to comment as
early as 1968, "Seen as a whole, West Indian literature is perhaps the
richest and most varied field of writing in English to have emerged since
the second world war."[2] The most immediate historical precedent can be
found in the Irish Literary Renaissance at the turn of the century; but
the cultural and racial mixture of the West Indies is far more complicated than that of Ireland. To begin with, there is the matter of geographical separation: Jamaica in the western Caribbean became part of the
British Empire in 1655; hundreds of miles away to the southeast (and
over a century later), Trinidad fell into British hands in 1797. Second,
the changing fortunes of international diplomacy and war put most of
the islands under a number of different flags at various times so that it is
not unusual to find the native populace of an English island speaking a
French patois, playing Spanish music, and sometimes living in villages
with Dutch names. Further complexity, perhaps the most important element, derives from the importation of foreign labor. It did not take the
Spanish long to realize that native Indians were not adaptable to
European working conditions. Thus in the early 1500s appeared African
slavery and the middle passage: the third leg of a triangular trade route
linking the continents of Europe, Africa, and the Americas. Despite the
rigors of the passage itself, disease, and dehumanizing treatment on the
plantations, Africans managed to endure, so that when emancipation
came to the British islands in 1838 they far outnumbered their white
masters. Emancipation found most Negroes moving to urban areas,
leaving plantations desperately short of hands. In order to supply the
needed laborers, the British turned to other parts of the empire: Indian
and Chinese peasants began arriving in large numbers.

It is no wonder, then, that the Caribbean is regarded as a social "melt-
ing pot." The label is convenient, although slightly inaccurate, since on
the larger islands especially racial groups have maintained their own
color and class barriers. Integration progresses, but the populace is still
something more of a conglomerate than a blended mixture, which only
upholds the legends of Caribbean variety and contrast. It is no wonder

either that the independence movements after World War II, followed by formal nationhood in the late 1950s and early 1960s, have brought out a deep-seated identity crisis. The abortive West Indian Federation held together only five years (1958–1962). Since then island nationalists have been pressing the former citizens of the British Commonwealth to become Jamaicans, Trinidadians, Barbadians, and so on.

Readers who approach West Indian literature unaware of these factors are in danger of receiving a distorted impression. Barbadian poet Edward Brathwaite expresses his fear that foreign readers will be entertained by the exotic surface and then miss the deeper loneliness and rootlessness underneath. In the same article he calls for a greater understanding of the cultural matrix out of which West Indian writing grows.[3] The importance of this understanding is underscored by Edward Baugh's observation that "[m]ost of our literature has so far concentrated on defining and assessing the society out of which it grows. It is directly concerned with questions of West-Indianness, of the values and aspirations of the society."[4] When Arthur Drayton attempts to define the essential qualities of a Caribbean literature, his emphasis is on the sociological: "The sense of humor which imparts a certain lightheartedness to this writing; the frankness of it; its raciness of style; the peasant interest; the almost complete absence of an 'African' theme or, for that matter, of an 'Indian' theme—and, as a corollary to this, the theme of racial and cultural synthesis; the social criticism and the analysis which such criticism necessitates, and in general the sociological nature of this writing: these are its dominant aspects."[5]

Whether, or to what extent, the writing of the area has distinguished itself from English literature remains debatable. What tradition exists at present is still in process of formation. Tradition, after all, is a product of time, and prior to the end of World War II only a few individual writers of note appeared here and there on different islands. Jamaican poet Thomas Henry MacDermot (1870–1933), writing under the pseudonym "Tom Redcam," could lay claim to being the father of West Indian literature, although his place in history is due more to his determination to initiate a local literature than to the quality of his work. Another Jamaican, Claude McKay (1889–1948), was the leading figure of the 1920s. As is the case with an unfortunate majority of writers who came later, most of McKay's life was spent in metropolitan exile. From the 1930s, the name of historian-novelist C. L. R. James (born 1901) stands out for his support of the West Indian independence movement and for his early novel *Minty Alley*.

Literary Developments after 1940

In the 1940s the essential groundwork was laid for the renaissance of the following decade. Of inestimable value to the development of an indigenous audience and to the encouragement of native artists is the opening of avenues of communication between the writer and his community. The openings came with the introduction of local periodicals: *Bim,* edited by Frank Collymore, began in Barbados in 1942; Edna Manley's *Focus* came out of Jamaica the next year; in British Guiana A. J. Seymour published *Kyk-over-al* in 1945; then in 1949 the University of the West Indies followed with *Caribbean Quarterly.* In addition to these printed outlets, in 1942 Una Marson's and later Henry Swanzy's BBC program "Caribbean Voices" afforded another medium for expression. Practically all the writers who have established themselves in West Indian literature appeared in one or another of these venues or are at least indebted to them for opening the way.

Prominent figures during the 1940s and 1950s include Roger Mais (1905–1955), Edgar Mittelholzer (1909–1965), Victor Reid (born 1913), Samuel Selvon (born 1923), and John Hearne (born 1926). Riding the crest of that wave through the 1960s and 1970s is a more recent surge of writers who have brought to fruition the promise of their predecessors. There are, to name only a few of the most active ones, Wilson Harris (born 1921), George Lamming (born 1927), Andrew Salkey (born 1928), Edward Brathwaite and Derek Walcott (both born in 1930), Michael Anthony and V. S. Naipaul (both born in 1932), Earl Lovelace (born 1935), and Dennis Scott (born 1939).

One anomaly of this remarkable renaissance is that it is almost entirely concentrated in fiction: poetry and drama are conspicuous, with rare exceptions, for their scarcity and generally poor quality. The usual standard of verse up to the late 1940s is Georgian, belletristic, and too slavishly imitative to be distinctive. As late as 1973 William Walsh states unequivocally, "There is a body of poetry, and there is one significant poet, Derek Walcott, but the level of achievement, in spite of a medium fed from the impressively vivid and vital sources of West Indian language, will not stand comparison in scope or standard with the fiction."[6] Nevertheless, there are several good poets: Wayne Brown, Anthony McNeill, Mervyn Morris, Dennis Scott; and Edward Brathwaite deserves to be ranked as a major West Indian poet even if he has not been accorded the same international recognition as Derek Walcott.

Poetry fared much better in the French West Indies than in the British possessions. Louis James accounts for this fact by recalling that the French colonies became politically active long before the British islands did. There is the example in Haiti after 1915 of poetry rising out of nationalist resistance to the presence of the United States: works by Bélance, Brierre, Depestre, Durand, and Laleau. James also points out a major difference between French and English colonial policies. The French attempted to incorporate their colonized people as completely as possible into metropolitan France. The major cohesive factor was a thorough grounding in European culture.[7] It would be unfair to say that the English pursued a policy of "benign neglect," but artists in their islands faced a bewildering array of ill-defined choices. The absence of a local tradition created a vacuum that pulled into itself the foreign traditions of Europe and North America and the folklore of Africa: the Anansi story, folksong, and picong. In addition, the British West Indian poet faces a spectrum of "voices" ranging from popular dialects to academic English. As James indicates, the artists and intellectuals of the French-speaking Caribbean face problems, but not such acute dilemmas as their English counterparts. In support of James's thesis, it is worth noting that Derek Walcott, the finest English-language poet writing in the West Indies, has not only immersed himself in a classical European education in St. Lucia, but his birthplace remains deeply rooted in its earlier French heritage: the island is predominantly Catholic in religion; its geography is mapped out in French place-names; and the native dialect is a French patois.

St. Lucia: Walcott's Milieu

Derek and his twin brother, Roderick—sons of Warwick Walcott, the artistically gifted father who died when the boys were hardly one year old, and Alix, the mother who served as headmistress to a Methodist grammar school—were born in Castries, the capitol of St. Lucia, in January 1930. St. Lucia may seem an unlikely place to have produced a leading contemporary poet: it is a small volcanic island of only 238 square miles situated in the Lesser Antilles about halfway between French Martinique to the north and English St. Vincent to the southeast. In 1950 when the brothers were collaborating on their first amateur drama production, Walcott estimated the island's population to have been only 80,000, but in spite of the obscurity and smallness of St.

Lucia, when he recalls his boyhood he likes to draw comparisons with Yeats's and Synge's Ireland. To his mind the physical environment with its mountains, mist, trees, animals, and imaginary beings is mysterious and strange: "Depending on how primal the geography is and how fresh in the memory, the island is going to be invested in the mind of the child with a mythology which will come out in whatever the child grows up to re-tell."[8] Nurtured on oral tales of gods, devils, and cunning tricksters passed down by generations of slaves, Walcott should retell folk stories; and he does. On the other hand, since he has an affinity for and is educated in the Western classics, he should retell the traditional themes of European experience; and he does. As inheritor of two vitally rich cultures, he utilizes one, then the other, and finally creates out of the two his own personalized style.

Walcott confronted the same schizophrenia that plagues nearly all West Indians. Descended from a white grandfather and a black grandmother on both the paternal and maternal sides, he is a living example of the divided loyalties and hatreds that keep his society suspended between two worlds. Although it may be painful enough to the man in his ordinary life, the poet, fortunately, can elevate personal crises into art. The most frequently quoted passage from all of Walcott's work illustrates the point:

> I who am poisoned with the blood of both,
> Where shall I turn, divided to the vein?
> I who have cursed
> The drunken officer of British rule, how choose
> Between this Africa and the English tongue I love?
> Betray them both, or give back what they give?[9]

It is the succinctly expressed thought contained in these lines more than their aesthetic worth that catches the reader's attention. Since this question of identity is one of the most frequently recurring themes in West Indian literature, it is fitting that Walcott should take it up and that his own people should appreciate it. Since questions of identity, personal meaning, and the individual's role in society are also important to intelligent men everywhere in the postexistentialist world, it is understandable why he (although he is the product of a colonized, isolated culture) should strike responsive chords in a far greater audience.

Necessity does indeed beget invention, and the absence of an audience of sufficient size in the West Indies is itself enough to require aspiring writers to seek readers in foreign markets. Granted this fact, it may be a positive advantage rather than a misfortune that West Indian artists find themselves cast away on obscure islands. Forced to live on intimate terms with the dilemma of existence that is frequently merely a philosophical exercise for metropolitan intellectuals, the West Indian writer comes naturally to the deepest psychological and sociological issues at the heart of modern literature.

Another apparent disadvantage that proves upon closer examination also to have a positive side is the strategic location of the Caribbean islands. In the days of discovery and exploration the islands were outposts of an empire, suitable for exploitation, and as way stations less important for themselves than for what lay beyond them. As colonialism entered its period of decline, they became burdensome wards, regarded as not worth the cost of their upkeep. This is one way to view their placement in geography and history. But like the Greek islands of the Aegean Sea they form a vital link between two great continents. They are also the front porch of the New World, latent with all the mythical potentials of Columbus, Crusoe, and a new Eden.

These two considerations are just as authentic as the more obvious reality of slavery and colonial neglect. Walcott seizes upon them both explicitly in his 1970 article "Meanings." As to the prospects for literature in the islands, Walcott thinks "that an archipelago, whether Greek or West Indian, is bound to be a fertile area, particularly if it is a bridge between continents, and a variety of people settle there."[10] Here are echoes of Henry Swanzy's prophetic observation from as early as 1949, that "of all the English-speaking world, the West Indies may be revealed as the place most suited for maintenance of a literary tradition."[11] Swanzy's prediction is based on the potentials of cultural crossfertilization among European, African, and Asiatic strains mingling in the West Indies just as they had converged in ancient Greece.

As for "maintaining" tradition, Walcott goes on in "Meanings" to speak of the old ideas in terms of the New World's fresh perspective. In his opinion the greatest bequest of the British Empire was education, which, in spite of some weaknesses, "must have ranked with the finest in the world. The grounding was rigid—Latin, Greek, and the essential masterpieces, but there was this elation of discovery. Shakespeare, Marlowe, Horace, Vergil—these writers weren't jaded but immediate experiences."[12] As Walcott indicates in "What the Twilight Says," the introduction to his collection *Dream on Monkey Mountain and Other Plays* (1970), this background is very important to West Indian artists: "[T]he writers of my generation were natural assimilators. We knew the literature of Empires, Greek, Roman, British, through their essential classics; and both the patois of the street and the language of the classroom hid the elation of discovery. If there was nothing, there was everything to be made. With this prodigious ambition one began."[13]

"Assimilation" is the key term that needs special consideration here. Unfortunately it is sometimes narrowly interpreted as synonymous with imitation. Walcott passed through a youthful apprenticeship phase wherein he consciously traced the models of established masters. He was humble enough to learn from example and honest enough to disclose his intention to appropriate whatever stores he found useful in the canon of world literature. There are traces in his poetry and his drama of James Joyce, T. S. Eliot, Sophocles, Andrew Marvell, Tirso de Molina, Bertolt Brecht, Baudelaire, the Japanese Kabuki and Noh theaters, and West Indian folktale and dance; but Walcott does not stop with imitation. *Assimilation* means to ingest into the mind and thoroughly comprehend; it also means to merge into or become one with a cultural tradition. Walcott's culture as a West Indian is fed by multiple tributaries. He not only accepts that fact, he is inspired by it.

In practical terms, most of the critics who decry Walcott's assimilative tendencies are disappointed, first, that he is not more thoroughly West Indian (whatever that may be); and second, they are alienated by his predilection for Western rather than African influences. It is difficult at best to separate social from aesthetic concerns, and in newly emerged countries nationalism tends to weigh heavily in any value judgment. When Walcott's assimilation is at its best, it may be said of him as Dryden says of Ben Jonson's literary borrowing: "He invades authors like a monarch; and what would be theft in other poets, is only victory in him."[14] On aesthetic grounds, it is not the artist's source that matters so much as the use he makes of his material.

Not only is Walcott an erudite writer, but he also has a facility with language that allows him to move with ease from dialect to standard English to Miltonic eloquence. His proven ability to turn a fine phrase that displeases sociologically interested critics at the same time exposes him to becoming what Michel Fabre calls "one of the sacred monsters" of our time. At the hands of formalists and critics of the rhetorical niceties of language, Walcott's broader skills as a poet are likely to be

disregarded. "Overpraised," Fabre suggests, "by British critics and sometimes shunned by other Black critics as too close an adherent to the
Western ethos, the Caribbean poet's relation to his classical aesthetic heritage has been unduly construed as exclusive of his equally strong (if not
stronger) ties with the folk culture he is heir to."[15]

Agonizing choices must be made, but Walcott is gifted enough to be
in the enviable position of having several options available. He freely
admits that his first poems and plays reflect his yearning to be adopted
in the line of Marlowe and Milton.[16] More recently the temptation for
his contemporaries has been toward the folk, the popular forms being
the folksong and the calypso.[17] In "What the Twilight Says," Walcott
describes three types of writers: one is the entertainer,

> "I will write in the language of the people however gross or incompre-
> hensible"; another says: "Nobody else go' understand this, you hear, so le'
> me write English"; while the third is dedicated to purifying the language
> of the tribe, and it is he who is jumped on by both sides for pretentious-
> ness or playing white. He is the mulatto of style. The traitor. The assimi-
> lator.[18]

This latter has obvious personal reference. In a *London Magazine* article in 1965, Walcott argues that the complex challenge and the thing
that is most frustrating to the West Indian poet is finding a natural
form. He believes the raw spontaneity of dialect allows a potentially
richer expression, but to achieve it he must sacrifice the syntactical
strength of English.[19] In the *Trinidad Guardian* in 1962 he complains
that poets like himself must of necessity seem precocious and artificial to
local audiences because the society is in a state of transition. Its Protean
language is not sufficiently geared to a formal syntax and accent. One
solution, the one selected by Walcott, is to seek a median standard that
captures the vitality of the native idiom and yet retains the cohesive
solidity of a literary mode. An inevitable step toward the goal must be a
backward one: the poet cut off from his ancestral home must "explore
his origins before he can purify the dialect of the tribe." For the English-
speaking West Indian poet the ancestral voice is to be heard in a language acquired by imitation, "but the feelings must be his own, they
must have their roots in his own earth."[20]

To ring with authenticity, the poet's voice must be rooted in his own
being. The exploration of origins must not stop in the past, but must be
the prelude to forward movement. Some of the very critics who fear that

Walcott will lose himself in Western culture are themselves probably closer to abandoning their proper heritages in desiring a return to Africa. Walcott speaks in "What the Twilight Says" of an African phase, with its pathetic imitation carvings, poems, costumes, and artifacts that are no longer sacred, but have become art objects to be sold to tourists: the result is "not one's own thing but another minstrel show." Elaborating on the point, he argues that "[p]astoralists of the African revival should know that what is needed is not new names for old things, or old names for old things, but the faith of using the old names anew, so that mongrel as I am, something prickles in me when I see the word Ashanti as with the word Warwickshire . . . both baptising . . . this hybrid, this West Indian."[21] There is not the slightest hint, however, that the African past should be neglected, any more than European culture should be abandoned. It is not a simple choice between cultures for Walcott, but a matter of laying claim to his mixed heritage.

Chiron's Legacy

Ultimately, the true artist's apprenticeship never really ends, even after he becomes a master and is himself imitated by others. Walcott's sources of inspiration are wide ranging; he experiments continually; he tries on a variety of masks, and he passes through a number of evolutionary phases. His novitiate period may be said to have run until his late 20s; by this time he had completed his formal schooling, taught briefly in Grenada and Jamaica, and studied in New York on a Rockefeller Fellowship. His first school plays, dated between 1947 and 1950 (now extant only in fragments of manuscript), are justifiably overshadowed by his more accomplished pieces: the historical *Henri Christophe* (1950), admittedly Jacobean in style; *The Sea at Dauphin* (1954), modeled after Synge's *Riders to the Sea; Ione* (1957), a Grecian-influenced saga of familial conflict; and *Drums and Colours* (1958), a West Indian epic commissioned by the University of the West Indies for the opening of the first Federal Parliament of the West Indies. Also, by 1960 his earliest poems had been privately printed and sold: *25 Poems* (1948) and *Poems* (1951). His first commercial volume of poetry, *In a Green Night,* although dated in 1962, really belongs, as the title page indicates, to the period 1948–1960. In 1959, having returned to Trinidad from his Rockefeller Fellowship year in New York, he founded his second theatrical troupe, designated variously the Basement Theatre and the Trinidad Theatre Workshop. (The first group, the Arts Guild of St. Lucia, he founded with his brother Roderick at St. Mary's College, Castries, in 1950.)

Already, as a novice, Walcott revealed the complexity of his artistic makeup. In addition to the predominantly African folk culture acquired from the streets of Castries and country villages and to the European books read in the classroom, he was also impressed by the exploits of outstanding figures from West Indian history. Henri Christophe may have become a tyrant, but Walcott at the age of 19 saw him and Dessalines in mythological proportions. The black Jacobins of Haiti seemed to him tragic because of their blackness and because of the manic heresy that drove them to rise against the white god's universe. Writing of this boyhood feeling in "What the Twilight Says," Walcott appreciates their desperate revolution as the beginning of racial self-discovery. He remembers being moved also, as a young writer, by the revolutionary pronouncements of Frantz Fanon and Aimé Césaire. Their rhetoric made him feel deprived, that he was no blacker, no poorer, to share even more in their tragic anguish.[22]

Although the styles of this youthful period are predominantly Western—the Jacobean touch in *Henri Christophe,* Synge in *The Sea at Dauphin,* Greek tragedy in *Ione,* Marvell in *In a Green Night*—the material is inherently Caribbean. Paradoxically, the solution to the problems of fitting Old World style to New World content (if the two can actually be separated in more than theory) does not come through the expedient of sacrificing one for the sake of the other, or by simply blending them. Instead, a third influence comes into the formula. During the late 1950s Walcott began the transition into the second stage of his career. Not content with writing itself, the poet-dramatist shifted his focus toward directing and producing. As he moved into the 1960s, Walcott's greatest activity was in the theater, and it was the nature of his growing concern with stagecraft that distinguished this period. The two new books of poetry in this decade are of high quality and they open some new ground, but they are for the most part reprints of earlier poems: *Selected Poems* (1964) contains 16 poems not included in *In a Green Night; The Castaway* (1965) introduces only 13 new poems. The turning point for drama came between 1957 and 1958 in New York, while Walcott attended classes with José Quintero and studied at the Phoenix Theatre.

The Workshop Years

In 1958 Walcott seemed to have settled any debt he might owe to West Indian history by means of the extensive pageantry and broad character exposition of *Drums and Colours. Ti-Jean and His Brothers,* a vastly different kind of play produced in the same year, indicates a new direction. In "Meanings," Walcott refers to the work as his first "stylized West Indian play": out of it, he discovers the style he wants, the dynamic fusion that is essential for his creation of a viable West Indian drama. His catalyst came from the Orient: the Japanese Kabuki and Noh traditions. The play immediately succeeding *Ti-Jean and His Brothers, Malcochon* (1959), is a deliberate imitation of the Japanese film *Rashomon*. "[I]t was one of those informing imitations that gave me a direction because I could see in the linear shapes, in the geography, in the sort of myth and superstition of the Japanese, correspondences to our own forests and mythology."[23] Walcott, then, assimilates yet another "foreign" culture which is also an integral part of the West Indian milieu.

According to Walcott in "Meanings," the paramount difficulty with West Indian drama is its unbounded exuberance, its self-indulgence.[24] His model for a more tractable and at the same time more uniquely West Indian drama is intended to remove that difficulty. Since his Caribbean culture is an amalgam of African, Oriental, and Occidental races, Walcott draws upon them all to create a theater that will reflect his diverse world. From Europe he borrows the established but flexible language of classical literature; from Africa and parts of the Orient he borrows ritual dances, mime, and narrative; from the Kabuki and Noh plays he borrows the emphatic power and beauty of restrained gesture, rhythm, and form. Without enervating the vitality of the West Indian folk idiom and spirit, he wants to introduce discipline.

Bertolt Brecht's adaptation of Oriental techniques first led Walcott to realize their potential. Another of Brecht's ideas that appealed to him was *Verfremdungseffekt,* the distancing effect that forces the viewer of a play to reflect upon its meaning. Walcott is deeply conscious of the impact of a stage production. Those critics who accuse him of not being concerned enough with the folk ought to take into consideration the time-honored place of theater in communicating with people. An older poet-playwright, T. S. Eliot, asserts in *The Use of Poetry* that "[t]he ideal medium for poetry, to my mind, and the most direct means of social 'usefulness' for poetry, is the theatre."[25] Walcott continues to explore the medium of the stage so that he can broaden the base of the arts and reach larger audiences, but he guards his artistic integrity at the same time.

Fellow West Indian Kenneth Ramchand judges the situation in the following manner:

> [I]n the plays themselves we see him creating the West Indian social world, placing the peasantry at the centre, and making exciting use of

folklore and oral tradition, music, dance and the popular speech. The plays have been ignored in recent assessments of Walcott's work, but Walcott the poet is inseparable from Walcott the dramatist. . . . While tired new voices have been drumming about "the folk," "the folk language," "folk culture," and "bringing theatre to the people," Walcott has been demonstrating over the last twenty years how a serious artist whose primary interest is imaginative rendering converts these self-indulgent abstractions into art.[26]

It does not hurt to remember in this regard that folk culture is basically ephemeral. Since it involves human institutions, it is not static but is always in the process of becoming. Whoever wishes to describe a primitive society, an ethnic or racial group (whether he is an anthropologist, a sociologist, a nationalist, or an artist), engages in a sophisticated intellectual activity that has its own discipline and terminology. Walcott employs the conventions of the poet and the dramatist to re-create in a tangible and more permanent form the experience of living beings, not to preserve someone else's concept of an ideal community.

Ironically, the best method of preserving the energy and spirit of a culture sustained by oral tradition is to absorb it still alive into the artist's reality. According to Cameron King and Louis James in their joint article, Walcott's use of the Western cultural tradition is fortuitous because it transcends national boundaries. The country that isolates itself and looks only inward may inadvertently cut off the best means of knowing itself. "It is not simply chance that the greatest nationalist writers in French and Spanish as well as English, in modern Africa as well as the West Indies, have been those who have been able most fully to come to their own predicaments through mastery of the European literary experience."[27] Walcott advocates this culturally enriching interchange.

During the years between 1958 and 1967—from his taking permanent residence in Trinidad until the initial staging of his internationally acclaimed play, *Dream on Monkey Mountain*—the central thrust of Walcott's activities was the development of a professional West Indian acting company. His founding in 1959 of the Trinidad Theatre Workshop to complement the already established Little Carib Dance Company was the direct result of his need for a specially trained pool of actors who would be able to perform the new kind of drama he was exploring. An early setback came when the Workshop group was forced to separate from the Dance Company, with the result that instead of employing the mixed troupe of actors and dancers he had envisioned he was forced to recruit actors who would acquire dancing skills. For three or four years, as hopeful actors and actresses gathered around and came to know their strengths and weaknesses, Walcott concentrated on improvisations and attempts to instill discipline in the group through exercises in method acting. Gradually his Brechtian objectives and the company's talents began to synchronize and West Indian exuberance answered to precise control.

Attempting to locate parallels in better known traditions, Walcott, in a 1964 article, cites the American musical. It is based on dance, but its drawbacks include its sentimentality and its appeal to the audience's emotions rather than its intellect. Walcott also recognizes similarities in Japanese theater. The Kabuki comes closer to his conception than the Broadway musical because of its physical action, its underlying mythology, and its use of masks; yet it is not as spontaneous in its tradition-laden gestures and extended silences, as Walcott's calypso, calinda, and Shango-influenced drama.[28] Since the calypso (also called kaiso) and these other African musical forms invite broad improvisation, one of his primary tasks is to focus his company's energy. "We love rhetoric," Walcott explains, "and this has created a style, a panache about life that is particularly ours. . . . Combine that in our literature with a long experience of classical forms and you're bound to have something exhilarating."[29] This is the background of theory and practice leading up to the Workshop's opening productions of Edward Albee's *The Zoo Story* and Walcott's *The Sea at Dauphin* at the Basement Theatre in Port-of-Spain in 1966.

The success of its public debut may be estimated by the fact that in spite of the crude facilities in a theater with a capacity for seating only 60 patrons, the premier two-day run had to be lengthened into a full week. In October this minor victory was reinforced by the success of the Workshop's first repertory experiment, which ran before good audiences for 26 nights. Not only for the Workshop, but for Trinidad and the British West Indies as well, it was an historical achievement: the first production of a complete theatrical season by a company of West Indian players. Fittingly, the season's bill of fare exemplified the region's cultural diversity: *The Blacks* by Frenchman Jean Genêt, *Belle Fanto* by Trinidadian E. M. Roach, and *The Road* by Nigerian Wole Soyinka.

The Dreams of Men

Dream on Monkey Mountain, which Walcott had begun in 1959 but did not finish until 1967, caps the Workshop years of experiment in the

1960s. It brings to fruition one phase of development and initiates another. After a series of revisions and several productions of the play, Walcott at last realized the full accomplishment of a uniquely personal and yet a thoroughly West Indian vehicle of expression. The international stature of the accomplishment may be seen in the fact that it received an Obie Award in New York as the best foreign play of the 1970–1971 season.

Since *Dream on Monkey Mountain* is the mature work of an artist who has come into his own, it does not properly belong in the period of experimentation out of which it grew. Entering his 40s, Walcott seems more sure of himself and exhibits less need for the defensiveness that appears in many of his articles as reviewer for the *Trinidad Guardian* in the 1960s. This is not to say, however, that he could afford to drop his guard; some of his new directions (in his plays especially) continued to offend people from various quarters. The poetry of this period displays the expansiveness of his mind, both its centrifugal and centripetal motion. *The Gulf* (1969) does not really swing outward to parts of the foreign world that Walcott has missed before; instead, it explores the paradoxical nature of gulfs, both literal and figurative, that stand between men. Islands, like men, exist apart from each other; yet their shores and men's lives are washed by a common sea and thus they are inevitably linked by the space that intervenes. While *The Gulf* entails looking outward from a central experience, *Another Life* (1973), Walcott's long autobiographical poem, delves into the heart of that central experience.

Together the two volumes demonstrate the increasingly personalized use that Walcott is able to make of his varied materials. Complaints arose, in fact, that he was too egocentrically involved in his artistry. From Patricia Ismond's point of view, this is yet another manifestation of the European influence.[30] Lloyd King, acknowledging that to be an intellectual and a writer is to put distance between the poet and the plight of the common folk, refrains from suggesting that Walcott become a writer of social protest, but he expresses fears that Walcott's posture as a Western literary humanist is impotent. *The Gulf* for example "is unlikely to be greeted by genuine widespread enthusiasm," due to the fact that "the poet's vision is not of the purgatory or hell of the masses held in thrall by administrative and political devils but his own private definition of purgatory."[31] Walcott appears to have anticipated precisely these kinds of concerns back in 1966 when he was at work on *The Gulf* and *Another Life*. In speaking of every writer's need to struggle toward his authentic voice, he argued that it is the young poet's wrestling with temptation that makes his evolution interesting. Two of the primary temptations are to satisfy popular tastes and to imitate the literary lions of the day. "The search eventually ends in the discovery of other voices, and yet at its end the poet by acquiring all of these demons, becomes himself. . . . Great poets sound both like themselves alone and like all the great poetry written."[32] The needs of the oppressed masses are not denied: in "What the Twilight Says" Walcott asserts that "[t]he future of West Indian militancy lies in art."[33] Yet the artist must first of all heed his own peculiar genius; otherwise, because he becomes false to his own inner being, he will be of little service to his people.

In his dramas of the early 1970s Walcott deemphasized the musical element temporarily, broadened the racial mixture of his characters, and experimented with a more realistic style. The next two plays after *Dream on Monkey Mountain*—*In a Fine Castle* (1970) and *Franklin* (1973)—use little music and then only as part of the background. *The Charlatan* (1973) incorporates a musical score and more fantasy, but all three plays deal with the privileged classes and have white characters in major roles. Class conflict is nothing new to the West Indies, but Walcott refused to oversimplify complex issues by fixing the blame for inequities on the class usually held responsible for social ills. Consequently, critics interested in social causes were quick to focus their attention accordingly. Ralph Campbell charged that Walcott's plays are of no pertinence and are irrelevant to the people. *The Charlatan* and *Franklin* specifically have "nothing to do with building our image."[34] Perhaps it would be equally irrelevant to point out that Walcott's intention, to render an accurate portrayal of a very real segment of West Indian society, is a far more demanding and more valuable objective than image building.

Turning again to song and fantasy in *The Charlatan,* Walcott was fortunate in obtaining the collaboration of gifted musician Galt MacDermot. MacDermot, whose credits include the highly successful Broadway musical *Hair,* has since 1974 scored the music for four more of Walcott's plays: *The Joker of Seville* (1974) and *O Babylon!* (1976), published together in 1978, and two later unpublished plays, *Marie Laveau* (1980) and *Steel* (1991). *The Joker of Seville* and *O Babylon!* depart to such an extent from all that Walcott had written previously that they must be treated as part of a new stage in his career. These works, together with two less-ambitious plays, *Remembrance* (1977) and *Pantomime* (1978), two major volumes of poetry, *Sea Grapes* (1976) and *The Star-Apple Kingdom* (1979), constitute a formidable literary outpouring during the 1970s.

Although *Sea Grapes* draws as much upon personal experience as does *Another Life* and recalls familiar themes and motifs from earlier books, it is neither narrow in perspective nor repetitive. Walcott's controlling image in a variety of shapes is the New World. Just as he demonstrates in *The Gulf,* he reiterates in *Sea Grapes* the means by which distant points in space and time are joined in the Caribbean's unique culture. Not surprisingly, the plays of this period complement the subtle linkages developed in the lyrical poems. *The Joker of Seville* revives seventeenth-century Spain in an adaptation of Tirso de Molina's *El Burlador de Sevilla* (1630). By now the consummate assimilator and artist in his own right, Walcott seemed a natural choice for the Royal Shakespeare Company's commission to write a modern version of Tirso's masterpiece. Moreover, it is difficult to imagine a piece of literature that could better coincide with Walcott's varied talents. There are the poetry, the music, the flamboyant action, and the character of Don Juan. If Walcott must again bear the label of "imitator" because of *The Joker of Seville,* his vibrant adaptation has too much life of its own to suffer much from the stigma. His skilled utilization of another artist's invention in fact recalls the list of other literary "borrowers" such as Chaucer, Shakespeare, and Pope.

O Babylon! leaves the Old World and takes up a story within Jamaica's modern Rastafarian subculture. The setting and characters may at first seem well outside the mainstream of contemporary life, but the deeper human conflicts are just as far-reaching in their implications as are the central themes of *Dream on Monkey Mountain* and *The Joker of Seville.* The following *Remembrance* and *Pantomime* (published jointly in 1980) are spartan productions in comparison with the musicals immediately preceding them. Here Walcott appears more introspective; with limited action and a sharp reduction in cast, he is able to concentrate on character exposition. Perhaps the subdued aspect of *Remembrance* is in part a reaction to impending divorce in his second marriage. His life was changing: a May 1977 notice in *Caribbean Contact* that *Remembrance* was to be produced under his direction in St. Croix also mentions without elaboration the fact that he had just resigned from the Theatre Workshop.[35] After termination of this long-standing relationship, he moved to the United States to teach at several prestigious universities before finally settling at Boston University.

If anything, since he began dividing each year between his residence in Massachusetts and the Caribbean, the pace of his work has increased. Not counting the unpublished plays, uncollected verse, and incidental prose, he has five volumes of poetry and one book of plays between 1980 and 1992, when he received the Nobel Prize. *The Fortunate Traveller* (1981), being separated into sections entitled "North," "South," and "North," reflects the polarities of Walcott's annual migrations from New England to the Caribbean. While a few poems relate to specific climates—for example, "Old New England" and "American Muse" on the one hand, or "Hurucan" and "The Spoiler's Return" on the other—selections such as "The Hotel Normandie Pool" and "The Fortunate Traveller" exploit the ironic interrelationships of the New World. As is evident from "The Hotel Normandie Pool," the linkage is historical as well as geographic, for the self-conscious poet draws parallels between his sense of alienation and that of Ovid, the Roman poet exiled to the provinces under Augustus. The title of his next collection, *Midsummer* (1984), extends the metaphorical amalgamation of environments. This book's sequence of forty-eight numbered poems is more crucially self-reflexive than *Another Life,* yielding as much Walcott's sense of his function as poet as it does his vision of the physical world.

In the 1980s, the textuality of expression itself becomes increasingly important as subject matter in Walcott's poetry and plays. The evolution of this tendency is made even more apparent with the publication in 1986 of his *Collected Poems 1948–1984.* Whereas earlier poems bear the imprint of wide-ranging influences from John Donne to Robert Lowell, more and more of the later verse refers to the process of converting experience into art, whether it be the printed word or the painted canvas. Reprinting poem "L" from *Midsummer* Walcott speaks of his father Warwick's hand moving in his:

> . . . Now, when I rewrite a line,
> or sketch on the fast-drying paper the coconut fronds
> that he did so faintly, my daughters' hands move in mine.[36]

Traditions of culture and blood coalesce in such lines, and they are manifest in Walcott's drama as well. In 1986, Walcott also brought out *Three Plays.* Each of the works collected in this volume deals with the recent history of Trinidad and Tobago: the political independence movement from 1948 through 1970; problems of post-independence economic development; and finally, the ongoing struggle for cultural authenticity. Significantly, the first of these plays *The Last Carnival* (which is an updated version of *In a Fine Castle* from 1970) is permeated with allusions to the rococo style of Antoine Watteau. The pastel wash of

Watteau's *Embarkation for Cythera* (1717–1719) captures the nostalgic surrender of imperial rule to provincial independence. The second work, *Beef, No Chicken* (from 1981), bears an equally poignant political message; however, with its farcical dramatization of the socioeconomic impact of modernization on a rural Trinidad village it seems to be an interlude between the two more serious plays in the book. *A Branch of the Blue Nile* (from 1983) derives its title from the fact that one of the plays within the play is Shakespeare's *Antony and Cleopatra* (1606–1607). Despite the influence of Shakespeare, and the benign neglect of art in their provincial colony, a struggling theatrical company attempts to "creolize" its productions so that they reflect their immediate culture more accurately. Personal entanglements, artistic contentions, and the scripts of separate plays provide intertextual layers of meaning as the plot unfolds. No great stretch of imagination is required to detect vestiges of Walcott's Trinidad Theatre Workshop in this fictional company.

Walcott's interest in the confluence of distant times and places continues in his next poetry collection, *The Arkansas Testament* (1987). Subsections entitled "Here" and "Elsewhere" convey the reader from the isolated West Indies to backwoods Arkansas, from Walcott's St. Lucian roots in "The Light of the World" to classical allusions in "A Propertius Quartet." The juxtaposition of such disparate points of reference has grown familiar enough in Walcott's work, but nothing heretofore approaches the scale of his epic-length *Omeros* (1990). In this 325-page poem, he does for the dispossessed peoples of the New World what epic poets from Homer to James Joyce have done for their countries. Yet despite the presence of certain traditional literary conventions, Walcott avoids ennobling characters beyond the enduring beauty of their simple lives. It is an eloquent tribute to the island of his youth.

Even before publishing his epic *Omeros* and his subsequent receipt of the Nobel Prize for Literature in 1992, Walcott had fulfilled the promise of his early years. Fellow West Indian Denis Solomon claimed as early as 1973 that *Ti-Jean and His Brothers, Dream on Monkey Mountain, In a Fine Castle,* and *Franklin* "constitute a body of work as complete and as immediately related to our contemporary situation as any society could hope to have."[37] Through the assimilated cultures of Africa, Asia, and Europe that were bequeathed to him naturally as a son of the Caribbean, he has since expanded to an international scale. Despite the fact that he now moves in circles that include people such as Seamus Heaney and fellow Nobel laureate Joseph Brodsky, he has never lost touch with the rich native soil that continues to nourish his creativity.

In addition to his better known accomplishments as poet, playwright, director, and producer, he is also an astute critic and keen observer of the sociopolitical scene. During the formative years of the Workshop he contributed regularly as an arts columnist to the *Trinidad Guardian*. His miscellaneous essays—on his life, on aspects of living in the West Indies, on literature, and on the status of the arts in general—appear in journals and books. The cumulative value of these articles is that they record in Walcott's own words (taken out of context) the "interesting evolution" of a "poet assailed by temptations."[38] The fact that his latest work has grown intensely self-reflexive makes this discursive commentary all the more significant. The creative writing and the expository prose together shed invaluable light on the ingenuity of Walcott's artistic processes.

Chapter Two

Apprenticeship Years: 1948–1958

Early Poems and Plays

Derek Walcott's debut as a writer in 1948 was an auspicious one. No less a figure than Frank Collymore—longtime editor of *Bim,* established critic and poet in his own right, and one of the fathers of West Indian literature—hailed his small collection, *25 Poems,* as the work of an accomplished poet.[1] Making such a pronouncement about a poet's first volume would involve risks under any circumstances: what is remarkable in the case of *25 Poems* is that the author of this highly competent work was only 18 years old.

This early collection not only revealed something of Walcott's poetic skill, it was also indicative of his enterprise and ambition. The necessary $200 to have the book privately printed came as a loan from his mother, who could ill afford it. Walcott then took it upon himself to hawk his poetry in the streets of Castries until he had repaid her investment.[2] His youthful ambition was tantamount to audacity. Later, looking back at his first poems and plays, he said, "I saw myself legitimately prolonging the mighty line of Marlowe, of Milton."[3] He yearned to belong, aspired to their achievement.

At his best, Walcott exploits to great advantage his own personal gifts, but when he wishes to he can assimilate the desirable qualities of various writers so skillfully that his language and theirs become indistinguishable. Examples of his developing ability on both counts are available in the poems selected for inclusion in *25 Poems,* in his extended 12-canto *Epitaph for the Young* (1949), and in *Poems* (1951), his second locally published collection. These are difficult to obtain; yet a few of the most important poems, those that after due consideration Walcott wished to make more readily available, are reprinted in his first book to be accepted by a major foreign publishing house, *In a Green Night* (Jonathan Cape, 1962).

Of the minor poems, the "juvenilia" that were not included in this important work, several deserve brief notice since they indicate Walcott's

earliest interests in technique and subject matter. In *25 Poems,* the generally somber tone shows up in titles such as "Elegies," "The Yellow
Cemetery," "A City's Death by Fire," "The Rusty Season Colours the
Leaves," and "In Death Are All Honourable." In "Elegies" the idea is
that innocence is stillborn or soon wrecked. He wonders when a Lazarus
will publish the unspoken tales of men who were quenched by harsh
existence before they had reached their goals. He indicates that a line of
tragedies extends from "naked and dead Greece" to a London flat, to
Castries and Kingston. The final couplet, a note of personal reference,
makes him heir to European tradition: "I am as young as they died, and
am proud in a trade of fames, / I fear death, inmate of my hand, leaps
wall to join their names."[4]

"The Yellow Cemetery" is headed with lines from Walt Whitman to
the effect that there really is no death.[5] The poem then proceeds to elaborate on the living death of men who have lost faith. Just as Whitman
found "letters from God dropt in the street, and every one . . . sign'd by
God's name," Walcott concludes that even if there is no life after death,
there remains the beauty of nature and art. In the first section of "The
Yellow Cemetery" the inverted syntax, the mixed parts of speech, and
the rigid economy of metaphor are reminiscent of Gerard Manley
Hopkins or Dylan Thomas. Walcott observes of the decadent present,

> . . . Could they speak more than bramble, they'd be
> One in the language of the sun and the bibleling [*sic*] froth.
> Their now bread is broken stone, their wine the absent blood
> They gave to days of nails.
>
> (ll. 8–11)

The only hints that this poem was written by an islander are the ever-
present references to sun, beach, and sea, all of which were as important
to Whitman as they are to Walcott.

Epitaph for the Young,[6] a poem in 12 cantos, which appeared shortly
after *25 Poems,* despite the suggestion of its title, has nothing to do with
death except that it recounts the dying away of innocence as experience
transforms the adolescent into a mature adult. Looking back at the
poem, Walcott stated in an interview in 1975 that it is full of the deliberately quoted influences of Joyce, Eliot, and Pound.[7] The borrowing is
so visible, in fact, that in his detailed review of *Epitaph for the Young* Keith
Alleyne says that Eliot is not simply an influence on Walcott, "but a

complete formula."[8] Alleyne feels that Walcott has assumed the role of a poet of crisis, that there is an uneasiness in many lines that discloses an embarrassed self-consciousness that is unresolved within the poem.

Little need be added to Alleyne's analysis of the poem's basic allegory except to point out that the voyage motif that serves to unify the cantos is a circular journey, and that the hero is pursuing an illusive quest that may be viewed on at least five levels. First, there are personal references: to the father whom he had lost just as Telemachus lost Ulysses (cantos 7 and 8); to the painting lessons he enjoyed on Saturdays in the studio of Harold Simmons (canto 2); and to his own writing, "My soul . . . / Is spread . . . / By 25 gestures of a lame mind" (canto 10). Second, he touches on the problems of West Indian society: as listed in canto 4, they are color prejudice, the governing mentality of clerks, and a lack of identity. On another level, European tradition comes into focus: there are direct quotations from Homer, Shakespeare, Eliot, Baudelaire, Dante, and Pound; the names of Buck Mulligan, Stephen Dedalus, Icarus, Don Juan, Hamlet, and Cyrano are introduced. Then, on the fourth and fifth, the artistic and spiritual levels, the separate threads come together. The voyager is an artist in search of a source of authority: it may be his actual father or an authentic tradition that should have been passed on to him naturally. Being told that he has no culture, as in the caption of canto 4, "There is not a West Indian Literature," the gifted boy has to absorb:

> A classical alas,
> For naked pickanninies, pygmies, pigs and poverty,
> Veiling your inheritance . . .
> You practise the pieties of your conquerors,
> Bowing before a bitter god.
>
> (canto 4)

At the end of this heavily satirical section, the narrator separates himself from the herd of civil servants, determined "to take up arms" as a writer. Then in cantos 5 through 9, the poet enters the depths of despair. His spiritual descent and ultimate reemergence parallel the movement of Eliot's "Ash Wednesday."

In place of Eliot's staircase image from "Ash Wednesday," Walcott borrows from James Joyce—first, Buck Mulligan's seaside tower and then the myth of Icarus as symbols of the artist's private struggle to sur-

vive harsh experiences (canto 9). Having been purged by fire and bap-
tized in the sea as Icarus was, the poet is able to resume his private journey on a new ship, this time without the imposed burden of the Old
World's furniture. Ironically, however, when he returns to his original
island home, he finds that nothing there has changed. The old forces are
potent and he cannot disengage himself from the conflicting claims of
Venus, daughter of the sea—representing nature—and Mary, mediator
for God's infinite mercy. Conveniently the oppositions blend in a visionary revelation as Neptune and Mary's colors, blue and green, become
one. Yielding at last to the inevitable, the wanderer hangs up his oars.

Considering the amount of anguish packed into this relatively brief
poem, such an abrupt, tame resolution comes off a bit too easily. When
Hamlet's "Alas poor Yorick" becomes "Alas poor Warwick" (the name of
Walcott's father), the five senses become "census" (for no apparent reason other than the pun), the cry "O my Sun" accompanies Icarus's fall to
the sea, and the titles of two Eliot poems are transformed together so
that "burnt nothing" is "A Little Giddying," the verbal tricks rather than
the poem draw most of the attention. Despite these shortcomings,
Epitaph for the Young is an intellectually provocative experiment.
Furthermore, Walcott has described it as an *Ur*-text for his later work,
the largely autobiographical, book-length poem *Another Life.*[9]

Two years elapsed before Walcott released his second collection, *Poems,*
in 1951. It came during his first year of study at the Mona campus of the
University of the West Indies. Between 1949 and 1951 his horizons,
which had always been broad through his education and reading, were
extended by his personal experience of living in Jamaica. The larger
island exposed him to urban blight, to new landscapes, and to a wider
audience for both his plays and his poetry. While his outward surroundings changed, Walcott's inner world remained fairly constant. His poet's
eye was attuned to the underlying sameness beneath the superficial differences of locations, faces, and institutions he encountered.

Much of what he writes seems intellectualized and abstract because of
his desire to elucidate the universals within particular instances, but with
Poems his movement is definitely toward concrete specifics; or perhaps it is
more accurate to say that he seeks a balance between the integrity of a
given moment and the myriad implications that radiate from it. The
satire—which in *Epitaph for the Young* dealt generally with the West
Indian's cultural ambivalence—is more pointed in its attack. Tourists, the
latest wave of colonialist invaders, are the subject of three poems: "The
Sunny Caribbean," "The North Coast at Night," and "Montego Bay—

Travelogue II." This last poem, while less probing in its analysis, shows the dual edge of his attack. Here the "assassins of culture" come to view the "picturesque fisherman's picturesque poverty," to "grin at cricketers on equality's field," and to throw coins to divers. When they arrive "Wrapped in the hundred thousand dollar charm," they are met by local sycophants who will do anything to please.[10] Pursuing money and approbation, these flatterers conduct tours, create exotic waiters' uniforms, and gloss over the slavery of the past and the racial tension of the present. One last target is the colonial politician. "The Statesman" is a prescription for the kind of government by clerks that was mentioned in canto 4 of *Epitaph for the Young*. In five short stanzas, each beginning "Thou shalt . . . ," the statesman is instructed to be piously indecisive, to accept bribes, to revolve around the proper club, to import sophistication, to educate his children at foreign universities, and to select by complexion.

These poems illustrate Walcott's tendency to give particular emphasis to larger issues, but their satirical thrust is only a minor note struck occasionally in *Poems*. Far more prevalent, in half of the total 31 poems, are explorations of the themes of love and the artist's struggle to create. He also touches on racial conflict, the problems of coming of age, exile, and death in his effort to bring out the complexities of human relationships. "Letter to Margaret," for example, is basically a subdued expression of love. It is very personal, though not necessarily based on Walcott's own experience. The speaker is a poet writing to reprimand his sweetheart, whom he has somehow offended, for not answering his last letter. He opens unexpectedly with the description of a cricket match, not for the sake of the sport itself but to remark on the racially mixed crowd. They sat and through "the language of applause" spoke together, "As though the gunman, Duty, behind them stands" (26). He resents the innocent laughter of other blacks in the crowd who do not understand the prejudice that is masked by social amenities. Then quite smoothly he ties the cricket match into his appeal to Margaret. He suggests that habits of praise ought to compel "Applause to talent on cricket field or pages." It seems that his "dark prose" in the past had disturbed her; so in deference to what he suggests is her youthful innocence he now swears to restrain his "choleric adjective" and behave "As poets should, insipid as their fruits" (27). For the reader, the light touch of self-deprecating humor at this point should be quite effective. He has not sacrificed his potential for deep indignation, as his observations on the cricket audience demonstrate. At the same time his restrained reaction should also prove to Margaret that he can curb his emotions.

As is characteristic of speakers' voices in many of Walcott's poems, the persona in "Letter to Margaret" is that of a mature person addressing someone younger. The advantage of this approach is that the speaker possesses the knowledge of experience. Having acquired that knowledge, he speaks in sadness. It pervades "Notebooks of Ruin," Walcott's combination of Thomas's "Fern Hill" and "The Force That Through the Green Fuse Drives the Flower." The lost joys of feckless youth, "When summer in the muscle pulsed your age, / And you were drowned in green on the green" (16), are recounted for three stanzas. In the last three stanzas time and regret take their toll. Just as certain lines recall Thomas's driving "force," other phrases echo his refrain, "I am dumb to tell," recognizing man's final inability to articulate his deeper feelings.

"The Cracked Playground," placed immediately after "Notebooks of Ruin," is a more effective poem. It is another exposition of the maturation process and it follows a highly regulated structural pattern, but the ideas seem fresher and as a result the structure is not unduly apparent. There is but one flaw, where form twists thought out of its natural line: in the second stanza a tutor is described as working between shelves "with assured vertigo" (17). The image does not seem true; it seems strained merely to rhyme with "studio" two lines above. Otherwise, the strength of the poem is in the memorable expression of its connected ideas.

Significantly, "The Cracked Playground" is the longest selection in *Poems*. The poem balances, as is typical of Walcott's developing style, the specifics of clearly autobiographical references with the outward implications of larger meaning. Readers familiar with Walcott's early life will recognize that the green-shuttered bungalow described in the first two stanzas houses the studio of painter Harry Simmons, and that the two boys—the "I" and "you"—of the third and subsequent stanzas stand for Walcott and his friend Dunstan St. Omer. Walcott, a writer, "took more easily to the talkative agony," while St. Omer, a painter, followed "the grammar of the instructive brush." They both spent many pleasant Saturdays painting and discussing art with Harry Simmons. Walcott describes them as "three black acolytes at the feet of Pater."

In the first of the four sections of this poem, the speaker discusses the way their youthful fire, spurred on by dreams of fame, had dwindled. He notes that it did not occur suddenly like a wreck, but slowly diminished through the working of time. Since they lived in a colony, their image of fame grew out of England; but even that lost its power as the foreign island's old cathedrals, evenings pictured by Turner, and manicured parks came to seem the "last infirmities for noble minds." In reaction they made quixotic charges as though the enemy could be met head-on. Section 1 ends on a note of despair, their vision broken, their chalice become a cocktail glass, their spear diminished to a spoon.

Section 2 applies the lesson learned from personal experience to mankind as a whole. Failure teaches that there is a "cracked playground" in the heart of every man. To avoid broken dreams, men seek to escape: to other islands, to the sea, to women, or to death. All this running serves only to prove more conclusively that, since there is no perfection anywhere, there is also no true escape. Section 3 shows that implicit in dreams of both fame and escape is an element of faith, faith that leads time and again to loss. "Rooted in childhood, faith cracks a hundred ways" (19), goes the first line. This leads to a list of failed ideals: godfathers, fathers, God, love, and chastity have each in turn proved inadequate. He points grimly at the founders of "Society" and the villas with imported roses, against the backdrop of cardboard shacks and illness. It would be appropriate at this point to note that references to religious faith are scarce in the entire collection of *Poems*.

"The Cracked Playground" reaches, in the final section, a crescendo of defeat. In the process Walcott aligns the present with past civilizations. We race like the Greeks "To the grave the international issue" (20). Just as the Renaissance had to endure the inevitable grief of time, endurance is all that remains for man in the present. In a somewhat self-pitying tone the world-weary spokesman notes that it is only human to long "To cage the truth in mica or in marble," but notes that "desires all grow old." His authority for this insight, he claims, is "the authority of despair" (21).

Lest anyone be left with the false assumption that Walcott denies the value of man's endeavors, it is necessary only to glance at the central idea of the poem that follows on the same page the lines just quoted. "Too Young for Remembering, Too Old . . ." argues that though stone wears away, a gesture never grows old. Drawing again upon Icarus, one of his favorite images, he insists, "That we tilt at suns is what is worth being told" (21).

There are no really new themes in *Poems*. The earlier influences remain: Joyce, Eliot, Pound, and Thomas. As to style, the finish of many of the works is rough, but obtrusive puns such as "the limb shall lie down with the loin" from "Ex Ore Infantum" (23) are not so numerous as they were in *25 Poems*. Walcott also demonstrates his increasing ability to synthesize abstract thought with concrete experience. In spite of

the improvements in this direction, when he made the selections to represent his early work in *In a Green Night* (which is subtitled *Poems:
1948–1960*), he chose only one poem, the satirical "Margaret Verlieu
Dies," from *Poems*. He reprinted five from *25 Poems*.

In a Green Night

With the appearance in 1962 of *In a Green Night* came proof at last
that the West Indies had a poet who could stand alongside their considerable list of established novelists. As Gordon Rohlehr put it, "*In a Green
Night* . . . was a landmark in the history of West Indian poetry, liberating it at once from a simple mindless romanticism, a we[a]k historicism,
over-rhetorical protest and sterile abstraction."[11] Just as Frank
Collymore had endorsed the privately printed *25 Poems*, Robert Graves
now spoke his appreciation of Walcott's first major collection: "Derek
Walcott handles English with a closer understanding of its inner magic
than most (if not any) of his English-born contemporaries."[12]

Rohlehr's comment indicates the fact that *In a Green Night* broke with
an old exotic tradition; Graves clearly judges Walcott on an international scale. These are crucial distinctions because, from the very beginning,
critical appraisals of Walcott have divided over the question of his cultural identity. In an early review for *Bim*, A. N. Forde warned that some
nationalists might be tempted to claim *In a Green Night* as another proof
of the existence of a uniquely West Indian poetry. Forde's position is that
Walcott writes as a sensitive individual within an established English tradition, the only literary tradition available in the British Caribbean: "A
West Indian poetry will only emerge when we attain the self-respect that
comes with being practitioners equal in sensitivity and purpose with any
other poets practising in the English tongue."[13]

If it proves nothing else, *In a Green Night* testifies to Walcott's versa-
tility. There is sufficient evidence within the book to identify his birthplace, but beyond that he exploits the multiplicity that, for better or
worse, is West Indian culture. P. N. Furbank admits the aptness of
Walcott's echoes of Villon, Dante, Catullus, the metaphysicals, and modern poets, since "history has made him a citizen of the world."[14] Variety
is the key term. Within the mixture of disparate elements pervading
both Walcott's poetry and his society lie the strengths and weaknesses of
In a Green Night. In addition to the plethora of familiar literary influences, themes range widely, scenes shift from the Caribbean to both sides
of the northern Atlantic, time encompasses the prehistoric past as well as

the present, and language glides through the spectrum from rhetorical elegance to patois. There is richness, beauty, and skill, but there is no consistent aim to his poetry before 1960. It is as though, lacking a clear picture of what role he should assume, he sets out to define the possibilities that are available.

Tacit admission of such a stance comes in "Prelude," the first poem in *In a Green Night,* one of his selections out of the earlier *25 Poems.* The speaker is a young poet who chose to make his life in his native island. Because of that choice, he suffers the indignity of knowing that his people are lost except to tourists who, in their ignorance, "think us here happy."[15] His boyhood has ended quickly, before he could pretend maturity, and his calling as an artist forces him to restrain his feelings until they conform to "accurate iambics." His defense, like that of the self-effacing J. Alfred Prufrock, is to wear a disguise:

> I go, of course, through all the isolated acts,
> Make a holiday of situations,
> Straighten my tie and fix important jaws,
> And note the living images
> Of flesh that saunter through the eye.
>
> (11)

At the moment of his speaking he has reached "the middle of the journey through my life." This is the same point, it should be noted, where Dante stood in the first lines of *The Inferno;* and crossing his mind is the same animal Dante first encountered, the leopard—Dante's symbol for the sins of self-indulgence. If the parallels were merely accidental they should be the more intriguing for their psychological implications. The point, however, concerning the relationship between "Prelude" and the rest of *In a Green Night* is that Walcott creates a persona who controls his reactions to the world that passes before his eyes; and he turns his eye inward as well, to analyze the mysterious workings of his own soul.

"A City's Death by Fire," also reprinted from *25 Poems,* is about the devastating fire that swept through Castries when Walcott was a child. With its obvious debt to the style of Dylan Thomas and its prevalent Christian references, it is a good representative of the first stage of Walcott's creativity. It begins: "After that hot gospeller had levelled all but the churched sky, / I wrote the tale by tallow of a city's death by fire" (14). In stark images—"the bird-rocked sky," clouds as "bales /

Torn open by looting"—nature reflects the torment of men whose lives have suddenly been snapped. In the closing sestet, however, through faith and Christ the fiery death is transformed into a redemptive baptism.

Even with the literary borrowing in this poem, there is a feeling of honest sincerity in the expression. In some poems, like "Choc Bay" and "A Sea-Chantey," the prettily smooth flow of language and glib imagery convey the impression of travel posters. In "Choc Bay" a hawk is a mote in the sun's eye and there are "herds" of bright fish in the spray. "A Sea-Chantey" is a catalog of alliterative names, scenic vistas, sounds, and conceits. Neither is bad poetry, but they are too light to carry conviction. At least "A Sea-Chantey" makes no pretensions to being more than an evocative picture. The thought in "Choc Bay" reduces to the plaintive,

> All that I have and want are words
> To fling my griefs about,
> And salt enough for these eyes.

(25)

On their own, poems like these that concentrate on the physical environment are sufficient. It is just that they do not stand as well in comparison with a poem like "Nearing La Guaira." Here, casual inquiry into the meaning of a place-name—he is told it means nothing—triggers in the questioner's mind a series of associations between specific things and the meanings attached to them. Even when he wants to play with an idea, as he does in "A Country Club Romance," description economically becomes a delightful blending of metaphor and fact. This Audenesque poem, which was entitled "Margaret Verlieu Dies" in *Poems,* takes on a more immediately recognizable social cast with the title change. The "Club" is as much an institution as is tennis, the polite game about which this poem revolves. Another welcome improvement is more concrete language. In the revised text the lines "Her vigour, tanned and bare / Was pure as Govt. Bonds,"[16] become "Her thighs, so tanned and bare / Sounder than Government Bonds." Logic dictates that thighs tan far more easily than vigor does; the satiric thrust of the poem makes "sounder" rather than "pure" the preferable term. Miss Gautier, whose thighs are the subject of comparison, concentrates her highly proper life on tennis. Her fatal mistake is to fall in love with and marry a black Barbadian player named Harris. The fact that she is ostracized soon makes their life together unbearable. The breakdown is unfolded in a series of tennis puns exaggerated so far as to constitute an elaborate conceit. She bears him twins, "a fine set / Of doubles"; when she takes refuge in whiskey, he gives her his "backhand"; at night he admits that it "serve" us right; at her funeral the Archdeacon will deliver a "powerful service." The puns, the fast-moving rhymed quatrains, and the wry humor all turn "A Country Club Romance" into fine satire.

It is the only sample of pure satire in *In a Green Night*. The closest thing to it is a bit of double irony in the fifth sonnet of the sonnet sequence "Tales of the Islands." The entire sequence deserves attention because it contains many vignettes of island life, but the fifth with its irony and the sixth because of its use of dialect are especially noteworthy.[17] In sonnet "Chapter V" an ancient blood sacrifice is reenacted for the benefit of a visiting anthropologist. The speaker comments on the irony of an occult rite being performed in a Catholic country; there is even a priest present who is "a student / Of black customs" (28). What doubles the irony in the commentator's eye is the fact that the practitioners are really putting on an act; it is the anthropologist and the priest who take the ceremony most seriously: "The whole thing was more like a bloody picnic. . . . Great stuff, old boy; sacrifice, moments of truth." The sonnet "Chapter VI" is perfect in its utilization of both patois and standard English. Exuberance marks the account of a wild party, from "Poopa, da' was a fête!" (28) in the first line through a drunken writer's misquotation of Shelley in the eighth verse. A second tone of voice, reflecting contempt for the writer's affectation, is inserted parenthetically in line 10: "(Black writer chap, one of them Oxbridge guys)." Should any reader undervalue the keen intelligence of the speaker because of his use of dialect leading up to this 10th line, he had best be wary. After this deft transition, the rest of the poem is written in standard English, up to the last lines, where dialect provides a final touch of levity.

> And it was round this part once that the heart
> Of a young child was torn from it alive
> By two practitioners of native art,
> But that was long before this jump and jive.
>
> (28)

The only regionally limited vocabulary words in the first verses are "fête," "pan" (steel drum), and "tests" ("sports" in American slang). Even with the syntactical inversions of the patois, the meaning is clear and the spoken idiom is captured exactly.

Concerning the occasional appearance of patois mixed with formal English in some of Walcott's poetry, Mervyn Morris has noted that there is nothing unnatural or contrived about it. Many West Indians interweave dialect and standard forms in their daily speech.[18] That being the case, Walcott's practice cannot be dismissed as merely exotic or a sop to partisans of the "folk." In this connection, John Figueroa has expressed the fear that many people may attempt to find Walcott's "true voice" only in the nonstandard passages.[19]

A different, equally authentic voice sounds through "A Letter from Brooklyn." This straightforward, unembellished poem illustrates Walcott's increasing ability to separate himself from the influences of Dylan Thomas and the metaphysicals. It begins:

> An old lady writes me in a spidery style,
> Each character trembling, and I see a veined hand
> Pellucid as paper, travelling on a skein
> Of such frail thoughts its thread is often broken.

(53)

These lines are far removed from the calculated images and rhetorical flourishes of "Choc Bay." The spider's web metaphor for the frailty of thought is fresh and convincing. It approaches the new style Walcott mentions in "Islands":

> . . . I seek
> As climate seeks its style, to write
> Verse crisp as sand, clear as sunlight,
> Cold as the curled wave, ordinary
> As a tumbler of island water.

(77)

As "A Letter from Brooklyn" continues, it becomes evident, however, that the heart of the poet is not "cold" even when his adopted tone is "ordinary." Mable Rawlins, the correspondent, writes that she knows his family, and she speaks of his father's death as his having been "called home." Through her genuine simplicity, his lost faith is briefly restored.

Walcott's mask in "A Letter from Brooklyn" is obviously transparent. The device, more and more central to his poetic expression, is crucial to the kind of balance that characterizes his maturing work. His personal voice, like Walt Whitman's, is at once his own and that of a representative spokesman. In "A Far Cry from Africa" he defines not only his dilemma but that of all men whose heritages of blood and culture are divided. The mulatto, descendant of slave and enslaver, must settle with himself his own degree of innocence, of guilt, as is the case with every son of Adam:

> The gorilla wrestles with the superman.
> I who am poisoned with the blood of both,
> Where shall I turn, divided to the vein?
>
> (18)

One possible solution is carried by "Ruins of a Great House," perhaps the finest poem in *In a Green Night*. There is a subtle play on "Great": the main house on a plantation, and a magnificent structure. All that remain are tumbled stones, and an axle and coachwheel silted over with cattle droppings. The acrid smell of dead limes, the original crop on the estate, strikes him as the odor of a leprous empire. Passing references to Greece's marble and Faulkner's South broaden the application of his meditation to include other places and more ancient times. Approaching the ruined house, he meditates that guilt may not have burdened the owners, but they had not been protected from "the worm's rent, / Nor from the padded cavalry of the mouse" (20). His mind then shifts to thoughts of Kipling, who witnessed the ebb of empire, and to the "Ancestral murderers and poets" Raleigh and Drake, who lived during the world's green youth. Another English name, that of John Donne, rises to his attention as he thinks of death and ashes. When it occurs to him one moment that some slave's remains may be buried nearby, he is enraged. But the anger subsides as quickly as it sprang up: his wandering thoughts, laced with fragments of Donne's prose, arrive at the conclusion:

> . . . Albion too, was once
> A colony like ours, "Part of the continent, piece of the main"
> Nook-shotten, rook o'er blown, deranged
> By foaming channels, and the vain expense
> Of bitter faction.

All in compassion ends
So differently from what the heart arranged:
"as well as if a manor of thy friends . . . "

                                                              (20)

Anger, nimble intelligence, compassion: each in its turn contributes to
the clarification of interlocking relationships; but there is no final
answer.

"Ruins of a Great House" contains the sensuous images, the ringing
lines of some of Walcott's more rhetorically indulgent poetry, and yet he
never loses the guiding purpose in this poem. The literary and historical
associations are indispensable, as are the borrowed quotations and the
archaic phrases in the last verses. The "ashen prose" of Donne belongs in
the West Indies, as does the green night of Andrew Marvell's
"Bermudas," the poem that provides the title of Walcott's book.
Marvell's lush New World has aged and the fabled Eden has not fulfilled
its promise. Walcott says as much in the title poem, "In a Green Night"
(73). He is perceptive enough to recognize that the fault is assignable to
humanity, not just to European imperialists.

Many sources feed into Walcott's poetry, but when they merge as
they do in the context of "Ruins of a Great House" and "In a Green
Night" the question of their "Europeanness" seems unimportant, little
more than an academic matter. It would be far more profitable, as
Mervyn Morris suggests, if critics would attend more disinterestedly to
what Walcott has to say, whatever his chosen style: "The central content
of Walcott's verse is not much examined. The accusers [who claim he is
not West Indian enough] get stuck with allusions to world literature or
with stylistic influences. Poems which happen to be about death, love,
evil, art, the loss of faith, are not relevant enough for those who find
compassion or complex ambiguity decadent luxuries in our emerging
society, and call instead for poems which speak stridently of politics, class
and race."[20] Walcott deals with internal issues, which are usually far-
reaching, rather than with causes, which have a habit of turning out to
be rather limited. Jamaican playwright Errol Hill, in fact, seizes on this
point to argue that it makes Walcott the major force that he is in both
poetry and drama: "Whereas most other playwrights begin with a locale
cluttered with images of temporal value, Walcott begins with a vision of
man. It is this vision that gives his plays a dimension lacking in many
playwrights of the region, it is this that makes him not only a major poet
but the major dramatist of the West Indies."[21]

Henri Christophe

Although critical opinion has accorded Walcott's poetry greater acclaim than his drama, from the outset he has shown commitment to both genres. As a matter of fact, many of his plays are written in verse or in a prose that evokes at times the sound of poetry. He has said that his first real involvement in theater was in 1950, when at his brother's request he wrote *Henri Christophe,* a play about the Haitian revolution.[22] That would make his career in drama commence some three years after the appearance of his first collection of poems. The dates are close, but Walcott's claim disregards at least six other plays he wrote between 1947 and 1950.[23] Some of these have become lost completely, and others remain only in incomplete manuscript form. Out of necessity, then, the study of Walcott's career as a dramatist must begin with the play he regards as his first, *Henri Christophe*—and it is written in verse.

Errol Hill's observation that Walcott begins with a vision of man is well taken. This starting point is both a strength and a weakness in his early plays. Just as the youthful Walcott had envisioned himself following in the poetic line of the metaphysicals and Milton, he sought high models for his plays as well. When he reflects back on the writing of his first play in the essay "What the Twilight Says," Walcott recalls the dilemma he faced: "At nineteen, an elate, exuberant poet madly in love with English, but in the dialect-loud dusk of water-buckets and fish-sellers, conscious of the naked, voluble poverty around me, I felt a fear of that darkness which had swallowed up all fathers. Full of precocious rage, I was drawn, like a child's mind to fire, to the Manichean conflicts of Haiti's history."[24] He felt the call of negritude in Césaire and Fanon at the time, and he suffered over what he considered to be the tragic blackness of the heroes of the Haitian revolution. His ambivalence arose out of the European perspective from which he viewed the events of history, and his use of the English language, the only medium of expression that he felt was adequate for recording his thoughts. Looking back, he admits the fustian of his Jacobean style in *Henri Christophe,* "its cynical, aristocratic flourish," yet he explains that it came naturally to him.[25] He conceived of one race rebelling against the god of a more powerful race.

Had his loyalties not been divided in this manner, he might have chosen Toussaint for his protagonist. Instead he chose Henri Christophe, whose exploits were no more heroic than Toussaint's, but who also possessed hamartia, an essential element for classical tragedy. Christophe's tragic flaw was pride. He and Dessalines resorted to intrigue and betray-

al to remove Toussaint from their path to power. *Henri Christophe* opens
with these treacherous generals awaiting news of Toussaint's death. It
follows the basic historical events of Dessalines's bloody rule, culminat-
ing in his being unseated by Christophe and ending with the tyrannical
Christophe commiting suicide in the final scene. Growing beyond the
simple chronicle of slaves in revolt, it becomes an account of racial
vengeance, of man's egomanic desire to impose his will on others. The
plot unfolds in Haiti and concerns black characters for the most part but
there is little else to mark the play as West Indian. A quotation from
Hamlet and another from *Richard III*, heading respectively each of the
two parts of the play, are in keeping with the language Walcott puts into
the mouths of illiterate ex-slaves. Dessalines bids a messenger to proceed
with his tale: "Be eloquent without elaboration; / Talk quickly."[26]
Christophe's effusion is even more overblown when he speaks of
Toussaint's death:

> Fold up your hopes to show them to your children,
> Because the sun has settled now
> Behind the horizon of our bold history.
> Now no man can measure the horizon
> Of his agony; this grief is wide, wide,
> A ragged futility that beats against these rocks, like
> Sea-bell's angelus.
> The man is dead, history has betrayed us.
>
> (10)

The major problem with the play is the Jacobean polish on words and
images that seems inconsistent with the rough-hewn dignity of the characters being portrayed. When Christophe utters fine poetic lines about
his grief, the sentiment rings hollow more because of his archaic language than for the fact that Christophe himself plotted Toussaint's
destruction. Even allowing for poetic license, there is nothing in this play
to show the bodily sweat that Christophe celebrates shortly before his
death: "The nigger smell, that even kings must wear / Is bread and
wine to life" (50). Nevertheless, G. A. Holder reports that the February
1951 BBC radio broadcast under Errol Hill's direction was captivating
for the beauty and vividness of its poetry.[27]

Harry Dernier

Noticeably lacking in Walcott's first play are modulation of feeling and differentiation of character. In his second drama he avoids these weaknesses and also the problem of the discrepancy between character and style of presentation. *Harry Dernier,* a tour de force for radio production, though markedly literary and metaphysical in tone, achieves greater unity by the expedient of having only one player and placing him in an unidentifiable location. The reduction in cast does not signal the narrowing of Walcott's scope, as it might at first suggest. Instead of drawing imposing figures from history, he projects into the future to create the last man on Earth. His classical affiliations are evident as well: an introductory quotation from *The Inferno* on the torment of carnal sinners, the approximation of T. S. Eliot's language from *The Waste Land.* With all other men dead, Dernier, the ultimate wastelander, is left alone to contemplate the existential questions about the essence of life, death, sin, God, and his own particular being.

Performance time is a brief 20 minutes, but the history of mankind passes through his mind in a catalog of names from Adam to Einstein, ranging over artists, scientists, philosophers, and the Greek gods. Dernier's greatest temptation, provoked by a female voice, is to re-create life. The voice of "Lily the Lady" represents the life force and also the principle of civilization, which paradoxically has driven man toward his own destruction. The confirmed misanthrope Dernier repudiates Lily:

> Haven't you seen plagues, explosions, man's knowledge?
> Surely the womb is the meaning of war.
> Repent, repent . . . I will not be tempted again.   .   .   .
>   .   .   .
> Our sin is flesh.[28]

He and Lily search for causes of the holocaust using terms from Christian tradition. He suggests pride. Punning heavily, Lily refers to the biblical tree of knowledge:

> .   .   . Why did the world end?
> Sin, I suppose, they new too much,

Aeonstain, and Openhimmel . . . It's a nightmare, like one of
    those
Desert island gags. But I'm alive.

(7)

Dernier is frustrated with the divergent attractions of the positive–negative forces that will not let him rest. Lily is not actually alive; her voice is
but one side of his own thinking. Even though he cannot bear his loneliness, he will not accept the responsibilities and guilt inherent in the
choices of life.

Walcott's themes and attitudes in the plays, as in his early poetry, are
predominantly weighty and somber, probing psychological motivations
and philosophical questions. It is as though he skirts the middle ground,
feeling comfortable only with the high seriousness of Jacobean English
or the wry intellectualism of more recent European writers. The spelling
puns with words and names in *Harry Dernier,* for example, have to be
seen and contemplated rather than heard to be appreciated. There is an
emotional restraint, an abstract dryness, about *Henri Christophe* and
Harry Dernier that prevents their taking on a full-bodied life.

The Sea at Dauphin

By comparison, Walcott's third drama, *The Sea at Dauphin* (1954), is
vibrant with the sounds of life. *The Sea at Dauphin* is Walcott's first folk
play and it is also the most perfectly executed of his early dramas. It
would be tempting to assume that the effectiveness derives from his turning to the setting of St. Lucia and to the language he has heard spoken
since childhood. These are important factors; but far more crucial to him
during this apprenticeship phase was his discovery of a precedent-setting
model in the work of Irish writer John Millington Synge. Walcott has
admitted his debt to *Riders to the Sea,* and he could hardly have found a
more instructive example to follow.[29] Synge, in prefacing *The Playboy of
the Western World,* acknowledges the influence on his work of the language
and folk imagination of the fishermen, peasants, and ballad singers along
the Irish coast: "In a good play every speech should be as fully flavoured
as a nut or apple, and such speeches cannot be written by anyone who
works among people who have shut their lips on poetry."[30] In the West
Indies, as in Synge's Ireland, the folk idiom and imagination continue to
thrive. There is a current in plays like *Riders to the Sea* and *The Sea at
Dauphin* that is elemental, close to the sources of life.

In these plays the sea represents the unpredictable forces of nature with which men have to contend for their lives. Theirs is a daily battle which, if unspectacular, is still no less heroic than the Promethean theft of fire from the gods. Such a comparison is not as unwarranted as it sounds on the surface. Walcott's Afa, a fisherman, works hard and receives little return; he recounts the litany of his failures and of the fishermen who have died, but even in the face of inevitable defeat he defies the sea and the god who ignores his prayers.

> God is a white man. The sky is his blue eye,
> His spit on Dauphin people is the sea.
> Don't ask me why a man must work so hard
> To eat for worm to get more fat. Maybe I bewitch.
> You never curse God, I curse him, and cannot die,
> Until His time.[31]

The name of Afa's boat, *Our Daily Bread,* is both metaphor and literal fact. Afa's recitation of the names of fishermen who have lost their lives at sea is a chronicle of the village's past. Growing out of this blending of metaphor and reality is an image of the cyclical nature of existence. Individuals come and pass; their legacy is the name and the memory they leave behind. Their collective record spells out the terms of Dauphin life. During the action of the play one aged man, Hounakin, chooses death in the sea over continued suffering. What saves the plot from tragedy and sends it off into yet another cycle is the appearance of young Jules. Jules, son of Habal, the man who first took Afa out to sea, comes to him seeking work. At this point Afa, childless, an intractable curmudgeon, begins the initiation of the next generation. Delivering his acceptance to Jules's advocate he says, "tell the boy it make you sour and old and good for nothing standing on two feet when forty years you have. . . . Ask him if he remember Habal, and then Bolo. If he say yes, tell him he must brave like Hounakin, from young he is. Brave like Habal to fight sea at Dauphin. This piece of coast is make for men like that. Tell him Afa do it for his father sake" (76). With its fullness of character and theme and its terse, simple development, *The Sea at Dauphin* is a fine one-act play. According to Slade Hopkinson, the problems of comprehending the St. Lucian French-English patois are readily overcome through enactment on stage.[32]

Ione

Ione (1957) moves deeper into St. Lucian folk tradition with the introduction of a greater number of characters, including an old prophetess, Theresine. Passions run high in this play, and the presence of the supernatural is emphasized not only by Theresine, but also by the almost casual manner in which Ione, her sister Helene, and others court disaster. They function according to drives and feelings that are greater than they can control. The central conflict is between two mountain families over land. Their uneasy peace turns to violence because of marital infidelity, pride, and the thirst for revenge. Several details such as talk of the remnants of noble African ancestry, the rights of the stronger rival to dominate the land, the appearance of a "civilized" black schoolteacher who claims immunity to the tribal conflict, and the blond American who has abandoned Ione with his unborn child, all contribute to the definition of place in this drama.

At the same time, in spite of the concreteness of local setting, character, and idiom, there are also elements that generate a pervasive tone reminiscent of Grecian classics: the inevitability of brooding fate (personified in the oracle Theresine), the chorus of women, and the Greek names of several of the characters. Like Teiresias, Theresine can foresee but is helpless to prevent impending doom. The brothers Victorin and Alexandre have hated each other too long for there to be reconciliation. One of the two lines of action concerns the Alexandre faction's demand for blood revenge over the death of Diogene at the hands of Achille Victorin. Achille had caught his wife, Helene, with Diogene and in his rage killed not only his rival but his own infant son as well. The second line of plot follows Ione's growing anguish as it becomes obvious that her American lover will never return to legitimatize their union. The interwoven action rises steadily to Ione's face-saving suicide and the catastrophic battle that will annihilate both tribes. Theresine's judgment in the final line provides a curt epitaph: "The bravery has begun."[33]

Walcott treats marital infidelity, familial strife, and personal pride within a remote mountain settlement with the same tragic high seriousness he accords Christophe. Such lofty elevation could degenerate into melodrama if, in production, the deep-seated emotional forces are not convincingly portrayed. Walcott ventures beneath the external simplicity of lives narrowly circumscribed by accidents of birth and history to explore their potential for great drama. The actions of despotic slave-kings and of downtrodden fishermen may be disparate in the impact of their influence on history, but they are equal in what they reveal about the dimensions of human behavior.

Drums and Colours

Drums and Colours (1958), Walcott's fifth play, exploits these dimensions by presenting characters of legendary proportion side by side with representatives of countless little men whose legacy is their ability to survive. The juxtaposition is subtle but effective, and quite revealing. Scene 1, set in 1499, has Christopher Columbus returning to Europe in chains, wondering what will become of the world he discovered. A passenger on his ship is Paco, a half-breed Amerindian who is learning that the conqueror's faith is valued in gold.[34] An officer gives him a coin that becomes a linking device throughout the drama. Ten years later in Cadiz, Paco comes into contact with slave traders on their way to the New World. Among the slaves is a dying tribal king. He does not live through the middle passage, but he is survived by his son Mano, who becomes one of the thousands of African transplants in the West Indies.

The second legendary figure to enter the drama is the young Walter Raleigh. Leaning on poetic license, Walcott has him discover the fable of El Dorado from the lips of Paco in his dying moments. Paco leaves Raleigh with his old Spanish coin and the prediction that searching for the golden city will cause his death (40). When Paco's coin next appears, it is in the possession of Jeremy Ford, an insignificant carpenter who dies along with Raleigh's son off the coast of Guiana. Pointing up the irony of these men wasting their lives in pursuit of fame and wealth, a Spanish captive muses:

> Again and again, the plot of conquest follows
> The hollow carcass of the drum of reputation,
> Who weeps for Jeremy Ford?

(53)

Part 1 of the play ends with a split interlude. In one comic situation a Barbadian servant, house-proud and jealous of the dignity of imperial rule, castigates a drunken British seaman for conduct unbecoming a guardian of colonial decency. The second scene is Raleigh's death cell in the Tower of London. Humor again enters in the form of puns and wordplay to lighten the dark moment. Raleigh's image as a courtier makes

believable his joking about losing his head; but there is no excuse when
Raleigh's priest suggests that he prepare "for the fatal sea, / To that
Virginian voyage, death's *New Foundland*" (56, italics mine).

The second half of the play, entitled "Rebellion," begins with the
Haitian revolution. Napoleon's brother-in-law, General Leclerc, reflects
the disillusionment that often follows the erosion of fond dreams. He has
seen what came of the French Revolution and he predicts the result of
the slave rebellion:

> There will not be liberty but mere patterns of revenge.
> The history of man is founded on human nature, and
> We cannot exorcise the guilt of original sin.
>
> (61)

Leclerc's foresight is borne out when in scene 12 the victorious slave-
generals Christophe and Dessalines are plotting to betray Toussaint to
their French enemies.

From Haiti the scene passes next to Jamaica. In 1833 there are no
more discoverers and conquerors, no more brilliant campaigns like those
of Toussaint. The circumstances of Jamaica's rebellious leaders are considerably reduced. George William Gordon, a white man, is hanged
from a yardarm for publicly advocating emancipation. The leader who
gets more attention is a Maroon guerrilla named Mano—direct descendant of the orphaned slave who made the middle passage in 1510.
Another link with the past comes through Calico, one of Mano's recruits.
Calico has inherited Paco's Spanish coin, which has been passed down
through his family since it was discovered on the body of Jeremy Ford.

Mano's band is a cross section of West Indian society: Calico, a ruined
white planter; Yette, his mulatto mistress; Pompey, a black fugitive;
Ram, an East Indian; and Yu, the Chinese cook. In a brief skirmish with
a detachment of English soldiers, the band is temporarily driven off, but
they return to search for Pompey, who did not make his escape. The
entire last scene is played in mock-seriousness so that the battle,
Pompey's apparent death, and his impromptu funeral ceremony become
not a catastrophe but the prelude to final celebration. The humor does
not, however, preclude an underlying truth. Over the body of his fallen
comrade, Mano asserts that "Pompey was as good as any hero that pass
in history" (98). When Ram becomes maudlin and searches for words to
explain Pompey's universal significance, Walcott's good sense in leaven-

ing the script with comedy is borne out. Yette shatters Ram's self-congratulatory rhetoric by reminding everyone that they are merely actors in a play. Pompey attempts to play his death longer than he is supposed to, but his game is ruined when Ram criticizes his acting. Unable to bear the gibes, Pompey leaps to his own defense. The curtain closes on a jubilant Carnival.

Drums and Colours, which marks Walcott's departure from the earlier apprenticeship plays, is a West Indian historical pageant commissioned for the opening of the First Federal Parliament of the West Indies in 1958. Because of the requirements of spanning 400 years of history, the play ranges too broadly to be truly unified. To aid continuity, Walcott utilizes for the first time an element of West Indian life that has never entered into his earlier plays. In addition to the coin as a linking device and the character names that recur, he frames the episodic action of the basic plot and provides interludes between scenes with a band of carnival dancers. The songs, dances, and antics of these celebrants exemplify the panache of West Indian life that rises above the brutal history of the islands. By including fundamental properties of Carnival—music, dance, masking, pageantry, mime, and parody—Walcott moves significantly nearer to the kind of drama that is adequate to express the rich diversity of his cultural experience.

Shades of Icarus

Walcott's next play, *Ti-Jean and His Brothers,* was conceived in the same year with *Drums and Colours,* but except for their closeness in time and certain technical similarities the two plays belong to separate stages of Walcott's career. *Drums and Colours* is a loosely constructed, somewhat didactic pageant. In spite of good character studies and convincing scenes, it lacks the kind of concentration that is desirable in drama. Such weaknesses may be unavoidable, considering the purpose for which the play was written. It is important in Walcott's career for two reasons: for the first time he opens his stage to a vast array of visual and audile experiences; second, he brings together his most prevalent character types. Walcott's little men, Mano and Pompey, call forth the unsuspected strength and grace residing in the lowest stations of life—as in *The Sea at Dauphin.* On the other hand, his men of importance, Raleigh and Toussaint, reveal the intellectual and emotional ambivalence that drives men to greatness, and beyond, to failure—as in *Henri Christophe.*

These central characters give focal interest to the themes of Walcott's drama. It is not so easy to determine a similarly cohesive factor in his early poetry. He ranges widely, sampling the nuances of language and styles of expression. His themes vary from the difficult memories of youth to contemplation of the leveling effect of death. The most characteristic image is perhaps that of Icarus—an Icarus after Stephen Dedalus, whom Walcott claimed as his hero during the early 1950s.[35] Like Icarus, Walcott is the son of a craftsman. He chose to pursue the career of an artist, despite his obscure birthplace and the color of his skin. His presumption in defying the odds against success might be compared with Icarus's act of taking wing toward the sun and with Stephen Dedalus's blasphemous defiance of society and religion. Icarus and Dedalus are alluded to directly in several places; equally important are the recurring images of men daring bravely and suffering their losses. Like Icarus, Walcott is also inclined to experiment with the artistic inventions of his predecessors—to try their wings, until he has made them his own.

Chapter Three

Castaway in His Workshop: 1958–1967

New York and Trinidad

No particular event signals Walcott's emergence from his apprenticeship years, yet a definite new phase of his career began in 1958. It was in his capacity as playwright that Walcott most evidently advanced beyond his earlier work. During the 10 years from 1958 through 1967 Walcott continued writing—two books of poetry published, four new dramas produced—but, perhaps more important than such signs of his personal growth, he used these years to lay almost single-handedly the foundation for professional theater in the West Indies. By 1967 he had completed early versions of the play that has come to be one of his most famous: *Dream on Monkey Mountain*. In August of the same year a milestone was achieved when Walcott's Trinidad Theatre Workshop became the first company of West Indian actors to tour outside the Caribbean.[1]

The year 1958 is especially significant in Walcott's development. He spent a few days in 1957 and then several months in 1958 in New York on a Rockefeller Fellowship, studying under José Quintero and visiting theaters such as the Phoenix and the Circle in the Square. His experiences of the metropolis were both positive and negative, but he turned them all to advantage. During his first short stay in New York he wrote *Ti-Jean and His Brothers*. Loneliness and fear, he says, were what drove him to a period of frenzied writing. The results were the same as if he had been moved by inspiration. He had never written so rapidly and he was astonished: "For the first time I used songs and dances and a narrator in a text. . . . Out of that play, I knew what I wanted."[2]

Another negative factor that eventually proved helpful was that he discovered on the New York stage what he did *not* want. He did not want a literary play, with the emphasis on words; and he did not want detailed psychological character exposition.[3] Coupled with this recognition, he sensed the absence of stage material suitable for black actors in general. Out of growing despair with this situation, he determined to cut short his stay in New York, return to the West Indies, and establish an acting company according to his own design.

When Walcott left for Trinidad in 1958 he knew what he was reacting against and he also had definite ideas about the requisites for an indigenous West Indian theater. The inveterate assimilator, he found the necessary elements to complete his design in the culture of his native islands; in the stagecraft of Bertolt Brecht, which he studied carefully during his months in New York; in the Broadway musical; and through Brecht, in the conventions of Oriental theater. All of these disparate elements are cast against Walcott's education in the European classics, and Brecht was the catalyst allowing the process of assimilation to proceed smoothly. Fortunately for the critic who is interested in the development of Walcott's version of West Indian theater, the process is touched on frequently in his articles and particularly in the regular newspaper column he began writing for the *Trinidad Guardian* in 1959, the same year in which he founded the Trinidad Theatre Workshop.

Blending Carnival and Brecht

What he had discovered almost by accident, in the writing of *Ti-Jean and His Brothers,* came into focus while he was in New York, and gradually took definite shape over the following years. The folk legend that provides the story for *Ti-Jean and His Brothers,* the narrator, the songs, and the dances originate in his native islands. He remembered the African storyteller tradition from St. Lucia, "a slave tradition adapted to the environment, the slaves kept the strength of the stories about devils and gods and the cunning of certain figures."[4] Also prevalent in his background are the pageantry of Carnival, the sounds of calypso and picong. Carnival, which was adopted from European religious ceremonies, is infused in the Caribbean with the special rhythms and slave-originated raillery of calypsonians. Reflecting on this pre-Lenten celebration in an article entitled "Carnival Spirit a Contempt for Material Treasures," Walcott observed that slaves and their descendants ridicule (or "picong") each other in mock quarrels that are in reality indirect attacks aimed at their owners, high society, or government. In his opinion, therefore, Carnival becomes the opposite of a religious rite: . . . "[I]t is a gigantic, deliberate folly. . . . The polysyllabic, surrealist, free-form rhetoric of robber talk is a parody of Biblical or English literature, just as the involved, infinite spelling examination of the Pierrot Grenade is a parody of mission school education and the magistrate's court."[5]

As Errol Hill has noted, calypsonians and other members of their masked bands are expected to sing, dance, make speeches, enter into set confrontations, act out dramatic situations, engage in conflict, parody current and historical events, and execute mimed sequences.[6] Hill contends that the history of Trinidad Carnival is the history "of a common people's struggle for freedom of expression," and that by the year 1919 "[w]ithout question, carnival had become a symbol of freedom for the broad mass of the population . . . rooted in the experience of slavery and in celebration of freedom," and was thus no longer dependent on its European antecedents.[7]

The culture in which Walcott grew to manhood was, like the area's calypso, derived from a variety of sources. When he envisioned himself and his role as an artist, he took this basic duality into account. "I am a kind of split writer. . . . The mimetic, the narrative, and dance element is strong on one side, and the literary, the classical tradition is strong on the other." Furthermore, he continues on the same subject, "Our most tragic folk songs and our most self-critical calypsos have a driving, life-asserting force. Combine that in our literature with a long experience of classical forms and you're bound to have something exhilarating."[8] By 1970, when he was recording these ideas, he felt that his acting company had achieved a significant fusion of styles: a powerful physical expression combined with classic discipline. Efforts toward that end began back in New York, in 1958.

At the outset he confronted what he considered to be the major flaw in West Indian art, "the sin of exuberance, of self-indulgence." To obtain the order, timing, and precision that were necessary to the kind of theater he wanted, his initial aim with the Theatre Workshop was to instill discipline. With a group of young actors and actresses he thus entered a period of instruction that was to last for seven years. His program included exercises in method acting and experimental improvisations whereby he and the company explored their potentials. The first strong point to emerge was the stage presence of his actors, their physical expressiveness.[9] In order to understand the use he wished to make of that powerful talent, it would be best to consider the lessons he had picked up from his study of Brecht.

Walcott respected Brecht's unencumbered clarity and his restraint. Brecht's theory of alienation (*Verfremdungseffekt*), the separating of "the actor from the role which he portrays so that its meaning, not its emotion, can be considered," provided the impetus toward discipline.[10] Equally important was the example Brecht set in utilizing Oriental techniques: "In New York, I came to the Chinese and Japanese classic theatre through Brecht." In reading the texts of classical Oriental plays, in observing the woodcuts of Hokusai and Hiroshige, then viewing films by the Japanese director Kurosawa such as *Ugetsu* and *Rashomon,* Walcott gained insight into working models.[11] All the parts did not fall into place immediately, but by 1964 in a *Guardian* article he could translate what he had learned in terms that applied to his West Indian company. In "The Kabuki . . . Something to Give to Our Theatre," he spells out some interesting parallels. Although the Kabuki is more rigidly set by tradition than is the calypso, which allows for freer interpretation and improvisation within the framework of a limited rhythm, they both assist narrative development through meaningful gestures and bodily movements. There are latent possibilities in the ritualistic steps derived from the Yoruban Shango cult or other ceremonial African dances transported to the Americas such as the belair, bongo wake dance, and calinda. The calinda, which grew out of call-response worksongs, can be quite belligerent and frequently accompanies stick-fight duels. In some of these the shuffle of the hands and the significant pauses resemble characteristic movements of Japanese dancers. Walcott saw in the bongo wake dance a momentary pause that is like the arrest of the Kabuki's "mie," where the actor's crossed legs signify controlled violence.[12] It was this bongo step that crystallized the kind of movement he desired. Building on it, he guided the company toward dances that were spontaneous, yet precise, having more to do with acting than with pure dance. Elaborating on the concept in "Meanings," he stresses the virility of the movement: "It is a very foot-asserting, earth-asserting, life-asserting dance. . . . there is all the male strength that I think has been absent for a long time in Western theatre. . . . In a theatre where you have a strong male principle, or where women aren't involved . . . [in its formative beginnings], a kind of style will happen; there will be violence, there will be direct conflict, there will be more physical theatre and there will be less interest in sexual psychology."[13] Elsewhere he expands the application, perhaps interpreting his mentor too freely. In his *Guardian* article "National Theatre Is the Answer," he says Brecht advocates a theater as physically exciting as the boxing ring, with audience participation as voluble as that which occurs in West Indian cinema houses. Never at a loss for finding precedent in other parts of the world for what he wants to attempt, Walcott foresaw a repertoire for local audiences that would be close to West Indian experience but would combine "the lyricism and savagery of Lorca, the Jacobeans, Brecht's 'Threepenny Opera.' " His national theater would have "the rawness and crudity of Elizabethan or Greek staging," and could be popular, fresh, and powerful.[14]

This prospect may appear somewhat grandiose, and the comparisons may seem to exaggerate peculiar aspects of foreign cultures, but it should be remembered that Walcott was addressing a skeptical public, people who have a provincial distrust of things produced locally and who typically prefer to rely on some form of authoritative precedent.

On a more basic level, Walcott has merely indicated the available resources. The underlying formula was at hand in the Kabuki dance-drama, in the bare stage and musical accompaniment of the Noh theater. The refined subtlety of Oriental art, he discovered, was not alien to his own culture. "What it parallels in our folk-lore and dance is its primitive mythology, its devils, thief-heroes, old-men and witch-figures, and most strikingly of all, its masks." Carnival masqueraders and the characters of local folk legend are as archetypal as the stock figures of Noh theater.[15] In the West Indies there is a ready-made audience, familiar with the traditional plots and figures of oral tales, accustomed to expressive gestures, mime, and the music and dance of the streets.

One of the dangers in adapting folk forms to staged productions is that the writer may settle for the pretentiousness of pseudo-African or nightclub folk routines. Walcott warns against this in "Patterns to Forget," a column he wrote in 1966, analyzing various approaches to an authentic West Indian musical. The first two approaches are through dances set to drum chants and "folk-ballets" with a strong narrative content. In the hands of amateurs, attempts may be made to re-create cultists engaged in their Shango and pocomania frenzies. Walcott draws a distinction between reenactment and a choreographer's imaginative simulation of spiritual possession. Conscious simulation "draws the dancer closer to acting, and acting emphasises dramatic development." The folk-ballet, in its sophisticated form, draws away from speech and song and is closer to mime: examples occur in the arrangements of Martha Graham and George Balanchine. West Indian choreographers influenced in their direction, at least according to Walcott, are afraid of losing the spontaneity, individuality, and elation that are the virtues of West Indian expression. Walcott trusts that the essential pattern is strong enough to survive the choreographer's translation of it into artistic metaphor. Successful productions have been carried off by Beryl

McBurnie in Trinidad and by Rex Nettleford and Eddie Thomas in Jamaica.

A third approach to the West Indian musical has been through the formula for American musicals. To work properly, the songs and dances should not be extraneous to the action: they should be "dance-dramatizations," the heart of the play itself. Finally, for Walcott's preferred approach, there is the classic Oriental theater. In Kabuki, each segment of the performance is equally relevant; neither plot, character, nor theme dominates. It differs from the folk ballet and the American musical in that a narrator-chorus dances the action.[16] He returns, then, in this 1966 article to the premise with which he began in 1958. It is worth noting also that 1966 was the same year in which the Trinidad Theatre Workshop opened its first official season.

Ti-Jean and His Brothers

Walcott generously credits Brecht and Oriental artists for his ideas and inspiration, but in fairness to his own creative abilities reference must be made to the fact that he had already begun to incorporate the elements of Carnival in *Drums and Colours. Ti-Jean and His Brothers,* the drama he says was his first experience of writing a "stylized West Indian play," was completed in 1957. Both plays in fact were written and one was even produced before his enriching period of study in New York. In the note on production history for *Ti-Jean and His Brothers* in the collection *Dream on Monkey Mountain and Other Plays,* Walcott places the original production date in 1958, although his brother Roderick and the St. Lucia Arts Guild had actually presented an early version of the play in December 1957. A second performance came at the Little Carib Theatre, Port-of-Spain, the following year, and other productions— including one by Joseph Papp's New York Shakespeare Festival Theatre company in New York, in 1972—have appeared in the 1980s in several countries.

Ti-Jean and His Brothers is based on a St. Lucian folktale, and Walcott succeeded well with his dramatized version in retaining the storyteller's simple, narrative force. At the same time the play is, as Walcott described it, "stylized." Vestiges of the African animal fable appear in the chorus of forest creatures: Cricket, Firefly, Bird, and their spokesman Frog. Lloyd Coke, whose commentary on a Workshop staging of the play in Jamaica offers valuable insight, argues that from the outset the chorus provides unique ambiguity: "Critics reared on Metropolitan theatre immediately see Greek chorus translated into folk-tale animals. Africanists recognise the village story-teller and keeper of legends, in which the frog is usually a model of sagacity. Both concepts fuse in the actor . . . as they doubtless fused in Walcott's heritage."[17] Walcott encourages the Greek connection when he has Frog enter with the lines "Greek-croak, Greek-croak." Frog sneezes, then excuses himself with the words "Aeschylus me!"[18] Such flippant allusions set a tone, and they are not likely to be missed by West Indians who from childhood become familiar with the rich puns, metaphors, and verbal play of fast-paced calypsonian rhetoric. The surface appearance is light: the movement is paced with music (composed by Andre Tanker), dance, emphatic gesture and pause, asides to the audience, and intervals of conversation among the animals about human behavior. Exposition is quick and varied, but nonetheless serious despite its deceptive simplicity. The allegorical meaning is enhanced, in fact, by the artifice conveying it.

Like the billy goats who meet the troll in the Scandinavian fairy tale, three characters—the brothers Gros Jean, Mi-Jean, and Ti-Jean—confront an embodiment of evil. Papa Bois (the devil) in Walcott's legend is far too formidable an opponent to be overcome by mere brute force as the troll is in the tale. The issues raised are also more complex and subtle. Theodore Colson finds a parable of mankind's various encounters with the devil, "more particularly of black man's confrontation with the white devil." Without overly stressing the color consciousness—the white planter's mask being only one of the devil's disguises, and the most logical considering the setting—Colson has good reason for indicating that the brothers and their mother are archetypal; the context of the play also supports his contention that another character, the Bolom (an unborn fetus), is symbolic of all suppressed human potential.[19] Albert Ashaolu sees no fewer than six levels of allegory: the artistic, historic, political, moral, Christian, and social.[20] Though these are not all of equal significance, they revolve around a focal center that is artistically unified through literary allusion, dance, and other stage conventions. The theme centers on the characters' methods of resisting malignant authority in their struggle to survive and to improve their lot.

Whatever the levels of meaning, the play is mythic in its proportions. The devil, so jaded that he can no longer enjoy his own vices, challenges three brothers to a duel of wills. The one who can move him to rage and pity will be rewarded with wealth, fulfillment, and peace: failure means death, and his flesh will serve as a feast for the devil. As is usual in life, the devil cannot really lose. If none of them can satisfy his desire to experience human emotions, he will at least have three free meals. When the Bolom delivers the devil's proposition to the family, the mother, an earth figure closely attuned to nature, senses evil before it discloses itself. In her capacity as nurturer of living beings, she offers love and compassion even to this aborted creature. The Bolom refuses because the devil has promised him eventually the gift of life.

Gros Jean, the eldest son, is the stereotypical black buck. His mother's admonitions about patience are ignored because, as Frog puts it, he is big but very stupid. Relying on the power of his arm, he also rejects the friendly advice of the animals. Interpreting the contest in terms of success and fame, he assumes that power is the answer. When the white planter (devil) sets him to counting the leaves in a cane field and collecting fireflies, he becomes discouraged after two days, but it is not the work that defeats him. His patience runs out when the devil continually forgets his correct name. This insult to his prowess is beyond endurance.

Mi-Jean, second in size to his big brother, is only half as stupid. His fatal pride resides in his book knowledge. Frog puns on his mental capacity, accompanied by comical music:

> When he going and fish,
> Always forgetting the bait,
> So between de bait and debate . . .

(87)

It is debate that finally undoes Mi-Jean. Flattery does not move him. He manages most of the planter-devil's assigned tasks well except for tying up an especially obstreperous goat. His main defense is to answer with silence the devil's annoying attempts to draw him out. It works until his opponent argues that the goat thinks and has as much a soul as man. Barely controlling his exasperation, Mi-Jean responds, "when you animadvertently imbue mere animals with an animus or soul, I have to call you a crooked-minded pantheist. . . . No, I'm not vexed, you know, but . . ." (129). Bush scholar to the end, he reveals the speciousness of his learning through his inept use of ostentatious words and his reversion to a dialect when the devil seizes him.

Ti-Jean has neither physical power nor extensive learning. His strength, ironically, is in his very lack of outstanding attributes. Humble rather than puffed up with pride, and willing to learn, he listens to his mother's voice of experience and to the instinctive wisdom of nature's lowest animals. When the Bolom warns that Ti-Jean must die in turn, the mother only admits that by giving birth she also assured the death of each of her sons. Firefly and Frog explain that although life is hazardous, and natural law decrees that one animal sometimes eats another, nature is not basically evil. By the time he meets the devil, Ti-Jean has developed the ability to face adversity with equanimity and even good humor. Confronted with his brothers' graves and the prospect of his own death, he responds, "Whatever God made, we must consider blessed" (139).

Comfortable moralisms and common sense alone are no match for the devil; at one point, he relishes his anticipated next dish of "man-wit." What he cannot properly calculate is Ti-Jean's irrepressible sense of humor, his nimble trickery. Ordered to tether the goat that kept evading his brother, Ti-Jean simplifies the task by castrating the goat. Sent to the fields to count and classify leaves, Ti-Jean settles for the expedient of burning the plantation before taking his count. Not only does the devil lose his house, but to add insult to injury Ti-Jean roasts his ill-fated goat on the flames. Ti-Jean's roguery causes the devil to laugh and rage in turn. Thus he wins the contest. The devil, however, always a poor loser, concedes grudgingly, threatening to break his agreement unless Ti-Jean can manage to sing while his mother dies. His voice falters as he sings her farewell, but his pain moves the devil to tears. At this point the Bolom, who has begun urging the devil to honor his bargain, pleads with Ti-Jean to request on his behalf the gift of life. The beauty of Ti-Jean's humanity is nowhere more evident than when he unselfishly uses the one wish offered by the devil to help the Bolom. The ambiguity of that gift is that it delivers the fetus into mortality. In spite of the paradoxical linkage of death and life, the Bolom chooses mortality with its joys and sorrows, and he claims Ti-Jean as his brother. Their victory, nevertheless, is a temporary respite. As the devil exits, he cautions Ti-Jean that they will meet again.

Fulfilling the tradition of many animal fables, the action closes with a moral. Frog, the storyteller, has the final word: " . . . so it was that Ti-Jean, a fool like all heroes, passed through the tangled opinions of this life, loosening the rotting faggots of knowledge from old men . . . brother met brother on his way, that God made him the clarity of the moon to lighten the doubt of all travellers through the shadowy wood" (166). No prose summation does justice to the color and movement, the dance, music, and humor of *Ti-Jean and His Brothers*. Since its message and manner of presentation are so uniquely West Indian in flavor, this play stands as Walcott's first technically integrated West Indian drama. It incorporates the major ingredients of his varied culture, including the prominent figures from Walcott's emerging gallery of character types. Overweening pride in strength and knowledge follows the same pattern introduced by the clansmen and the "civilized" teacher in *Ione*. Also, like Theresine the seer in *Ione,* the mother is as closely attuned to the processes of nature as any earth mother. Evil, rather than appearing as a disembodied force or a subconscious drive within a character, is personified in the devil, who in turn assumes the guise of an old man and a white overlord. There to recount the story is the omniscient narrator of oral tradition. More important than all of these, Ti-Jean himself embodies the character of the trickster hero, one of the most popular figures in West Indian stories. Unable to overcome by force of knowledge or physical might, he can endure like his enslaved ancestors by outwitting those who have power. Overall, the play exemplifies the kind of foot-, life-, and earth-asserting force that Walcott called for in "Meanings." It is perhaps his best play between *The Sea at Dauphin* and *Dream on Monkey Mountain.*

Malcochon

Walcott candidly admits that his next play, *Malcochon* (another product of his fertile year in New York, first performed by his brother's company in St. Lucia in 1959), was a deliberate imitation: . . . "[B]ut it was one of those informing imitations that gave me a direction because I could see in the linear shapes, in the geography, in the sort of myth and superstition of the Japanese, correspondences to our own forests and mythology. I also wanted to use the same type of figure found in this material, a type essential to our own mythology. A woodcutter or charcoal burner."[21] After *Ti-Jean and His Brothers,* Walcott's dual focus is still on St. Lucia and increasingly on his recently discovered Oriental models. He had seen Japanese director Akira Kurosawa's film *Rashomon,* a lurid murder story set in feudal Japan. In the film Kurosawa emphasized atmospheric setting and explored the subjective quality of "factual" explanations. His cinematic experimentation provides an ironic sidelight on cultural cross-fertilization because just as he utilized techniques and motifs out of John Ford and Howard Hawks films, American movie makers copied his works in return. His *Seven Samurai* and *Rashomon* became the popular westerns *The Magnificent Seven* (1960) and *The Outrage* (1964).

Kurosawa's influence on *Malcochon* is less pervasive than it was on popular cinema. As Errol Hill points out, Walcott's play opens like *Rashomon,* with a group of people forced to shelter together out of the rain, and is similar in spirit.[22] His imitation began with corresponding primitive character types, an austere setting, and an atmosphere of mystery where things are not always what they seem. Then the play assumed a direction of its own. As Walcott described it,

What I wanted to do was reduce the play almost to an inarticulateness of language. . . . a play made up of grunts and sounds which you don't understand, like you hear at a Japanese film. The words would be reduced to very primal sounds.

But in writing the play another more literary tradition took over, so that I made the figures voluble.[23]

This development was quite natural considering the verbal richness of the public for which he writes, and considering his own preoccupation with the written and spoken word.

Malcochon, subtitled "The Six in the Rain," carries an epigraph from Sophocles: "Who is the slayer, who the victim? Speak!"[24] The characters introduced by the storyteller, the Conteur, include the old man Charlemagne and his nephew Sonson; Popo and his wife, Madeleine; and the aged woodcutter Chantal with his companion, a deaf-mute called Moumou. Because Chantal (the slayer-victim of the epigraph) is old, ugly, and a feared criminal, he stands as a test case for Ti-Jean's statement, "Whatever God made, we must consider blessed" (139). At the time of the action of the play, Chantal's exploits have achieved legendary status. Only old Charlemagne recognizes him and reminds Sonson of the stories about his madness. Popo laughs at his physical condition and wonders if life really holds any monsters since this one has been reduced so far. His levity is cut short by the appearance of a body in the rain-swollen stream nearby. It is the body of the white planter Regis, whom members of the group assume must have been murdered by Chantal.

Taking advantage of their fear, Chantal decides to play a macabre game. In a situation reminiscent of the trial-by-fool scene near the end of Brecht's *The Caucasian Chalk Circle,* the mad woodcutter decides to pass judgment on those who so readily condemn him. What they do not yet know is that he killed Regis to defend Moumou. He intervened just as

the planter would have shot the deaf-mute for having stolen his silver-
ware. Before beginning his interrogation, Chantal warns that the truth
they claim to care about will not be as palatable as they believe.
Threatened with a cutlass, Madeleine confesses her adultery. Pressed to
declare the sentence on his wife, Popo instead declares that in spite of his
mistreatment of her, his love, flawed as it is, will not permit him to condemn her now. Charlemagne has no undisclosed sin to confess. For years
he has borne openly the guilt of having committed adultery with his
brother's wife. He suffers too because he can no longer endure the hatred
of a boy who could be his own son.

Satisfied that he has made his point about guilt and truth, Chantal
ends his mock trial with acquittal. Ironically at that point, the deaf-
mute, whose life he had saved, misinterprets Chantal's intentions and—
believing that he is saving the entire group from murder—stabs Chantal
in the back. Mortally wounded, sensing Moumou's motivation, Chantal
reinforces his point about the deceptive nature of life's appearance: "You
see how a man can have a good meaning and do the wrong thing?"
(202). In this way, layer by layer, the play's complex meaning unfolds.
The slayer who acted to save someone else becomes the victim of the one
he saved.

The truth, of which so much is made in the dialogue, can never be
fully disclosed. All but old Charlemagne desert him in his dying
moments, and by leaving they never get to know the soul within
Chantal. Asked if he needs a priest, Chantal answers in a way that indicates the unsuspected depths of love and beauty that lie buried under his
offensive exterior: "I don't want to shock the priest and make him
believe man can be so wicked. The priest might lose his faith listening to
the madness of an old thief. Only God, who have a strong stomach and
who is a very old man, an old rascal like me who frightening the world,
could understand that. . . . sometime in the morning . . . I did only feel
to roar like a mad tiger. 'Praise be God in His excellence!' " (204–5). In
his final moments Chantal the outcast reveals feelings that he had never
before shared with his fellow man.

Chantal's confession is moving, but it is no more convincing than the
usual deathbed testimony. No attempt is made to explain how he
acquired such sterling philosophical views; and there is nothing to reconcile his underlying thoughtfulness with his lifelong history of antiso-
cial behavior. The plot also suffers in that the catastrophe hinges vitally
on a deaf-mute. Chantal could not have been stabbed so conveniently by
a person capable of hearing the merciful judgment he was in the process

of delivering. The action is possible, but it does not seem as plausible or as well motivated as Walcott is capable of making his drama. Chantal is important, however, in that he is the precursor of Makak in *Dream on Monkey Mountain.*

Selected Poems

In addition to training his young company and writing his regular column for the *Trinidad Guardian,* Walcott also devoted time to poetry during the Workshop years. In 1964 his second major volume, *Selected Poems,* was published. Sixteen of the poems were written after 1960; the remaining 23 are reprinted from *In a Green Night.* One of these latter, "Bronze," which concludes the first section of the book, provides an excellent stepping-off place before the newer poems. "Bronze" is also representative of the period in the late 1950s when Walcott was debating whether to stay in the West Indies and while he was writing plays with characters like Ti-Jean's mother and Chantal. It is a poem about a bronze mask with lineaments in eye, cheek, and bone structure of mixed Amerindian, West African, and perhaps of Egyptian stock. The mask is female, and in comparison with the marble representations of Western beauty—Aphrodite, Diana, Leda—her sexuality is fierce, cunningly sibylline. Hers is the coloring of earth, the earth that eventually swallows all men. She combines the experiential knowledge of Ti-Jean's mother with the elemental savagery of Chantal in a

> . . . monolithic, unforgiving face
> Wrought in a furious kiln, in which each race
> Expects its hundredth dawn.[25]

Her "unforgiving face" signifies not indifference but the relentless comprehension of immortal nature.

"Bronze" and "Origins," the first of the new poems in the book, are related in tone and spirit. Their common theme is the disparate cultural heritage and the foreign racial lines that merge in the West Indies. By the time "Origins" appeared in 1964, Walcott was committed to living in his native Caribbean. In that the poem sorts through foreign influences and goes back in time to seek out a personal history, it is fittingly dedicated to the author of *Cahier d'un retour au pays natal,* Aimé

Césaire. Mervyn Morris reports a comment by Walcott that he wished the poem to be reminiscent of Césaire, Saint-John Perse, and the best of French West Indian poetry.[26] At least he intended to echo artists closer to home. In the same seminar that Morris mentions, however, another poet in attendance, Edward Brathwaite, contended that poems as sophisticated as "Origins" do not address themselves directly enough to the society out of which they grow. Morris, a poet as well as an astute critic, argues that the crucial point is the "level and mode of communication," not the immediacy with which Walcott speaks to a general public: "[I]f we restrict our poets to speaking directly to this [West Indian] society in general, we will never get any deeper than Louise Bennett or The Mighty Sparrow, both superb performers and sharp-eyed, ironic critics but both, by the immediate clarity to which they are committed, limited to external satiric comment. . . . [T]he modes in which they work preclude any deeply personal human expression."[27]

"Origins" is deeply personal while it is at the same time evocative of other poets and far-ranging experiences. Reviewer Robert Mazzocco detects the prophetic quality of Perse's rhetoric, especially in the italicized portions of the poem.[28] Winston Hackett finds "an odyssey through a haze of myths, that culminates in the explorer's passionate self-discovery at green beginnings."[29] Childhood memories of St. Lucia are interspersed among the names of men—Columbus, Hector, Achilles, Ulysses, and Moses—and among places such as Egypt, Guinea, Greece, and Troy. The major difficulty in the poem is that the narrative flow is discontinuous, the voice of racial memory journeying back into the recorded and the unknown recesses of human history.

The point of origin is the sea. For West Indian islanders, the sea is not merely the mythological source; it is the pathless road of no return, "Trace of our exodus across its desert / Erased by the salt winds" (53); it is a surrounding gulf. Columbus made the crossing and in his wake the presence of the original natives was obliterated by European culture. Invoking the name of Moses, another exile, in the second section, the speaker finds himself a "lost animist" having the task of naming things on his own "Between the Greek and African pantheon" (52). Stanza 6 gathers force for the conclusion as the twin-souled people—having the memory of African river spirits and the spirit of the salt ocean—rise from their quietude to shed

> *. . . colonial languor, their old Egyptian sickness, their imitation . . .*
> *. . . The surf has rased that memory from our speech, and*
> *a single raindrop irrigates the tongue.*
>
> (54)

In the final section fresh rain and dew, the natural distillations of rivers and the sea, symbolize the potential for man in his new world. The racial memory, having fathomed its origins, now consecrates man where he finds himself: the sower of grain, the fisherman, those "Whose sweat, touching earth, multiplies in crystals of sugar" (55). The closing lines are Blakean in their vision; the dewdrop prism discloses the multiplicity of color making up white light, and in so doing it annihilates race for those who have earned their place in the world; "Those who conceive the birth of white cities in a raindrop / And the annihilation of races in the prism of the dew" (55). It would be mistaken to interpret this image to mean that racial distinctions should be destroyed. Had the order been reversed, this could be true. As it is, the thrust of the idea is that in the single drop of water, a microcosm of nature, all individuals are part of the whole of mankind. The dewdrop acts as a prism. The sunlight passing through the prism reveals its multiplicity, but the light itself refracted in the water remains intact— the paradox of the one and the many. The contemporary fate of the individual who realizes this existential paradox becomes the subject of the remainder of this book and of Walcott's next book as well.

"Origins" bears a heavy thematic burden. Winston Hackett considers it "immense and amazingly sustained," Walcott's major achievement between *In a Green Night* and *The Castaway*.[30] It is given added prominence by the fact that it alone constitutes part 2 of *Selected Poems*. The title of the first poem following it in part 3 supplies the key image for all of Walcott's poetry during this second phase of his career: "Castaway." In reading this and the poems that follow, it is impossible to avoid the perspective of the artist. Cast away on an island, in the first line the speaker scans the horizon for a sail. Cast away in life, he faces a new beginning on his own: "We end in earth, from earth began. / In our own entrails, genesis" (58). As the creator of his own new life he is in God's position:

> Godlike, annihilating godhead, art,
> And self, I abandon
> Dead metaphors like the almond's leaf-shaped heart.
>
> (59)

"The Swamp" has another kind of exile. Walcott alludes to Hemingway's hero in the short story "Big Two-Hearted River" who is attempting to rebuild his war-shattered life. Hemingway's character is confined to fast, clear shallows in his fishing because the nearby swamp is too black and sinister for him to enter. The unknown future is like the swamp, "Like chaos, like the road / Ahead" (61).

Raw material for construction of the new life depends on the inner man and on his surroundings. "A Tropical Bestiary" indicates some of Walcott's surroundings, each of its subdivisions headed with the name of an exotic animal. Several of these are pointedly aphoristic: "Ibis" uses the captive bird's fading plumage to comment on domesticity that lacks motivating passion; "Man O'War Bird" uses the bird's high-flying observation to muse that "somewhere is an Eye / That weighs the world exactly as it pleases" (65). Each of these makes effective use of imagery and rhythm, but "Sea Crab" is especially interesting because of what it says about style:

> The sea crab's cunning, halting, awkward grace
> Is the syntactical envy of my hand;
> Obliquity burrowing to surface
> From hot, plain sand.

It too voices a moral, one that confirms Walcott's roots in the Caribbean:

> Keep to your ground, though constellations race,
> The horizon burn, the wave coil, hissing,
> Salt sting the eye.
>
> (65)

"Obliquity burrowing to surface" is a far more applicable description of Walcott's style than his earlier assertion in "Islands" (from *In a Green Night*), that he seeks to write verse that is crisp, clear, and ordinary.

"Tarpon" illustrates the increased particularity of description as well as the deeper intricacy of Walcott's poetry. In strict detail the dead fish is examined until, in its every part, it takes on a pervasive beauty. Mervyn Morris cites poems like "Tarpon" and "Sea Crab" in contending that Walcott strives to prune his earlier rhetoric in favor of a verse of greater complexity beneath a surface of more natural-sounding explicitness.[31]

Cameron King and Louis James are impressed that Walcott has grown increasingly objective and that "Not intellectual concepts, but the physical environment of the Caribbean, has become more and more the bedrock of his imagination."[32] As evidence, they quote from "The Swamp," "A Tropical Bestiary," and "Coral."

"The Wedding of an Actress" and "The Glory Trumpeter" turn from the environment to people. Old Eddie blows his trumpet like "Joshua's ram's horn / . . . Of patient bitterness or bitter siege" (73) toward Mobile and Galveston. Across the separating gulf is the speaker's uncle, whom he will never see. The horn blows "For all whom race and exile have defeated." In church for "The Wedding of an Actress," the poet speaks of a spiritual rather than a physical exile. Unable to enter into prayer, the speaker is a detached observer; he meditates on the illusory nature of customs and of life itself:

> We too are actors, who behold
> This ceremony. We hold
> Our breath, defying dissolution;
> Faith, we are told, like art,
> Feeds on illusion.
>
> (75)

Imagination, indispensable to the artist, is a kind of faith that makes life possible even for one "divorced" from belief.

In the final poem of the volume, "Crusoe's Journal," the themes of lost faith, art, and the island setting again emerge. Walcott's presence is identifiable in the poem, but the personal element telescopes into the figure of Robinson Crusoe, the paradigm of castaways. Personal details include the mention of Walcott's deceased father, his own age, his need for rest, and his son's illness at the time of his writing. The setting is Tobago (the place Daniel Defoe selected for his fictional treatment of Alexander Selkirk's shipwreck), where the poet has sought peace and quiet. As a chapel bell tolls, he reflects that he cannot recapture the childlike faith he has outgrown. There is regret at the loss, but pride will not allow his return. No substitute is ever as sufficient as what he has given up, not even his poetry.

Watching a group of worshipers pass, "Friday's progeny, / The brood of Crusoe's slave," he acknowledges his inadequacy to do for them what their own simple faith can accomplish:

> And nothing I can learn
> From art or loneliness
> Can bless them as the bell's
> Transfixing tongue can bless.

(85)

For its candor, its plainspoken images, and its directness, this is the unembellished poetry of things as they are.

From "Castaway" to "Crusoe's Journal," Walcott demonstrates a remarkable degree of balanced objectivity while delving into the heart of what it means to be West Indian, and more than that, what it means to live as an artist in the West Indies. A poet, naturally isolated to some extent from the audience he addresses, is successful only to the extent that he can translate his personal experiences into less private terms. Robinson Crusoe is important to a greater extent than Icarus and Dedalus were as symbols in the 1950s. He is the archetypal center of all Walcott's poetry during the early Workshop years.

Crusoe: The Castaway

Walcott's conscious exploration of the castaway image is emphatically brought out in a lecture entitled "The Figure of Crusoe," which he delivered on the St. Augustine campus of the University of the West Indies.[33] In leading up to his exposition, he speaks of his objective as being the reconciliation of the isolated poet and the world around him. Adopting the Crusoe image for this purpose, Walcott reserves the privilege of using him in a variety of shapes because "they represent various problems organic to West Indian life":

My Crusoe, then, is Adam, Christopher Columbus, God, a missionary, a beachcomber, and his interpreter, Daniel Defoe. He is Adam because he is the first inhabitant of a second paradise. He is Columbus because he has discovered this new world, by accident, by fatality. He is God because he teaches himself to control his creation, he rules the world he has made, and also, because he is to Friday, a white concept of Godhead. He is a missionary because he instructs Friday in the uses of religion. . . . He is a beachcomber because I have imagined him as one of those figures of adolescent literature, some derelict out of Conrad or Stevenson . . . and finally, he is also Daniel Defoe, because the journal of Crusoe, which is Defoe's

journal, is written in prose, not in poetry, and our literature, the pioneers
of our public literature have expressed themselves in prose. (6)

It would be difficult to find better words to explicate "Crusoe's Journal,"
one of the poems Walcott quotes in his lecture, and one of the best
poems in *The Castaway.*

"Crusoe's Journal" describes how the survivor of shipwreck learns to
accommodate himself to a strange environment. Another poem, "The
Almond Trees," touches on the fact that whatever the castaway con-
structs he must build where there is no historical precedent. In his lecture on Crusoe Walcott comments, "I have tried to show that Crusoe's
survival is not purely physical, not a question of the desolation of his
environment, but a triumph of will. . . . We contemplate our spirit by
the detritus of the past" (13). Two of the most prevalent aspects of that
past surface in poems like "Laventville" and "Veranda." Laventville is one
of the hillside shantytowns overlooking Port-of-Spain. As the poet
climbs the hill to attend a christening, he considers the degradation surrounding his fellow inheritors of the middle passage: they are crowded
five to a room like their ancestors massed in the holds of ships. There is
bitter irony in the fact that as he ascends higher above the city, he
descends further into areas of poverty. "Veranda" concerns the divided
ancestry that causes internal splits within Walcott and many of his countrymen. Addressing his white grandfather, he assures him that "your
genealogical roof tree, fallen, survives, / like seasoned timber through
green, little lives."[34] His contemplative, gentle mood in this poem contrasts with the bitterness of "Codicil," the last poem in *The Castaway.* In
the lines "Schizophrenic, wrenched by two styles, one a hack's hired
prose, I earn / my exile" (61), Walcott's personal anguish over the divided aims of his own writing are abundantly apparent. The broken ends of
history, the fate of other writers in his situation, the feeling of nothingness in his heart: all these accumulate to an intense blankness, and "All
its indifference is a different rage" (62).

Nothing significantly new is introduced in *The Castaway.* Most of it
consists of the final section of *Selected Poems.* Of the 13 new poems, several depict experiences in the United States: "A Village Life," "God Rest Ye
Merry Gentlemen," and "Lines in New England." "Goats and Monkeys"
and "The Prince" touch melodramatically on Shakespeare's *Othello* and
Hamlet. These two and "The Flock" recall some of the Jacobean polish
and verbal excesses of Walcott's earlier style. They are exceptions that

point up the tighter images and the more natural, precise economy of rhythm and meaning in the best poetry collected in *The Castaway*.

Walcott's protean Crusoe figure is adequate to the many burdens it must bear. Louis James is correct in assessing the social relevance of the poetry, although Walcott seldom writes political verse: "Walcott's vision is largely an excoriating one, the burning up of clichés and muddled thinking about the Caribbean situation."[35] James refers to his explosive, transforming power. On the other hand, according to James Livingston, "What finally constitutes Walcott's proper claim to the New World, what finally delivers him from colonial servitude into independent consciousness, is the forging of a language that goes beyond mimicry to an elemental naming of things with epiphanic power."[36] Perhaps the primary achievement of *The Castaway* in this regard is the sustained coherence of the point of view. With the clear understanding of his central image, he seems to be able, with few minor exceptions, to retain his own poetic voice no matter what the setting of the poem and no matter how abstract or universal his underlying theme.

Opening the Workshop

In 1966, the year following publication of *The Castaway*, Walcott's theatrical company opened its first official production. After successful runs of Walcott's own *The Sea at Dauphin* and Albee's *The Zoo Story*, the Workshop, which had by then also become known as the Basement Theatre Workshop because of its location in a converted bar in the basement of the Bretton Hall Hotel, decided to attempt an extended season of repertory theater. Thus in October 1966 it began a four-week run of three plays: *Belle Fanto* by Eric Roach, *The Blacks* by Jean Genêt, and *The Road* by Wole Soyinka. Since the experiment played to large audiences nearly every night, more plays were scheduled.

If attendance is any measure of success, the Trinidad Theatre Workshop succeeded very well. Therese Mills reports in the *Guardian* (July 1967, a year after its initial opening) that the company continued to play to full houses at home and that it was in the midst of a series of foreign tours.[37] Walcott was understandably busy as a director and producer during this period, 1966–1967, but in the same article Mills discusses a new play he had written, *Jourmard*.[38] It was a light farce, with plenty of dialect and humorous action, which is generally overshadowed by *Dream on Monkey Mountain*.

Jourmard is significant only for its lack of depth. It is unusual for Walcott to write unrelieved comedy. The action centers on a group of vagabonds who attempt to get money from churchgoers on Easter Sunday by conducting a mock burial and resurrection scene. In the end Jourmard's accomplices flee to avoid arrest, leaving him nailed shut in his coffin. The play is merely a harmless, comic interlude; interestingly enough, it also happens to be another of the several works that Walcott wrote during his Rockefeller grant year in New York. There is exuberance in *Jourmard* and lively characters, but the play falls short of the precise movement, the economy of expression, that Walcott looks for in other writers and claims to want in his own drama.

Chapter Four
Dreams and Revolutions: 1967–1973

A Dream

Walcott seems an unlikely candidate for the title of revolutionary. His tendency to delve into all sides of complex issues, his balanced handling of sensitive questions, and his opposition to extreme solutions mark him as anything but violent. Yet he is no reactionary, either. In articles, poems, and plays he not only chronicles but promotes growth and changing orders. He considers the writer to be a special kind of revolutionary: "[A]ny West Indian writer, any colonial, is immediately, synonymously a revolutionary even when he puts himself in a defensive position and says: 'There are certain values here that regardless of the violence of the revolution, we need to preserve if we want the society to work.' "[1] Unlike some of his more strident contemporaries in the third world, he is concerned more with the quality of change than with mere change for its own sake. His highly acclaimed *Dream on Monkey Mountain,* for example, depicts not only the Negro's righteous rebellion against the white master: it goes further, to the heretical extent of having the protagonist reject the equally oppressive role imposed by black racists. The extension of meaning is an important one, and not only for this play: to overlook it would be a gross misinterpretation of Walcott's contribution to third world culture.

Dream on Monkey Mountain was completed especially for the Trinidad Theatre Workshop's first tour outside the Caribbean, to Toronto in 1967. Subsequent productions—at the Eugene O'Neill Memorial Theatre in Connecticut in 1969; the Mark Taper Forum in Los Angeles in 1970; NBC television's adaptation in Trinidad in 1970—were crowned in New York when the Negro Ensemble cast won the prestigious Obie Award for the best foreign play of the 1970–1971 season. Since then various companies have performed it in Canada, Europe, the

United States, and throughout the West Indies. Walcott himself directed a 1985 revival at the Astor Theatre in Port-of-Spain.

In spite of the fact that Errol Hill pronounced *Dream on Monkey Mountain* to be "a tangled, incoherent piece,"[2] it has been well received by audiences and critics in general. Difficulties with the play are due partially to the multiplicity of interrelated themes, but the very form of presentation—within a dream framework—underscores its complexity. A production note reminiscent of Strindberg's preface to *A Dream Play* warns of the play's "illogical, derivative, contradictory" nature. Walcott suggests that his source is metaphor and that producers will need the kind of disciplined actors, dancers, and singers who perform in Kabuki theater.[3]

Characters exchange roles, assume aspects of the protagonist's dominant personality traits, and serve as symbols; one who is twice killed returns alive again in the epilogue. Without actually defying logic, but complying with the subliminal continuity of dream sequences, the plot unfolds piecemeal as Makak attempts to explain the vision he has seen and the events that led to his arrest on charges of being drunk and disorderly. Makak's assistant in the charcoal-burning trade, named Moustique, the mulatto jailer Lestrade, and two fellow prisoners, Tigre and Souris, merge with his hallucination and participate in his experiences. The very names of these men suggest fable: Lestrade, neither black nor white, is a straddler; Makak means monkey, taken from the name of the mountain where he lives; the others are mosquito, tiger, and mouse. The fable is pushed to the forefront as soon as the conteur, chorus, and actors begin discussing Makak's condition in the prologue.

Corporal Lestrade's words and actions, leavened with comic turns, show his stereotypical house-Negro prejudices. He ridicules backward savages and proudly upholds his master's standards. Gloating over his presumed superiority, he proves through interrogation that Makak is an ape, an imitator who must be told how to behave and what to do. Throughout Lestrade's grandiose exposition he is served by Tigre and Souris, who sit in mock judgment, miming at appropriate moments the gestures of hearing, seeing, and speaking no evil. It becomes clear by the close of the prologue that they all exemplify the "mimic men" made notorious in V. S. Naipaul's novel. Unsure of themselves, they know only how to play assigned roles. Makak does not recall his legal name; when asked to declare his race, all he can answer is "tired." When he is at last allowed to account for himself, his own words disclose the root of his problem: an apparition of a white woman has told him that he is descended from warrior kings and should return to Africa. Lestrade concludes, "this rage for whiteness . . . does drive niggers mad" (228).

Scene 1 is a flashback to the morning when Makak announces to Moustique that he has been commanded to regain his African birthright. Moustique does not believe in the cause, but like Sancho Panza he decides to accompany his quixotic leader. In scene 2, their first adventure calls forth Makak's new spiritual power. Through prayer, calling on the people first to believe in him and then in themselves, he is apparently instrumental in restoring a dying man to life. Moustique is quick to seize any opportunity for gain. Thus he advances Makak's reputation and like many another trickster hero of West Indian folklore converts faith and trust into a profitable enterprise. But his fraudulent career ends abruptly when he is beaten to death by a crowd of villagers who discover that he is impersonating the miracle-worker Makak.

What gives Moustique away is his superstitious fear of a small spider. The man who first discerns the truth behind the disguise is Basil the carpenter, maker of coffins, and an appropriate symbol of death. Makak arrives in time to gaze into Moustique's dying eyes in hopes of catching a glimpse of what lies beyond. All he finds is empty, black nothingness.

An interlude in the dream opens part 2. Back in jail while Makak puzzles over Moustique's betrayal and the blackness that his death portends, Lestrade engages in a pointedly contradictory defense of white justice. He has hardly finished complaining that law adjusts its price according to color when, without blinking, he is incensed that Makak should offer a bribe for his freedom. The incident points up the corporal's ambiguous feelings about his position and his color consciousness. The hint of a bribe also inspires Tigre and Souris to humor Makak's delusion so that they can lay hands on his money.

Reentering the dream state, Makak and his two new accomplices overpower Lestrade, escape from jail, and open the way to revolution. As the corporal sets out to recapture his prisoners, he voices the perspective of his acquired power: "There's nothing quite so exciting as putting down the natives. Especially after reason and law have failed. . . . Then I'll have good reason for shooting them down. Sharpeville? . . . Attempting to escape from the prison of their lives. That's the most dangerous crime. It brings about revolution" (286–87). Although the thrust of the play is couched in terms of black consciousness, words such as these in the mouth of a racially mixed character move the deeper meaning of the fable onto a broader plane. Up to this point in the play none of the characters manifests any sense of self-awareness. Each one relies on a racial identity. Significantly, while he is pursuing his escapees, the corporal "goes native" and becomes the most fanatic convert to Makak's back-to-Africa movement. In a dramatic reversal, Lestrade becomes the unyielding advocate of the black race's law.

Makak foresees in the wrangling that develops among his followers the rising level of violence that lies ahead, but as the tempo of the play's action increases he is caught up in the frenzy for power and revenge. The last scene before the epilogue, a scene described by Walcott as an apotheosis, is a dream within the dream. Transported to Africa, Makak sets up court and judgment is passed on all the history of racial oppression. Lestrade will brook no patient reforms. He insists on death for all the accused, including Makak's white goddess. In one of the wittiest passages in the script, Basil reads a list of the offenders: Noah (but not the son of Ham), Abraham Lincoln, Robert E. Lee, Mandrake the Magician, Al Jolson, and others—all of whom are guilty of being "indubitably" white (312). Moustique is also executed (his second death) for having betrayed the original dream. He offers no defense, but before he is carried away he argues that Makak's own good intentions have been corrupted by his group's lust for power and revenge. There is no longer room for personal relationships; there is only racial retribution.

At last the bloodletting climaxes with Makak's beheading of the white apparition. By this heavily paradoxical gesture Makak is finally free to be himself. The visionary goddess may have been white, but the inspiration she brought of African identity was as inauthentic and limiting as the one she was replacing. When in scene 1 Makak discovered the possibility of beauty within his aged, black body, he advanced one step. His journey back to Africa was a necessary intermediary step toward personal liberty. The final step came when he outgrew his need for the racial crutch.

Walcott's attitude on this point is explicit in the essay introducing the volume containing *Dream on Monkey Mountain:* "Once we have lost our wish to be white we develop a longing to become black, and those two may be different, but are still careers. . . . The depth of being rooted is related to the shallowness of racial despair" (20–21). His dramatization, because it is a more subtle statement, is likely to be overlooked by those wishing not to see it. In the epilogue, which makes it clear that all the play's action had been real only in Makak's fervent imagination, Walcott gives the audience a protagonist who has cut through illusion to discover his essential self. With his first words in the epilogue, Makak recollects that his legal name is Felix Hobain. When Moustique picks him up at the jail soon afterward, he finds Makak to be a new man. Upon his release, he determines to establish himself where he belongs: "The branches of my fingers, the roots of my feet, could grip nothing, but now, God, they have found ground. '. . . Makak lives where he has always lived, in the dream of his people.' Other men will come, other prophets will come, and they will be stoned, and mocked, and betrayed, but now this old hermit is going back home, back to the beginning, to the green beginning of this world. Come, Moustique, we going home" (326).

Certain rich ambiguities within the play leave it open to broadly dive·gent interpretations. Theodore Colson talks about the need to go back, even if only vicariously, to primordial beginnings as a corrective to the myths and stereotypes that undermine man's humanity.[4] Victor Questel points out the many ways characters manipulate each other throughout the play.[5] Denis Solomon argues that in addition to problems of black identity *Dream on Monkey Mountain* examines "the elaborate antithetical structure of ideas relating to man's inward and outward existence—dream and reality, essence and substance, passivity and action, purity and corruption."[6] Selden Rodman takes Walcott to task for having permitted the New York production to become a weapon in the hands of antiwhites.[7] Walcott admitted in conversation with Rodman that the attitude of the Negro Ensemble presentation disturbed him. His intention was not to promote confrontation.

Dream on Monkey Mountain ends in fact not with a beheading, but with a man reaching an accommodation with his environment. In spite of the violent, political overtones of the action, the resolution of the play is in personal, perhaps religious terms. Despite the moments of humor and the framework of the dream, as Lloyd Brown has indicated, the play offers a serious prescription for change: "The dream-fantasy about revolution involves and confirms a very real revolutionizing of self-perception."[8] Makak returns to his mountain retreat a new man because of his increased insight. His seclusion is not going to have a dynamic impact on society, but as Walcott indicated to Rodman, Makak fulfills his function in West Indian society as a charcoal burner, and he will no longer be misled by spurious chimeras. It is an authentic foundation on which to begin.[9]

Living Apart

That Makak should work out a separate peace is not unusual for a Walcott character. More often than not the individuals he portrays, like his native islands, live separated by one kind of gulf or another. The title of his fourth major collection of poems, *The Gulf* (1969), suggests the significance of this theme in his work. Gordon Rohlehr considers the unifying theme of *The Gulf* to be "the general chasm separating peoples, cultures and even individuals within the closed unit of a family."[10] Continually the speaker views scenes through glass, sometimes from a plane or a train, detached from the things he contemplates. In "Codicil," the concluding poem of his preceding volume, *The Castaway,* Walcott refers to indifference as a different kind of "rage."

The Gulf's predominant air of poetic detachment expresses that classically restrained rage. Restraint extends to the intended style of language: in "Nearing Forty" the poet begins to judge his efforts by

> the household truth, the style past metaphor
> that finds its parallel however wretched
> in simple, shining lines, in pages stretched
> plain as a bleaching bedsheet under a gutter-
> ing rainspout, glad for the sputter
> of occasional insight. . . .[11]

Such "plainness" demonstrated in these lines embodies the crisp, clear, and ordinary language he called for in *In a Green Night*;[12] but even at the time he writes he has reservations about becoming too obvious and simplistic. Talking with poet Dennis Scott in 1968, he confessed concern over the clarity that seemed to be encroaching on his work.[13] He told Scott that he read poetry not for enjoyment, but to be terrified: "And people who terrify me from their size and the grandeur of their imagination now are people like Pasternak and Neruda . . . Lowell—very few English poets."[14]

To the confusion of many of his critics, Walcott's style pulls in two directions. One of the major unambiguous statements that carries from the Scott interview into his later poetry is that he wants to cultivate a private, close attentiveness to objective reality, after the example of Thomas Hardy and contemporary West Indian novelists.[15] The critical opinion as to how well he succeeds in executing his design varies considerably. Reviewing *The Gulf,* Roy Fuller suggests stricter forms and more revision as remedies for the syntactical clumsiness and obscurity of attitude and situation in some of the poems, "Mass Man" and "A Change of Skin," for example.[16] Conceding that Walcott is a powerful writer, Denis Donoghue argues that because of his weakness for grandeur, and his attempt to speak both as private poet and social observer, some poems in *The Gulf* suffer from rhetorical excesses: "He writes everything so large that the reader is inclined to deduct something, to keep the situation reasonable."[17]

Verbal dexterity and rhetorical flourishes verging on the excessive are nothing new in Walcott. According to Edward Baugh, however, *The Castaway* and *The Gulf* show a more mature control than is typical of his early verse: "Walcott has not abandoned the ringing line, and it would be a pity if he did, but he has come to use it with less prodigality and a greater functional discretion. He has been moving towards sparer yet, in a way, subtler rhythms, more angular perhaps, nearer to normal speech and prose rhythms. . . . The rhetorical flourish and the rich melody are used now more discreetly, with more specific functional point."[18] In spite of reservations about other selections in *The Gulf,* Fuller finds the title poem entirely successful. Baugh describes it as "a model of a firmly controlled blend of eloquence and rhythmic emphasis on the one hand and the plain-sounding and low-keyed on the other."[19]

"The Gulf" incorporates most of the important themes and motifs from the entire volume. Aloft in a plane high over Texas, the speaker contemplates things as disparate as bad coffee, Borges's prose, John Kennedy's assassination, his own detachment, racial violence in the United States, and the gulfs—real and symbolic—that stand between men and anything that might seem like home. Subdued in the beginning, the voice catalogs passing thought until in the concluding lines it achieves a tense climax:

> I have no home
> as long as summer bubbling to its head
>
> boils for that day when in the Lord God's name
> the coals of fire are heaped upon the head
> of all whose gospel is the whip and flame,
>
> age after age, the uninstructing dead.

(62)

The dead are uninstructing, of course, because the living never learn from their mistakes.

His voice, in the final analysis, is not really dispassionate, but he is on the move and is looking at things from a distance. Other poems in the volume are set in the Caribbean, in England, in North and South America, and toward the end return to the West Indies again. By the time the geographical circle is completed back in the Caribbean, images and references become intensely personal.

One of the early poems in the book, "Mass Man," an acerbic commentary on the Trinidad Carnival, probes behind the gay masquerade to the clerks "making style" and one forlorn child. In anticipation of Ash Wednesday, the poet recognizes within his heart a different kind of abandonment from theirs, "my mania is a terrible calm" (48). "Exile" and "The Train" speak of England as "home." In the latter, he settles on the fact that the mother country is merely half-home because his "randy white grandsire" came from there a century ago. "Elegy," drawing on the brutal execution of Che Guevara, ties American clichés about liberty, Miss America, and cherry pie together with the genocide the country perpetrated against native Indian tribes. "Washington" and "Negatives" paint verbal pictures in the colors of war: one the Vietnam War, the other the Biafran rebellion in Nigeria.

Nicely rounding off *The Gulf,* the last few poems narrowly circumscribe Walcott's most private concerns. "In the Kitchen," touchingly but without sentimentality, reunites the poet's long-deceased father with his mother: "this woman who has waited / since her first death for this" (101). "Love in the Valley" is about love, love of literature and of life made more vivid by the likes of Pasternak, Hawthorne, Hardy, and their heroines. Love, literature, and the life he knows most intimately come together in the final poem, "Hic Jacet." Claiming that "Before the people became popular / he loved them" (110), the poet accounts for his decision (at least prior to 1977) to remain at home rather than seek refuge like other writers in metropolitan exile. In a tone Edward Baugh describes as "petulant and arrogant, but magisterially so,"[20] Walcott candidly spells out his motives:

> I sought more power than you, more fame than yours,
> I was more hermetic, I knew the commonweal,
> I pretended subtly to lose myself in crowds
> knowing my passage would alter their reflection.

(111)

In answer to those who are bothered by the seeming contradiction between Walcott's professed desire to lose himself among the people and his actual practice of maintaining his unencumbered individuality, it should be pointed out that he only "pretends" to lose himself in crowds. The distinction he intends to draw is between those who use the "people" for their personal advantage and one who, without sacrificing his integrity, would learn at first hand what is moving his society at the most basic level. Lloyd King is probably correct in assuming that because Walcott describes a more subjectively private than a conveniently public purgatory in *The Gulf,* the book is "unlikely to be greeted by genuine widespread enthusiasm."[21] Enthusiasm may be too much to expect, but *The Gulf* deserves widespread, close attention because of the accuracy of Walcott's cultural perception. According to Gordon Rohlehr, "The tensions . . . in Walcott's poetry are rooted in West Indian society—which is a much more gloomy and anxiety-ridden place than is normally imagined by anthem-and-flag enthusiasts."[22] Ironically, the gulfs that stand between individuals serve as well to link people together in the common experience of being alone in the world.

Playing Mass

Walcott's subjective microcosm with its symbolic and other more explicit implications for the larger world reflects the values he deems worthy of preservation and the problematic circumstances that give rise to the kind of revolution he wants to foment. In introducing the volume that contains *Dream on Monkey Mountain* in 1970, he declared that the future of West Indian militancy lay in art.[23] Three years later he emphasized the discretion that is necessary if a coherent, working order is to grow out of revolution.[24] Makak enacts a fantasy to emerge a more whole man. *The Gulf* delineates aspects of a world of broken and ineffectual relationships. Even the poet's race is no protection in the humorous poem "Blues," where a group of young Negroes "beat this yellow nigger/ black and blue" (67). *The Gulf* is a cohesive, well-rounded collection, but it offers no easy solutions.

The lesser known plays first produced in the early 1970s contribute significantly to Walcott's explication of the social illnesses in the Caribbean islands. Although *In a Fine Castle* (1971, eventually rewritten and published as *The Last Carnival* in 1986), *Franklin* (1973), and *The Charlatan* (1973) have never been published in their original form, they have all been staged internationally. *The Charlatan* has been presented at the Mark Taper Forum in Los Angeles, and performed in Barbados and Trinidad as recently as 1990. *In a Fine Castle* and *Franklin* tend to be slightly more realistic (in the vein of *The Sea at Dauphin*) than are the Brechtian plays since *Ti-Jean and His Brothers*. Music and comedy assume more prominence in *The Charlatan,* the first of several plays on which Walcott collaborated with Galt MacDermot, who provided lyrical scores.

In a Fine Castle, Franklin, and *The Charlatan* have in common their emphasis on identity crises and racial and social confrontations. Walcott anticipated that he would be criticized from some quarters for writing leading roles for white characters,[25] and several witnesses to local reactions verified the fulfillment of his expectation: Eric Roach, John Figueroa, and Denis Solomon in different reviews were moved to comment on the apparently racially biased outcries that were heard.[26] Walcott's excuse for risking sensitive racial and social mixes might well be the words he offered Selden Rodman: "There's no conflict between the color of my skin and the language I use. My great desire is to make the scene I write about as *true* as possible regardless of the consequences."[27]

Brown, the protagonist of *In a Fine Castle,*[28] is as his name suggests neither white nor black. In fact, he lives out the division he has inherited, being torn between the demands of his girlfriend Shelley, an ardent black nationalist, and his deeper impulse to come to a better understanding of the remnants of colonial society that are rapidly dying all around him. Not sure where he belongs, Brown uses his profession as a reporter as a means to enter the "castle" of the de La Fontaine family. It is Carnival in Trinidad and Brown's ostensible mission is to interview Clodia de La Fontaine, who has just astonished everyone by resigning her crown as Carnival queen in favor of a black girl.

Inside de La Fontaine's elaborate house, Brown encounters arrogance and prejudice, but also fear and exhaustion. Clodia confesses a desire for martyrdom as expiation for the sins of the past. Because the family's stability has declined in tandem with the rising forces of nationalism—there are hints of madness, of waltzing on the edge of an abyss—Clodia and others are on the verge of leaving the country. Brown and Clodia find themselves in love briefly, futilely, before they separate.

On the other side of the racial barrier, within the same first act, with the new set of characters simply moving into the same stage area, Brown steps into the planning session of a strike committee. There he finds more arrogance, intolerance, and a vicious disregard even for the feelings of long-standing friendships. In act 2 Brown finds himself alone, having chosen to relinquish his ties with Clodia and preferring noncommitment rather than blind allegiance to a cause such as Shelley demands. The final scene is a dumb show: as if in a dream, marchers, flags, banners, and former acquaintances pass by.

One immediate drawback to *In a Fine Castle* is the fact that Brown is not an admirable protagonist with whom an audience is likely to identify. His rational stance may be viable, but it is costly and unpopular. None of the characters creates a memorable impression. Two minor figures serve important functions, however, as they epitomize the direction of thematic development. George, the de La Fontaines' life-long servant, utterly defeats Brown's gibes about his servility with a profound, dignified silence. From him Brown learns the power of restraint. Elizabeth Prince, white wife of a black militant leader, wastefully sacrifices her life in order not to embarrass her husband. Finding herself ostracized by her former friends, she commits suicide. Dying with her (unknown to her husband) is the unborn child that was to have been the fruit of their marriage. The setting of the concluding demonstration march on Ash Wednesday (juxtaposed with the frenzy of Carnival) underscores the hollowness that is the point of the entire drama. That is perhaps Walcott's benediction on their kind of madness. Elsewhere he asserts that any revolution based on race is bound to become internecine, to be self-defeating.[29] In chapter 6, Walcott's extensively revised version of *In a Fine Castle*, entitled *The Last Carnival* (first produced in 1982) will be discussed in detail. The later text emphasizes Walcott's concern with the impact of independence not only on the lower and middle classes but on the deposed colonial aristocracy as well.

Franklin, his next play, is also about the burdens of complexion. In Franklin's case, a retired colonial wants desperately to become an accepted member of the island settlement that bears his name: "But this white hand puts up a struggle. / It won't turn black."[30] Antecedent to the action of the play he has undertaken a three-part campaign to establish himself in the face of a growing nationalist movement. He has successfully maintained his legal claim to the land on which he lives. His rival is a black agitator, Charbon, who protests that the land had been left to him by the former landowner, for whom he had worked. Franklin's second tie to the land is through Clive Morris, a young Negro whom he brought into his own home and who now serves as first mate on his schooner. The weakness in this relationship is that Franklin continues to regard Morris paternalistically even after he has grown up and earned his official captain's license.

His third move, which comes as the story opens, is to bring a native girl into his house as wife. From the outset this effort is unsuccessful. Maria, despite her Christian name, is not black, but East Indian. She elopes from her Hindu family and Franklin never fulfills his promise to marry her legally. Within a few months she finds solace with Morris, becomes pregnant, and after suffering the curse of her father drowns herself in the sea.

Franklin is capable of absorbing this blow. His first wife, who was also unfaithful, had been lost in a German submarine attack 10 years earlier, taking their small son with her. For some reason, perhaps to avoid the accumulation of melodramatic incidents, Walcott never allows Franklin to find out about Maria's pregnancy or about Morris's culpability. It is worth noting in this regard that an earlier typescript of the play stresses Franklin's pride to such an extent that his only honorable exit (like that of the heroine in *Ione*) is through death. This more spectacular version brings the curtain down on exploding oil drums, Franklin dying in flames, and a character moralizing that the conflagration represents the "final blaze of Empire."[31]

In the more restrained later version, Franklin's conscious burden is sufficient motivation for the action that ensues. His dream is to assimilate and become one with the indigenous environment. With Maria he fails miserably. He almost loses Morris because he suspects him of being involved in the labor agitation then moving through the island. After their argument, the single most important factor that brings reconciliation is Franklin's belated confession that he has never actually been legal captain of a ship. Subdued over Maria's suicide and saddened by his misunderstanding with Morris, he prepares to abandon his dreams and retire with his old companion Willoughby to England. When all seems lost, Franklin refuses Morris's offered resignation and cancels all obligations and debts of gratitude that Morris had felt and reclaims his honest identity.

Morris decides to accept his charge as captain of Franklin's schooner, and to round out the plot (almost too smoothly) Charbon enters to call off his land dispute. Charbon has acquired satisfactory proof that Franklin's deed is valid. Not only that, but because of Franklin's suffering, Charbon admits that after all his years of being envious his feelings now have turned to pity. On that note, Franklin resolves to take his losses and remain with the only vestige of home he has ever known.

Once again, in the pattern of *Dream on Monkey Mountain* and *In a Fine Castle,* the object lesson relates to the wake of empire. No matter what the person's race, amid disorder and fragmented relationships the individual's hope for survival lies in his ability to begin anew where he lives, without false illusions.

A more entertaining update on *Franklin's* setting in the preindependence 1950s may be found in *The Charlatan.* Galt MacDermot's score and Walcott's lyrics are aimed at capturing the spirit of Carnival in a more modern Port-of-Spain. Two struggling calypsonians, Mighty King Cobo and an ex-police corporal, open the play complaining about the way their country neglects its true poets of the street. An argument develops when they begin to review the great calypsonians of the past. When Cobo brands the Minstrel Boy a fraud, the dialogue brings into focus the significance of the title of the play. Cobo dislikes the way entrepreneurs can impose themselves on his countrymen: "So many people coming here and fooling them. / And the more they fooling them the more they admire them."[32]

Cobo is himself something of a fraud, since he is taking advantage of his friend Robert Martin, sleeping, eating, and drinking free of charge in his apartment. Another impostor is Dr. Voltore, a quack who passes himself off as a heart specialist. The principal charlatan of the play, however, is Theodore Holley, an Englishman pretending to be a spiritualist and a dealer in magic potions. Cobo is harmless, but Dr. Voltore makes a living by telling patients that they will soon die. Since he is lying in order to make them remain under his care, they can keep paying his fees indefinitely. Holley, a beneficent spirit, uses his tricks against other schemers and to the advantage of people he likes.

Robert Martin, the character in the play who comes closest to being a sympathetic hero, is Voltore's latest victim. Andrea Holley, the charlatan's daughter, supplies the romantic interest and thereby renews Martin's lease on life. Holley informs Martin that Voltore is a sham and that he must learn to want life rather than death. Spinning off humor, songs, and minor subplots, the action works its way to a mock resurrection in the last scene. In the end Robert and Andrea receive permission to marry; the corporal becomes engaged; both Dr. Voltore and Holley escape arrest by mingling with the Carnival crowd; and, elated with all the good feelings, Cobo pronounces the whole world man and wife.

If it proves nothing else, *The Charlatan* demonstrates that *Jourmard* was not merely an accident: Walcott sometimes enjoys writing a happy musical comedy. Although it touches more weighty issues than does *Jourmard,* the play still lacks the substance and deeper seriousness of his best drama. At its Los Angeles premier one critic had difficulty getting caught up in the theme—"the conquest of Death by Love"—when it was transmitted through the language of calypso and Carnival symbolism which seemed confusing.[33] As another of Walcott's continuing experiments in theatrical technique, *The Charlatan* is both interesting and valuable. It comes surprisingly close, in fact, to the kind of drama that *Guardian* columnist John Melser considers to be natural for Trinidad. Melser describes a combination of foreign and local influences that would result in

a total theatrical experience, capable of symbolising the energy and optimism of the world, as well as the stupidity of barren social forms and the occasional evil of political and economic institutions. . . . It draws on folk-culture, on the "musical," on dance, on the movie film, on the psychedelic light-show as much as on traditional drama.

And it is a theatre of celebration, a celebration of vitality, joy, gusto, sexuality, love, compassion and all the pity and wonder of being human.[34]

Walcott has established his career on that rich potential, both the misfortunes and the privileges of his environment.

In a Fine Castle, Franklin, and *The Charlatan* may be experimental and may not perform equally well on stage, but each with its particular difficulties is a sincere effort to dramatize crucial aspects of the revolution that has been essential to the development of Caribbean independence. Whether a man is playing mass, or undertaking revolution, he must with equal diligence mark the distinction between illusion and reality. Here the artist serves a crucial role which Walcott describes in "Mass Man" from *The Gulf*:

Upon your penitential morning, . . .
some mind must squat down howling in your dust,
some hand must crawl and recollect your rubbish,
someone must write your poems.

(48)

Another Life

In a powerful way Walcott fulfills that encyclopedic function in *Another Life,* an autobiographical account of his childhood and early career as a poet. In spite of its evident foundation in personal experiences, there is no self-centered egotism involved. Rather the impulse of the poem derives from universal resonances within particular events that obtain coherence in the presence of a recording intelligence. This is not to say that the verse is cold or without feeling, but that an admirable balance is achieved between emotional response and aesthetic distance. A measure of Walcott's advancement over the years can be made by comparing *Another Life* with the poem that he once designated as its prototype, *Epitaph for the Young* (1949).[35] Whereas the earlier work can be described as overly self-conscious and a pastiche of half-digested allusions and borrowed styles, *Another Life* is fully mature—its tone equally assured whether the perspective is profoundly reflective, gliding easily into wry self-mockery, or mounting to sharp invective.

Another Life recounts the evolution of an artist. Despite the forthright language and studied avoidance of elaborate metaphors, the thought development is intricate, moving circuitously with centers of meaning building as related ideas recur throughout the four major divisions.

Significantly, part 1 is captioned with a story from Malraux's *Psychology of Art* to the effect that it is never reality that inspires a Giotto to love painting, but rather his looking at the paintings created by such a master as Cimabue.[36] The first scene is of a boy (Walcott) finishing a landscape for the inspection of his teacher (Harry Simmons). The view given is that of the boy, lending a sense of immediacy; but simultaneously it is enriched by the more pervasive insight of the narrator reflecting back over his childhood. Thus the reader sees *with* the boy, and recognizes *through* the narrator, that because of his immersion in European ideas, "The dream / of reason had produced its monster: / a prodigy of the wrong age and colour" (3).

He is the "Divided Child" indicated in the title of the first subsection. The story takes in the people and things nearest him: his mother and her sewing, their house and its physical details, objects that held their places so definitively that they could no more be shifted in his memory than the parts of a finished painting could be altered (15). Domestic motifs of sewing, washing, and ironing clothes dominate pages 10 through 15, yet through subtly refined conceits the ordinary acquires poetic beauty. One line, "The week sets sail"—following a two-line description of Monday's washing fluttering in the yard—is sufficient to call up the image of a ship with canvas sails stretched from its yardarms (11). The silence of the sewing machine on Sunday is a tribute to the sacred day of rest, the sound of its stitching monotony left to cicadas rasping in the forests. The child remembers clothes made "from the nearest elements," laundry like "freshly ironed clouds," and his mother's "iron hymn" on the old machine (12). None of these images draws undue attention to itself. The young poet who wished to extend the line of Milton and Marlowe has learned to curb his metaphysical conceits. He weaves metaphors into the fabric of his advancing narrative far more effectively than he did in *Epitaph for the Young.*

Underscoring the power of memory to order things is a gallery of neighbors, arranged in alphabetical order, each tagged with some animal trait or classical association: Berthilia, a froglike cripple; Choiseul the chauffeur, who closes garage doors as if they were the gates of Troy; Janie (Helen), the town's only clear-complexioned whore; Auguste Manoir, a businessman with the Midas touch; and Zandoli, "the Lizard," extermi-nator of rats and mosquitoes—"they were the stars of my mythology" (22). What he learns in the classroom is translated in imagination to the streets, making Castries into his Troy. At times religious training converts the city to his New Jerusalem, but he is never far from the black practices of Obeah: "One step beyond the city was the bush" (25).

In the mind of an impressionable youth the confrontation of these two worlds—Europe and its neglected colony—could easily be magni-fied beyond reasonable bounds. To restore equilibrium, without destroy-ing the childlike sense of wonder, Walcott resorts to gentle, self-deprecating humor:

> Provincialism loves the pseudo-epic,
> so if these heroes have been given a stature
> disproportionate to their cramped lives,
> remember I beheld them at knee-height,
> and that their thunderous exchanges
> rumbled like gods about another life.

> (41)

The gift of hindsight permits that leveling editorial comment, but it relieves rather than undermines the primary point of view. Lloyd Brown, recognizing the natural connotations, interprets Walcott's use of the child image as archetypal reinforcement for the sense of newness and the possibilities for creative action in the New World.[37] In fact, Walcott is of the opinion that provincialism itself provides certain advantages for the colonial writer. It forces him into a "deeper communion with things that metropolitan writers no longer care about . . . attachments to family, earth and history."[38] It is not worth conjecturing about which writers he has in mind. The point is that vital resources await the colonial writer in his narrowly circumscribed world.

The closing chapter of "The Divided Child" section brings events through the 14th year. It is a climactic year. He remembers days of rustic seclusion with his poems and painting. His mind reeling with images of religion, Africa, and the latter-day legions ("pale, prebendary clerks") of colonial empire, "he fell in love with art, / and life began" (44). At the same time a blonde schoolgirl, Anna, enters to become another dominant force in his life.

Part 2, entitled "Homage to Gregorias," concentrates on Walcott's teenage years and on his budding friendship with an aspiring young painter, Dunstan St. Omer. St. Omer provides the model for "all the Gregoriases," all frustrated young artists struggling to unleash their pent-up energy. Dreaming, arguing, and carousing together, they undertook one primary aim: "Adam's task of giving things their names" (47)—the phrase was taken by Walcott from Alejo Carpentier's *The Lost Steps* for an introduction to this second part. Both boys were impressed with the weighty privilege of having a virtually unexplored world they could record, and by recording could immortalize in the framework of their art.

Their thinking was crowded with names from the masters of European tradition, but they had no precedent for expressing the island's primeval past. They faced a wall of amnesia between the present and the lost histories of Arawak, Carib, and the slave from Africa. Due to their dissimilar temperaments and styles they sought different approaches to the problem. Walcott felt that he was disciplined and humble enough to remain true to the visible reality he sought to capture, but he was hindered by his interest in paradoxes, ambiguities, and subtle metaphors that belonged more properly in the realm of literary tradition. Gregorias, on the other hand, "abandoned apprenticeship / to the errors of his own soul" (59). While he envied Gregorias's instinctive brush strokes, Walcott the poet was governed by "this sidewise crawling, this classic / condition of servitude" (59), and in the end they complemented each other: one on canvas, the other on the written page.

In the schoolroom his imagination was continually fed with romantic adventures of empire, and he envisioned himself alive in the Paris of the 1920s with Pound and Hemingway. Strong impressions were made by one of his teachers, an Englishman who loved Conrad's prose. In a later segment of part 3, Walcott recalls other teachers from Ireland who brought the atmosphere of their faith and their country to life for him (104–6). They were all Catholics and, like him, exiles in a distant island. He does not name them or the Englishman in the poem, but the originals—T. E. Fox-Hawes and the Irish Brothers of the Presentation—are easily recognizable from the more direct account given of them in Walcott's 1965 article "Leaving School."[39]

Such factual elements as these, which contributed to the inspiration of the poem in the first place, enter and enhance the meaning to a limited extent, but their presence should not be allowed to restrict interpretation. When asked whether the broader implications of *Another Life* might not suffer neglect in the hands of critics who attempt to read the life of the poet into his poems, Walcott responded that he could hardly have left out the particular details, but that his was not a physical chronicle so much as the biography of a West Indian "intelligence," using the word in the Latin sense of "spirit." He admitted that one friend had already researched and pointed out to him the many "errors" of chronology, places, and names that existed in the text.[40]

What is more interesting and more conducive to fruitful insight is to understand the artistic use the poet makes of his personal experiences. The conclusion of "Homage to Gregorias" is significant in this regard. The poet, in reflecting on the futile hopes, the difficulties, and the drunken revels he and his friend had known, declared: "Yet, Gregorias, lit, / we were the light of the world!" (78). There is nostalgia in the thought, and the mild pun is appropriate for the sentiment. Were there nothing more, the description would fit the moment; yet the image is enlarged to the proportions of a metaphysical conceit when within a few lines of this seemingly innocent expression these "inflamed men" who are upholding "the old sacred flame" witness the conflagration that burned away forever the Castries they had known in their youth.

Part 2 ends abruptly, but the major fire that swept through Castries when Walcott was a boy becomes the dominant symbol for the third section of *Another Life,* which is entitled "A Simple Flame." The same event is the subject of "A City's Death by Fire" from *In a Green Night.* This time the poet moves beyond the flames and the burned-out ruins to the decadent reconstruction that rose above the ashes. The personality of his

old world is buried under the modern "cement phoenix" (103).
Meanwhile his infatuation with Anna progresses into love and her presence passes into his art. She becomes his doomed heroine "all Annas,
enduring all goodbyes" (96). He envisions her departure, a nurse pursuing her dedication to the afflicted.

He fantasizes about her ministering to the war-wounded, and he a
maimed soldier; but World War II has no lasting impact on him or the
life of the island. Soon he has to take his leave for further education
abroad. Preparation for the trip includes a meeting with a representative
of the British Council (a meeting that again provides an opportunity for
Walcott to exercise his satirical wit):

> I am hoisted on silvery chords upward,
> eager for the dropped names like sugar cubes.
> Eliot. Plop. Benjamin Britten. Klunk. Elgar. Slurp.
> Mrs. Winters's cheeks gleaming. Polished cherries.
>
> .   .   .
>
> Down on her speckled forearm. More tea.
> Thank you my mind burrowing her soft scented crotch.
> First intimations of immortality.
> Other men's wives.
>
> (106)

The boy has grown to be a man. It only remains for him to take formal
leave of Dunstan, their mentor Harry Simmons, Anna's island, and to
cross the sea.

"The Estranging Sea," the final section of *Another Life,* rises at last to
an almost lyrical climax, but before Walcott reaches that peak he
indulges in some severe social criticism. The most obvious motivation for
his severity is contained in the plight of artists in the West Indies. He
comes to believe that brotherhood among the descendants of slaves
means struggling for escape, "spitting on their own poets, / preferring
their painters drunkards, / for their solemn catalogue of suicides" (123).
Dunstan informs him that he had failed in an attempt to commit suicide. Word arrives that Harry had succeeded in killing himself: his body
lay undiscovered in his home for two days.

Under the general title of "syntactical apologists of the Third World"
(127), Walcott singles out several culprits for particular attention.

Ministers of new governments, young radicals, and Uncle Toms alike stand in the way of authentic development. Some reject Christian names, campaign to prove to the peasant that he is really African, display old scars to prove who has suffered most. In the name of history, they continue to retain the old order under the guise of a new dispensation. They define and categorize:

> of toms, of traitors, of traditionals and AfroSaxons.
> They measure them carefully
> as others once measured the teeth
> of men and horses, they measure and divide.

> (128)

His is a "society which denied itself heroes"—here quoting V. S. Naipaul (130)—where simply to survive is a measure of success.

With this much negativism, it is only logical to ask why anyone would want to strive at all. Walcott himself raises the question. His answer evolves from the resiliency of the human spirit and, paradoxically, from some of the same experiences that have led others to despair. His points of reference, as usual, are very personal ones. In spite of his losses through death and separation, he has learned from a girl like Anna to love; he has married a woman who answers his needs; his three children refresh his memory of the world's continuing potential for renewal.

Having expended its fury, the narrative voice returns in a calmer mood to the problems of slavery and colonial servitude in West Indian history. Upon reconsideration he decides some good might possibly derive from those who inexorably dwell on the cruelty of the past; that is, if the search returns them to a time wherein their memory is wiped clean. From that primeval "nothing"—the word he stresses by repetition—a new beginning could arise (144–45). It may sound ironic, for a poet who has assimilated such a vast number of traditional influences as Walcott has, to find him advocating a tabula rasa. The apparent self-contradiction resolves itself when his special use of "nothing" is explained.

In his essay introducing the plays in *Dream on Monkey Mountain,* two crucial points are made manifest. First, Walcott does not advocate a back-to-Africa movement as an end in itself. The problem with that kind of fantasy is also spelled out in the introduction. He has found, and he illustrates through Moustique, Tigre, and Souris, that the New World Negro is

> . . . as avaricious and as banal as those who had
> enslaved him. What would deliver him from
> servitude was the forging of a language that
> went beyond mimicry, a dialect which had the
> force of revelation as it invented names for things.

(17)

The second point that grows out of Makak's experience is that his revert-
ing to the bush in order to purge his memory is a selective, reordering
process. What Makak must remove from his system is the overload of
hatred and the colonial thinking pattern that identify and evaluate men
by their complexions. As in Makak's case and as with the West Indian
"intelligence" in *Another Life,* the individual must overcome the shackles
that prevent his seeing himself for what he *is,* not simply what he came
from (as important as the latter may be). This is the heart of Walcott's
form of revolution.

A highly relevant extension of this thought is contained in a short
passage Walcott read to Selden Rodman in 1971:

> A great amount of the Third World literature is a literature of revenge
> written by the descendants of slaves bent on exorcising this demon [his-
> tory] through the word. Or a literature of remorse written by the descen-
> dants of masters obsessed by guilt. . . . The *truly* classic—written by those
> who practice the tough aesthetic of the New World—neither explains
> nor forgives history because it refuses to recognize it as a creative force. . . .
> The old style Revolutionary Writer sees Caliban as an enraged pupil. He
> can't separate the rage of Caliban from the beauty of his speech. . . . The
> language of the torturer has been mastered by the victim. Yet this is
> viewed as servitude, not as irony or victory![41]

This excerpt also covers the charge of mimicry that is frequently leveled
at writers who do not renounce the language and literature of their former masters.

Walcott sees mimicry as part of the process of beginning anew. He
contends in an article on West Indian culture that what some purists
condemn as demeaning imitation is actually "the painful, new, laborious
uttering that comes out of belief, not out of doubt."[42] Leading up to this
remark, he argues that West Indian creativity—his revolution—depends
on a man recognizing the positive value of his owing nothing to any previous source. In his own words, "[C]ultures can only be created out of
this knowledge of nothing, and in deeper than the superficial, existential

sense, we in the Caribbean know all about nothing. We know that we owe Europe either revenge or nothing, and it is better to have nothing than revenge. . . . Revenge is uncreative."[43]

Thus the emphatic repetition of the term "nothing" near the conclusion of *Another Life* may be understood not as a nadir of pain and despair but as an opening for growth. Immediately in the following verses, Walcott summarizes with important dates, local place-names, and images the background of his island experience. Ending on a note of exaltation, he rejoices in the Greek name he assigned Gregorias. He is delighted with the task the two of them had—like that of the Mediterranean Greeks—of giving to a virginal world new names.

In poem after poem and play after play—despite the negative sound of titles like *Epitaph for the Young, The Castaway,* and *The Gulf*; despite the shortcomings and defeats of characters like Makak, Brown, Franklin, and the artist Harry Simmons—Walcott is not a negative writer. The meticulous honesty with which he attends to the somber aspects of life attests not to a morbid pessimism, but to a profound faith in the undying worth of things in themselves, no matter how degraded or corrupt they may have become. Walcott's kind of revolution is grounded in that inner worth that is not his alone but is available to anyone with the strength to journey back to it.

Chapter Five
Natural Topography: 1974–1980

Spirit of the 1970s

When considering the roots of his own culture, Walcott turned to some basic elements: "Where have cultures originated? By the force of natural surroundings. You build according to the topography of where you live. . . . you create what you need spiritually, a god for each need."[1] Long before writing these words in 1974, he had established the fact that his cultural topography extends beyond continental boundaries. He knows first the Caribbean, but from there he has been receptive to influences from Africa, Asia, Europe, North and South America. What at first appearance might have seemed "foreign" in his earliest writing has evolved into a consistent style as he matured, and by the late 1970s became endemic to his work. Experiments continue—new adaptations of matter and form—but there is a growing sense of culmination, as though a plateau has been reached. For example, the disparate elements constituting Walcott's style in 1974 made him an ideal choice for the Royal Shakespeare Company when that organization was seeking a modern revision of Tirso de Molina's Spanish classic *El Burlador de Sevilla.*

While *The Joker of Seville* brings out one area of Walcott's world, the past of Europe, *O Babylon!* reveals the topography closer to home. In this play he focuses on the Rastafarian subculture of Jamaica, only to draw out far-reaching implications about man's spiritual potential. More varied and comprehensive than either *The Joker of Seville* or *O Babylon!* are Walcott's two major volumes of poetry from this period, *Sea Grapes* (1976) and *The Star-Apple Kingdom* (1979). Without benefit of the central, narrative voice that unifies *Another Life,* Walcott succeeds as never before in linking the individual poems of *Sea Grapes* into a pattern of meaning. Retouching familiar themes, he provides a mature, yet fresh, retrospective of the inner and outer worlds of his poetic experience.

Appropriately, the next work to follow *Sea Grapes* is entitled *Remembrance* (1977). Using a flashback technique, Walcott has the protagonist, a subdued, retired teacher, recall the events of his life. There is little of the Brechtian flair for color and action in *Remembrance,* and still less in *Pantomine* (1978). The latter is another kind of journey into Walcott's past. Characters in it resurrect his well-worn Crusoe–Friday theme. Some passion is generated, but it derives more from philosophical exposition than from dramatic confrontation.

The phase that begins with all of Walcott's talents on display in the *The Joker of Seville* assumes a reflective direction with *Remembrance,* is almost becalmed in *Pantomine,* and then rises to powerfully assured resolution in *The Star-Apple Kingdom.* In spite of their static quality, *Remembrance* and *Pantomine* are more than a mere summing up. Given Walcott's subsequent move to the United States and his prolific writing throughout the 1980s, they seem to be an interlude before fresh undertakings. It is significant that at the time *Remembrance* was entering its first foreign production in April 1977 an announcement in *Caribbean Contact* noted Walcott's resignation from the Trinidad Theatre Workshop, the company he founded and had been heading for over 18 years.[2]

El Burlador

When Walcott accepted the Royal Shakespeare Company's commission to adapt *El Burlador de Sevilla* in 1974, he confronted the task—both problem and opportunity—of reinterpreting the legendary figure of Don Juan Tenorio. The problem is that since he was introduced into literature by Tirso de Molina (pseudonym of Gabriel Téllez, 1571?–1648), Don Juan and his exploits have been molded by the hands of such giants as Molière, Mozart, Lord Byron, and George Bernard Shaw. Any artist might well be intimidated by this monument of their construction. On the positive side, however, with his established mythic proportions, Don Juan provides an ideal vehicle for demonstrating the fact that Walcott's West Indian experience is neither as isolated nor as unique as its exotic appearance might suggest.

While the majority of Walcott's leading characters are little men who rise up as circumstances demand—Afa, Ti-Jean, Makak—Don Juan works in the opposite direction. He is an aristocrat, the ultimate in masculine potency, the embodiment of supernatural impulse. Among the components of the Don Juan archetype are the lover, the archrebel, the trickster, the Dionysian liberator, and the sacrificial god. Walcott expands the field of action to include the New World, but rather than add to the number of these dimensions he prefers to amplify certain

facets and provide more character exposition than appears in Tirso's original. In spite of the added psychological insight, Juan remains provoca-
tively enigmatic. In order to understand his motivation, inquiry must be
made into four central issues: the nature of his quest, lessons provided by
the women he seduces, the parallels drawn between the Old and New
Worlds, and the meaning of his tragic fate.

Walcott discovered that he had to change very little of Tirso's basic
plot in order to develop specific elements of his protagonist's character.
The original and Walcott's version of the play open with the seduction of
Isabella by Juan, who is disguised as her lover Octavio. Isabella is rele-
gated to a convent for her indiscretion. Juan escapes, and at this point
Walcott makes his most obvious departure from his source. Whereas
Tirso puts the next seduction (of Tisbea) in a Spanish fishing village near
Tarragona, Walcott launches Juan across the Atlantic to a Caribbean
island. In Walcott's text, Tisbea drowns herself upon learning that Juan
intends to abandon her; she merely disappears briefly in the original.
There are minor rearrangements of details, but both versions place the
third major scene, the pivotal sexual encounter, in Seville, in the house of
Don Gonzalo. Gonzalo's daughter Ana is Juan's third victim, whose
favors he enjoys disguised this time as her chosen lover the Marquis de
Mota. A duel follows, with Ana's outraged father dying in defense of her
honor; but Don Gonzalo's sworn vengeance results ultimately in Juan's
destruction. The scene of his fourth and last conquest is a country village
where Aminta on her wedding day is tricked into believing that her
betrothed groom has given her up in Juan's favor.

After enjoying her, Juan appears to tire of his adventures. He seeks
sanctuary in the church until he can make peace with both his father and
his king, and he agrees to marry Isabella. It is at this point that the statue of Don Gonzalo miraculously intervenes to exact his revenge.
Gripping Juan's hand, he drains all life from his body, denying him the
final rites of absolution. Tiros's ending is severe, but the last words
uttered by the statue sum up his message: "Esta es justicia de Dios: /
<<Quien tal hace, que tal pague.>>"[3] That a man must "reap what he
sows" is too much of a cliché and the deus ex machina as a theatrical
device falls short of expectations created by the quality of the rest of the
story. Raymond MacCurdy singles out the major difficulty in his introduction to the Laurel edition of the play: as clear as his prosaic point is,
"Tirso unwittingly subverted it by creating a character whose vital
response to the challenge of life and death suggests a meaning beyond

the literal meaning: man's compulsion to travel paths prohibited to him."[4]

Walcott quite properly seizes on Juan's compulsion as the heart of his modernized revision. He uses Tirso's plot, he claims, like a rough map—allowing details to blur, taking care to retain primarily the pace of its scenes, and the patterns of meter and rhyme. Authenticity, not artificial imitation, is his major concern.

Walcott noted, "[t]he wit, panache, the swift or boisterous elan of his [Tirso's] period, or of the people in his play, are as alive to me as the flair and flourishes of Trinidad music and its public character. . . . Once its music entered my head naturally there was no artifice in relating the music and drama of the Spanish verse to what strongly survives in Spanish Trinidad."[5] It is this compatibility of life-styles and means of expression, perhaps, that gave Walcott the confidence to adapt the figure of Don Juan to his own intents and purposes. (Walcott's free use of the original may also account at least in part for the fact that the Royal Shakespeare Company has yet to produce the play it commissioned.) Whatever may be the cause of delay in London, since its premier at the Little Carib Theatre in Port-of-Spain on November 28, 1974, Walcott's *Joker of Seville* has been received with enthusiasm by audiences each time it has been staged. Patricia Ismond reports in her review of two Port-of-Spain productions that audiences were elated with the "sheer sensuous and aesthetic expression"; the musical sequences in particular brought on a spirit of communal participation.[6]

Each aspect of the play pushes the action forward: music, humor, dialogue—all are in keeping with the protagonist's driving force, his compulsive quest. Shortly before his fatal meeting with the statue, Juan comes as close as is possible to explaining his motivation. Reminded by a priest of the church's principles of penitence and grace, he responds:

> I serve one principle! That of
> the generating earth whose laws
> compel the loping lion to move
> toward the fallow lioness,
> who in this second embodied
> his buckling stagger! I
> fought for that freedom delivered
> after Eden. If I defy

your principles because I served
nature, that was chivalry
less unnatural than your own.[7]

There is dramatic irony in the fact that the man he addresses, thinking
him to be his confessor, is actually Octavio, Isabella's vengeful lover, in
disguise. One effect of Juan's impenitent stand is to prevent Octavio
from attacking him. Octavio is too merciful to dispatch a sinner who has
not confessed and asked forgiveness; he leaves that to Don Gonzalo's
unfeeling "justice."

Another important function of Juan's speech is to reveal character.
Several points emerge: Juan embodies an irrational force—the spirit
within man that urges him to obey subconscious impulses and to defy
prohibitions such as those imposed in Eden and in society. He is, as
existential, post-Adamic man, outside the pale of institutional values.
The terms of his quest, indeed of his very existence, require that he use
every trick in his arsenal to outmaneuver each man and conquer each
female he encounters. As it turns out, however, the men he outwits
often see in him the vicarious fulfillment of some of their own suppressed desires. While they secretly relish his liberty, they hate him
and that dark nature within themselves that conscience struggles to
keep under control. That subconscious conflict is made explicit in a
dream that keeps haunting Octavio. His nightmare is of a garden, a
woman, and a snake. In that garden he becomes the beast he abhors
and the woman he attacks welcomes her violation. Knowing this
aspect of his personality, Octavio suspects the purity of even his most
honorable actions. Reacting out of guilt, he plots to have Juan murdered. The instrument of his design is Rafael, the leader of an acting
troupe, who is hired to assume the role of Don Gonzalo's statue. In
this way, Walcott makes more credible the appearance of a moving,
talking work of stone. Yet the element of supernatural intervention is
still retained, for at the crucial moment when Octavio's resolve breaks
and he commands Rafael to let go, he discovers that Juan is in the
unbreakable grasp of real stone.

Octavio's ambivalent feelings continue to the end, for, as he says, "the
Christian / warrior must love his dragon" (148). Without his dragon,
that evil which necessitates moral choice, the knight would have no reason to exist. There is informing ambivalence centered on the women
Juan seduces as well. They are not entrapped, but are liberated through
his violent embrace. Ironically, each woman bears some of the responsi-

bility for her fate because of a weakness in her own spiritual armor. Isabella and Ana are deceived by darkness and Juan's disguises, but each of her own volition has invited a man into her room to make love. Tisbea, in the pride of her beauty, disdains all suitors from her own social station, and as a consequence of her pretensions is susceptible to the advances of a gentleman. Aminta allows herself to be won over by the argument that love from the heart transcends marriage vows (and his argument is not weakened by the prospect he offers of a noble match in the future).

In connection with his depiction of these women, Walcott takes advantage of the opportunity to comment on the status of women in a male-dominated society. After months of contemplation in enforced seclusion, Isabella comes to see her loss of maidenly innocence in light of the human awareness and freedom that were purchased by Eve when she disobeyed God by eating the fruit of knowledge in Eden. Speaking to her fellow sufferers Ana and Aminta, she explains how chastity, self-denial, and conformity to the dictates of propriety are antithetical to full life and freedom:

> .   .   . He taught us choice.
> He, the great Joker of Seville,
>
>   .   .   .
>
> Listen, Ana, don't you see
> that what he's shown the lot of us
> is that our lust for propriety
> as wives is just as lecherous
> as his? Our protestations
> all marketable chastity?
> Such tireless dedication's
> almost holy! He set us free!
>
> (114, 117)

Such a bitterly earned perspective assuages the grief of Isabella and Ana, and to some extent Aminta, but it comes too late to help Tisbea, who rashly committed suicide when Juan dashed her hopes of upward mobility through marriage.

When Juan first met Tisbea on landing in the New World, which he took to be an uncorrupted, virgin land, he mistakenly thought that a

second Eve and another paradisal Eden were in the offing. Hope soon
turns to bitterness when she begins to talk of marriage and he is bent on
no encumbered love affair.

> A wife! You calculating bitch,
> you're as heartless as the average
> virgin back there!   .   .   .
>
>   .   .   .
>
> God, you beasts must love your cages!
> Marry a man, Tisbea; I am a
> force, a principle, the rest
> are husbands, fathers, sons; I'm none
> of these.   .   .   .
>
>   .   .   .
>
> I'm going back on the next ship.
> Old World, New World. They're all one.
> Dammit! I hate a wasted trip.

(47, 48)

Following the same line of thought, Juan's servant Catalinion criticizes
several of Tisbea's friends because of their desire to emulate a European
life-style. In the published text Catalinion speaks satirically of the relationship between Old World Christianity and New World slavery, but
in an earlier manuscript the underlying meaning is much clearer.
Given the opportunity to break the established pattern, they have
settled for an imitation of "free Spaniards." In the manuscript
Catalinion warns,

> You're watching the rape of the New World, but you're
> too close to notice.   .   .   .
>
>   .   .   .
>
> .   .   . You have a chance to remake
> things instead you accept them. That's disgraceful.[8]

Catalinion's disgust at colonial subjugation and Juan's diatribe against
the institution of marriage gives more definite focus to the general rebel-

liousness that Tirso instilled in his prototype. Both writers convey insight, but whereas Tirso's purpose is to exemplify a moral, Walcott conscientiously develops characters and uncovers issues that bear critical examination. The practice saves him from didacticism, and it may account for his decision to excise Catalinion's overly explicit speech to the islanders (as well as a few other direct pronouncements) when he published it.

In his wake, Juan leaves many disappointed expectations and sometimes death, as is the case with Tisbea and with Ana's father, but one result of his chicanery is the revelation of truth. Octavio and Isabella, and through them the audience, come to a deeper understanding of Juan and of their own humanity. This is their privilege and their reward—a prize that is not reserved for Juan Tenorio. A song in the prologue carries the choral refrain "*sans humanité.*" Therein lies Juan's tragic epitaph. As Juan remarks on several occasions, he is a principle, a force larger than life; therefore, like the white planter-devil in *Ti-Jean and His Brothers,* he is incapable of experiencing love. He admits as much to Isabella in scene 6 of act 2 (136). Taking leave of his father in the first act, he describes himself as a mirror which, feeling nothing itself, merely reflects the emotions of other men (66). Underscoring that assessment after Juan's death, his former rival the Marquis de Mota observes that there is no greater suffering than to have lived as Juan did, without a center, unable to return affection (149).

Juan's unrelenting siege of maidenhood and all vestiges of authority is fruitless for him, though others benefit from his exploits. To compound the fatal irony, Juan the archliberator is himself a victim, trapped in the irreverent role he has chosen to play. In this respect he assumes characteristics that are Dionysian. Opposed to him are the protectors of Apollonian reason and order: church, state, and home. Reason on the one hand and feeling on the other may be opposites, but they are polarities of the same continuum: they are complementary aspects of the whole person. Between these poles ordinary men continuously work out their mundane lives: he who ventures too far to either extreme places himself in jeopardy. Juan is willfully off center, representing man's irrational side, the unknown area from which spring dreams, imagination, and the will to survive and procreate in spite of life's ultimate termination in death. On the subject of death, Juan predicts that beyond life he will become a legend (137). When Don Gonzalo's statue confronts him with the prospect of Hell, he answers that no horror equals that of the empty existence he has known (144). Having chosen his inhuman role, he denies to himself everything that makes life pleasurable. Like the god of the grape, he delivers the freedom of uninhibited pleasure and pain to humanity, but he too must suffer and return to the dry earth in season.

Yet death is not the final word. As Juan's corpse is borne off by Rafael's players to an insistent calypso rhythm, death itself is cast in the joker's role: "*If there is resurrection, Death is the Joker, / sans humanité!*" (150). Juan's reward, like Makak's in *Dream on Monkey Mountain,* is to become immortalized as a dream image. Unlike Makak, however, Juan cannot descend from the realm of the ideal to the mundane tasks of day-to-day living.

Rafael's troupe serves as a chorus at points throughout the drama, and as costumed characters they would be familiar to West Indian audiences as Carnival bands. In harmony with the protagonist's role as Joker, they are dressed as the Jack, the Queen of Hearts, and the Ace of Death. The music they bring to the play is also as vibrant, sometimes as risqué and sharply satirical, as the region's kaiso. Thus, in spite of the serious theme and the protagonist's inevitably tragic ending, a lighter, comic mood is an integral part of the overall impact. As might be expected, the play contains all the qualities of the kind of integrated theatrical performance that Walcott speaks of as being nec-essary for West Indian expression; nevertheless, the meaning and the language belong to a larger world. In 1975, while he was engaged in rehearsing and revising *The Joker of Seville* for yet another series of pro-ductions, an interviewer asked whether there were any danger that he might ever be tempted to sacrifice artistic quality to the cause of regional theater. Citing Clifford Odets and Harold Pinter as examples, he answered that a good writer is inevitably parochial in certain ways. As he sees it, "The more particular you get, the more universal you become."[9] Walcott's particulars, of course, are commonly attached to very serviceable images and easily recognizable themes: the existential condition of Adam's descendants, the influence of experience on cer-tain types, man's response to various forms of authority, and the worth of the individual.

There is no serious test of this theory when it comes to adapting an established classic, but it becomes a crucial matter when in his next dra-matic effort Walcott turns to the subject of Jamaica's Rastafarian coun-terculture.

Ras Tafari

While *Dream on Monkey Mountain* was being staged in New York in 1971, Walcott was quoted in an interview there as saying that the play was about the West Indian search for identity, and about the damage that colonialism does to the soul. He felt that the situation he described was true not only in the third world, but in any society where men have been reduced to a meaningless, purposeless existence. He feared that some people in attempting to find a way out of their predicament might end up escaping from reality itself. Such was the danger he saw in the movement popular among many Negroes of returning spiritually or physically to Africa.[10] In another discussion that same year, he expressed the opinion that his countrymen were mistaken in diluting "our real power, a human thing, with the hallucination of *sharing* it, either with Africa or America." His solution: to find a truly West Indian sense of belonging, "We must look *inside*."[11]

Dream on Monkey Mountain dramatizes that philosophy, which reappears five years later in the Trinidad Theatre Workshop's opening production of *O Babylon!* Walcott could hardly have selected a group that is farther removed than the Rastafarians are from the mainstream of modern Western culture. The sect practices abstention from the material trappings of civilization, making a virtue of poverty, until they can escape Babylonian exile and return to Africa. He had this to contend with, as well as their deliberately distorted language. To suit the material for the public stage, he could rely on two primary points of common reference: certain recognizable qualities basic to human nature and biblical scripture.

The setting of *O Babylon!* is a squatter community facing the harbor of Kingston, Jamaica, in 1966. The year is significant because it was then that Haile Selassie made his celebrated visit to Jamaica. There is sufficient documentary accuracy to assure realism of place, time, and character. Walcott stresses the peaceful intentions of the Rastafarian brethren, but he does not ignore the militancy and violence that seem to be an inevitable part of minority movements in recent years. Their unusual life-style, including their matted "dreadlock" hair and heavy use of ganja (marijuana), draws added attention from the authorities. Fortunately, Walcott does not overburden the text with arcane doctrine; necessary exposition occurs naturally. Rufus Johnson, the protagonist, becomes a convert early in the play, and since he has difficulty living down his criminal past he has to be reminded of his new faith. "Rude Bwoy" Dawson, a cynical outsider who wants only to become a popular singing star, is continually testing the values of his friends.

Rude Bwoy's rising career leads the scene to shift at times from the beach settlement to the alleys, dressing rooms, and stages of the night-club circuit. Music then (again scored by Galt MacDermot—some dri-ving reggae, some pleasantly lyrical, some spiritual)—becomes an important consideration. In one article Walcott is quoted as having described *O Babylon!* as the first "real musical" ever to be staged by his company; the crucial difference between it and a play like *The Joker of Seville* is that he had not previously attempted to incorporate song and dance so thoroughly into the very design of a text. He expects his per-formers to be judged by their singing and dancing as well as by their ability to act.[12] He may have a point in making this distinction, but whether the final product succeeds or fails depends on what he has writ-ten and how well he functions as a director.

Early productions (and the play has been restaged several times in Trinidad and Jamaica since its premier at the Little Carib in 1976) brought receptive audiences, but a number of critics—even as recent-ly as a 1988 London production[13]—detected what they considered to be serious flaws. Victor Questel, who has followed Walcott's career closely, found the acting to be uninspired and the construction of the play to be "without the fierce integrity that the Rastafarian cult deserves and demands." It is "too easily, too glibly put together," the music developing weakly and separately from the plot. Questel had reservations about the altered Jamaican dialect as well.[14] Sule Mombara attributes the breakdown in dramatic performance to a fun-damental incompatibility between the traditionally light European musical form and the African orientation of the beleaguered Rastafarian culture.[15] Raoul Pantin appreciates Walcott's translation of problematic social conditions into drama, singling out his satirical por-trayal of "Deacon" Doxy, the local politician who sells out to foreign entrepreneurs. He has high praise for the "immortal figures" sketched in the play, but considers the musical element to be too delicate to carry the vigorous tempo that is called for.[16]

Whether he regarded these opinions or not, Walcott made important changes in the text before *O Babylon!* was published in 1978. In 1976 the play opens with an elaborate nightclub routine in the plush New Zion Hotel.[17] It quickly turns serious as Rude Bwoy the "Big Black Star" reminisces about the shantytown yards where he and the reggae music that lifted him to fame originated. The revision for publication loses much of the glitter, but instead there is a stylized reenactment, behind a choral explanation, of the near-fatal event that thrust Rufus Johnson into the Rastafarian camp. The new version has several advantages: it captures the audience's attention with less wasted motion; it shows at the start, as the original did not, the process by which Rufus (who adopts the name Aaron) finds new faith and peace; and it sets immediately a more serious tone that is consistent with the central theme. The conclusion, another emphatic portion of any play, is also improved by revision. The older manuscript has an unconvincing parting scene between Aaron and his common-law wife, Priscilla, who is about to desert him for some indeterminate destination in Babylon. Claiming that her unborn child deserves a better chance in life, she picks an argument with Aaron and walks out. Her resolve breaks suddenly, however, and she rushes back to embrace her husband. Her timing is melodramatically perfect, for he is on the point of marching to his death in the sea, entranced with his vision of joining ancient African warriors.

In the published play the final scene is toned down. Priscilla is pregnant, but without dwelling on her misfortunes she simply tries to convince herself rather than the audience that she should return to her former life as "Electric Gyal" in Rude Bwoy's show. When her determination fails this time, she is locked in Aaron's arms and they resolve to work out their future together at a new settlement in the mountains. Both versions have uplifting conclusions; the later one is more down to earth, with hope for a future Zion and the will to make the best of their own world in the present. Other parts of the play are similarly refined, with greater care devoted to generating causal relationships between the action and the musical score.

Every aspect of dramatic tension in the plot centers on the conflict between the temptations of venal comforts and man's yearning for a spiritually fulfilling life. The most aggressive antagonist is the land-development corporation with Mafia ties in the United States that plans to build a resort hotel on the property occupied by the Rastafarians. The corporation purchases the services of the politician "Deacon" Doxy, his mistress Dolly, the white social worker Mrs. Powers, and Rude Bwoy. They are unsuccessful with Aaron and with "Sufferer," the leader of the squatter community. Much inner conflict develops because of the pressure—in the form of official harassment, physical abuse, and tempting bribes—to destroy the settlement. Matters are forced to fever pitch by the news of Haile Selassie's imminent arrival in the country. The brethren are elated to learn that a number of them will be repatriated when their emperor returns to Ethiopia.

All might have gone well except for the restriction that prohibited former criminals, like Aaron and his closest friend Samuel, and the elderly, like Sufferer, from being eligible for repatriation. Probably Aaron, Samuel, and Sufferer would have allowed the corporation to have its way in return for guaranteed passage. As it turns out, Aaron's frustration drives him to commit arson against his tormentors. He is apprehended, committed to jail, and thus because of his own weakness is prevented from seeing his God in the flesh. His rash act drives Priscilla to the verge of leaving him, but they both learn a valuable lesson from the experience and end up in a stronger relationship than they had known before. Unfortunately, because of his lawless action the Rastafarian brethren lose the government's permission to use the land. The corporation wins: Deacon becomes proprietor of the ironically named "New Zion Hotel"; Rude Bwoy is signed to a lucrative contract to play in the hotel's "Babylon Lounge"; those who could not sail for Ethiopia are forced to be absorbed by Babylon or to begin anew in the mountains.

As the various conflicts resolve themselves, the theme rises to the surface. One key to Walcott's underlying message may be found in Rude Bwoy's changing perspective. As he experiences success, his cynicism wears away until he admits to envy for Aaron's strength in battling the temptations that had been too great for him to resist. Aaron serves as a more positive example. Priscilla and the Rastafarians nurse him back to health after the gunshot wound he suffered in defending Rude Bwoy in the prologue. In scene 1 he assumes a new trade, that of a woodcarver, for subsistence. From the start his carving of a statue of the biblical Four Horsemen is more than a simple job. It takes on both spiritual and artistic significance, the Horsemen being duplicated and inserted symbolically into the action in the persons of the dancers Edwin, Elijah, Daniel, and Shadrach. Aaron pours his heart into the carving, and his chisel is especially precious. Ironically, it is his chisel, stolen and planted at the scene of the fire, that leads to his arrest, trial, and confession of guilt. The climax of the play comes in his defense lawyer's final summation, one of the most powerful musical sequences in the text:

> *Oh who in his heart has not wanted to burn*
> *the unjust city?*

> *The ghettos, the slums, the barrios, the dunghills,*
> *the shanty-towns, Laventilles, Harlems,*
> *from Rio to Kingston?*
>
> . . .
>
> *But if we who are the just*
> *lock him up in darkness,*
> *I know, in the depth of that dark,*
> *you will still see something burning,*
> *starlike, a diamond, unquenchable,*
> *a simple spark!*[18]

The sequence ends with a strident chorus, fire in the background, and the jail doors slamming shut on Aaron.

The play winds down to its conclusion three brief scenes later. The summary for the defense expands Aaron's plight to include the oppressed wherever they are found. In addition it signals that "unquenchable spark" which turns out to be Aaron's salvation. When he is released from jail days later, his sacred locks shaven, feeling that he has betrayed all that was valuable to him, his faith is still intact. He tells Priscilla that even though he has not seen God, his God still exists.

In the triumphant finale stress is placed on a heavenly Zion—perhaps too much stress, in light of Walcott's expressed concern about the hallucination of escaping from the real world. There are, however, explicit passages within the play where he makes it clear that Aaron's strength derives from his growing sense of belonging. Aaron spends two days walking in the clear air of the mountains and he comes to love that part of his native Jamaica. At the moment when it seems that he has lost everything, he finds peace inside—where Walcott insists man must look to find his authentic identity.

In spite of the leveling influence of that central theme, and the revisions for more unified structure, *O Babylon!* is still an unsatisfying, somewhat romantic play. The protagonist is better off than Don Juan because he discovers a center within his existence. Aaron makes the same adjustment to place that Makak makes, but he is not the fully realized character that either of these other figures is. Walcott would have done well to have developed those forces in Aaron's life that give him the strength to believe, rather than trail off into a nebulous vision of future rewards in Zion. There are fine poetic passages and moments of good theater, but in

O Babylon! Walcott seems to be refining formal techniques and rework-
ing old themes rather than exploring in any particular new direction.

Odysseus Revisited

Walcott's sixth major book of poetry, *Sea Grapes,* was published in 1976,
the same year *O Babylon!* first appeared. Although both works to a certain extent revive familiar material, *Sea Grapes* functions more successfully as an artistic whole. Whereas *Another Life* pays tribute to St. Lucia, the
birthplace that had shaped his childhood, *Sea Grapes* is an index, a virtu-
al compendium of every major influence on his poetry. Aside from
Another Life, which is one extended autobiographical poem, this is the
first of Walcott's many verse collections to exhibit a sustained, organic
unity.

There is a subtle but effective pattern in *Sea Grapes,* a pattern that
seems to have been overlooked by the *Nation*'s reviewer, who argues that
the book attempts to bring in too much diversity to be rounded off completely.[19] The initial sign that a metaphorical return voyage is in store
appears in the title poem. The opening image is of a Caribbean schooner
sailing homeward. In the observer's mind, that scene is telescoped to the
Aegean Sea and Odysseus's journey back from Troy. All the movement
runs full circle by means of a second classical allusion. The boulder
heaved at Odysseus by the giant Cyclops he had blinded creates a
ground swell that washes up in rhythmic surf on Caribbean beaches.
Anyone who knows Walcott's poetry will recognize the connection: as a
Western artist, he acknowledges his classical origins. "Sea Grapes" also
brings out the timeless theme of man's divided nature:

> .   .   . The ancient war
> between obsession and responsibility
> will never finish and has been the same
>
>   .   .   .
>
> since Troy lost its old flame.[20]

In Walcott's life as well as in his writing, this split between personal feeling (obsession) and public duty (responsibility) is compounded by his
divided heritage as a West Indian. His dual allegiance gives added
poignance to the concluding line, "The classics can console. But not
enough" (9). The story of his career has been the struggle to reconcile

such opposites as European thinking (its formal order and calculating reason) with African feeling (associated with "soul" and natural instinct).

In order to prove the endlessly rich possibilities latent in this kind of blending, he has developed a style that is as rich and varied as the West Indies itself. The title poem merely opens the door to a second look at many of the resources he has utilized. A review does not have to be repetitious. Redundancy never becomes a problem in *Sea Grapes*, for although much of the territory has been covered previously, a seasoned perspective and a mature style keep the expression fresh. Furthermore, there is evidence that Walcott has added control not only of the content of individual poems, but of interrelationships that extend through the entire collection. No physical subdivisions are made in the text, no arbitrary groupings; nevertheless, there are roughly three major movements within the book. They form units of unequal length, approximately 47, 23, and 17 pages, respectively, with little more than tangential ideas to suggest that they interconnect. Within the groups are lesser concentrations of closely related ideas that counteract any superficial tendency on the reader's part to stray from the integrity of any single poem. At key junctures a few poems provide incidental transitions from one major center of interest to the next so that overall continuity is maintained subtly.

Whether Walcott intended this intricate substructure, it exists nonetheless. The crucial dividing factor, as the title poem suggests with its transoceanic, cross-cultural references, is geography. The largest section, containing 21 poems beginning with "Sea Grapes," is devoted to the Caribbean and it culminates in a paean to St. Lucia. Three poems on the U.S. Virgin Island city of Frederiksted direct the reader's attention to the corruption that follows in the wake of tourism. Having established the idea of beauty despoiled, Walcott then inserts two coolly detached pieces on art: "Sunday Lemons," a verbal still life depicting a bowl of fruit beside a reclining woman, and "Schloss Erla," which conjures seasonal images of a Brueghel painting. Following this interlude are three philosophic poems on one of Walcott's favorite subjects, Adam in the Garden of Eden. "The Cloud" depicts Adam beside the sleeping woman who had proved to be the instrument of his death. As the shadow of a passing cloud falls across them, he names it "tenderness." "New World" comments on Adam's adjustment to the curse of earning a living by the sweat of his labor. Bitter humor appears in the closing lines:

> Adam had an idea.
> He and the snake would share

the loss of Eden for a profit.
So both made the New World. And it looked good.

(19)

"Adam's Song" makes the point that men still sing of the burden that
was acquired in Eden.

Adam's progeny, at least those who continue to betray their brothers,
become the subject of attack in the next eight poems. The evangelical
hyenas of "Vigil in the Desert" become the smiling betrayers who "exact
thirty pieces of silver / in the name of a cause" in "The Brother" (23–24).
Other targets include the guilt-ridden writer in "Preparing for Exile"
and the party hacks in "Party Night at the Hilton" who wrangle impo-
tently and without imagination. Against the politicians who are casti-
gated for forgetting about the people who elect them in such poems as
"The Lost Federation" and "Parades, Parades," Walcott offers a tribute to
Jean Miles in "The Silent Woman" (31). Hers was one voice that would
not permit the poor and needy to go unnoticed. "The Dream" (a song
that appears in *O Babylon!*) and "Dread Song" are concerned with current
spiritual degradation. The latter particularly focuses on the divisive
attractions of "Economics and Exodus." After a long history of changes
that make no difference, Walcott sees their credo as pointless suffering:
"let things be the same / forever and ever / the faith of my tribe" (34).

"Natural History" forms a bridge from the harsh bitterness generated in the political poems to the more constructive hope that comes to
dominate in the crucial poems that round out the first section of the
book. "Natural History" is about man's evolutionary growth, from the
time he emerges from the sea as a "walking fish," through his adaptation to a hostile environment, into his atomic age. The struggle has
moments of accomplishment and much brutality. Ironically, man's
beautiful aspirations often result in destruction and rapine. The next
poem, "Names," continues the image of the sea as the mother of life.
This time the sea gives birth to the West Indian "race," a people who,
having been cut off from their ancestral roots by the middle passage,
must assume Adam's ancient responsibility of naming the New World
in terms that will make it truly their own. "Names" is studded with references to broken shards of the Old World that have washed up on
Caribbean shores: Benares, Canton, Benin, Castile, and Versailles are
but a few. At the end of the poem an exasperated voice asks what the
stars look like if they are not Orion and Betelgeuse. A child answers,
"Sir, fireflies caught in molasses" (42).

This unsophisticated, earthy response is the perfect note to lead into the book's centerpiece. "Sainte Lucie" is not only the dramatic climax of the first section, the longest and most stylistically diverse poem; it is also at the physical center of the text. The first two of the five subdivisions of "Sainte Lucie" run through local place-names and the native dialect that give Walcott's birthplace its unique identity: "moi c'est gens St Lucie. / C'est la moi sorti; / is there that I born" (47). There follows in the third division a native song in dialect which is reproduced in the fourth section in standard English. The concluding part, subtitled "For the Altar-piece of the Roseau Valley Church . . . ," is constructed around a mural painted by Walcott's friend Dunstan St. Omer (the "Gregorias" of *Another Life*). The significance of the mural is that it functions as a spiritual focus for the island. In it St. Omer has depicted not unearthly saints, but the local people in their accustomed attitudes of living and worshiping. Walcott candidly admits that the Roseau Valley is not the Garden of Eden and that its inhabitants are not in heaven, but he sees faith in them, and "the real faces of angels" (55).

Combining realism and faith in "Sainte Lucie," Walcott displays the kind of balanced perspective that has kept him from being distracted from the restraint demanded by his art. He never loses himself either in fantastic illusions or the depths of self-pitying despair. There is in this regard a special kinship between him and Walt Whitman, another "national" poet, whose name appears in the first line of the poem that opens the second major ideological portion of *Sea Grapes*. As Walcott's reference to Whitman in "Over Colorado" suggests, visionary prophesies have also gone awry in places other than the West Indies. Several of the geographical fixes in this 14-poem section are clearly indicated by some of the titles: "Over Colorado," "Ohio, Winter," "California," and "Midsummer, England." Other locations are scattered liberally within the poems.

One of Walcott's objectives in this part, aside from the re-creation of foreign scenes, is to acknowledge gratitude to certain writers. "For Pablo Neruda" singles out the late Chilean poet as an example for third world artists, "a benign, rigorous uncle, / and through you we fanned open" (61). "Volcano" refers to James Joyce and Joseph Conrad as giants of another age whose thunder and lightning are now taken for granted by a generation that no longer distinguishes greatness. To his detriment, man has lost his sense of awe. The section contains several short poems on love, inner suffering, and personal loss; then it reaches a peak of intensity with two especially effective poems. "Midsummer, England" begins as a postcard landscape, turns bitter with the fearful newspaper accounts of the dark tide of immigrants corrupting the "imperial blood," then becomes reflective. The observer of the scene wonders at his hurt feelings: he had thought that he was immune.

Personal feelings remain the center of interest in "The Bright Field." His nerves fortified against the massiveness of London, the man in this poem absorbs visual details of the evening until his mind wanders from underground trains and cabs to bullock-carts in far-off canefields. Distances dissolve and images coalesce as he realizes that the wings of birds circling above him in London beat the same rhythm as pelicans in his native island. Edward Baugh finds "The Bright Field" to be reminiscent of "Ruins of a Great House," with a very important difference. The earlier poem from *In a Green Night* (1962) re-creates a West Indian's painful confrontation with history. "The Bright Field," on the other hand, "is most concerned with recreating the glow of the one dying light which illuminates and unifies all (seeming) opposites—past and present, the crowd and the individual, colonising conqueror and colonial victim."[21] The older theme is evident, but in its reappearance in the more recent poem it is extended significantly.

After touching points on the outer circumference of his broader world, Walcott returns with the intermingled images of "The Bright Field" to his original West Indies. The structure of the book, then, becomes circuitous. The calm reconciliation achieved in "The Bright Field" also brings the second phase of exposition to an emotional completion, preparing as it does so for the mood of the concluding section.

"Dark August" begins the final group of 11 poems in a tone of voice that sounds more somber than before; it denotes hard wisdom acquired by experience. In the pouring rain of a gloomy day, the speaker says that he is "learning slowly / to love the dark days . . . / and to sip the medicine of bitterness" (79). After complaining in "Sea Cranes" that the earth has claimed more of his loved ones than it has left, he recognizes that in return he has grown stronger. In these later poems, with one exception, there is no trace of the rancor that appeared fleetingly in "Midsummer, England." The exception is "At Last": addressing himself to "the exiled novelists" who have only disparagement to heap on their homeland, the writer asks them to consider the fact that an artist can survive in the Caribbean. With undisguised pride he cries that even though the "heartbreaking past" neither forgives nor is forgivable, "the net of my veins I have cast / here flashes with living / silver at last, at last!" (90).

No one should make the mistake of identifying the speaker in "At Last" with Walcott. A brief glance at the poem that follows it, "Winding Up," reveals a counterbalancing antithesis. The poet here resolves to quench feeling, to forget his gift, and to learn to live "rock-like" (91). Neither extreme, of course, is Walcott's. The attitude that dominates the final section of the book and leaves the last impression is more stable. In "The Morning Moon" and "To Return to the Trees," Walcott shows that he is indeed capable of the kind of crisp, clear, straightforward poetry that he speaks of in "Islands" over 20 years earlier. "The Morning Moon" expresses pleasure in change itself, down to the white hairs he discovers growing in his beard. The theme carries over into "To Return to the Trees," where the color gray has come to symbolize strength. As with the trees of the title, he secures his hold on the earth by sinking roots, by "going under the sand / with this language, slowly, / by sand grains, by centuries" (95).

In the final stanza Walcott settles unerringly upon the core of his strength. *Sea Grapes* proves once more his adept handling of each level of the spoken and written word. In her review of *Sea Grapes* for the *American Poetry Review,* Valerie Trueblood recalls the fact that Walcott has been "criticized at home for not making the break with the great tradition of English literature and writing in 'the language of the tribe.' " She correctly observes that "[h]is way is to find what we didn't know was there in English, while keeping its excellences."[22] What he has found is as much an outgrowth of the language he has heard, wherever spoken, as the words and concepts he has derived from the written page. His treasured resources have served him well both in poetry and in drama.

Remembrances of Things Past

Remembrance, the play that was first performed in St. Croix in April 1977, exhibits in its title the general tendency of Walcott's writing in the middle and late 1970s to conjure up the past. While he seems to be settling into a more concentrated form, he shows less diversity and a calmer, more measured pace.

Compared with most of his previous plays, there is not much physical action in *Remembrance.* The little music that occurs is primarily for supporting mood. Although the opening scene is a drawing room in contemporary Port-of-Spain, Walcott employs a flashback technique to start the main story many years earlier, before Trinidad became independent. His protagonist, Albert Jordan, has been induced after many requests from the editor of the *Belmont Bugle* to confide his thoughts to a tape recorder. Since Jordan—a retired, locally prominent schoolmaster and poet—was involved more or less inadvertently in the country's independence and Black Power movements, the *Bugle* wants a record of his views. With this convenient framework, Walcott accomplishes seamless transitions in time and place.

Looking back on his life, Jordan at first recalls only mistakes and failure. As schoolmaster, husband, father, and occasional writer, he contends he has had no positive impact. The students he taught with great conviction grew to taunt him as "Uncle Tom" because of his values. His wife carries on a running battle against his futile hopes of winning overnight riches from the lottery drawings. Both of his sons have wasted their lives, he feels, as a result of the inadequate model he provided them. Albert Junior was killed by the police during a Black Power altercation. Frederick has become a painter. Because of his own disappointments as a writer, Jordan sees his second son's career as an artist in a backwater colony as merely a slow form of death.

Jordan's assessment, of course, is not the only one available. As the story unfolds, it becomes apparent that Jordan deserves credit (that he refuses to allow himself) for having raised the consciousness of his ungrateful pupils so that when the time came they found the pride to take up the cause of Black Power. His sons' independent gestures may seem empty to him, but they show that each of them possessed the strength to pursue his own destiny. In a scene toward the end of the play his wife confesses that her constant antagonism had been her way of keeping up his waning spirits. The people who know him—the editor of the *Bugle,* his wife, Frederick, and others—respect him in spite of his own self-deprecation.

Walcott manages to include a great deal of rhetoric and exposition in this play by having Jordan disclaim the philosophical tenets that he had lived by. The primary vehicle for drawing his essential ideas together is Thomas Gray's "Elegy Written in a Country Churchyard." In several brief sequences Jordan is shown back in his classroom declaiming the virtues of Gray's message. Jordan's theme (Gray's and Walcott's as well) is that the individual human being is of worth despite his humble birth and provincial surroundings.

Jordan sought to instill that sense of value in his students, yet he guarded against letting them know that he loved them, thinking that they would see it as a sign of his weakness. This accounts in part for their later misunderstanding of his motives. Another factor that turned them against Jordan was that the literature he loved and the concepts he advocated were imported from England, the imperial oppressor. Jordan suffers to a degree from having been a colonial subject all his life. To his credit, he realizes that it was his own class consciousness that had denied him access to Esther Trout, the English girl he once loved. That is not sufficient reason, however, for his denying the validity of his own true beliefs. A degree of moral fortitude is discernible in the unpopular stand he took during the Black Power agitations. Had he been really weak, he could have followed the crowd; instead, he turned his quiet anger inward and allowed the revolutionary fury to expend itself around him in words and gestures.

In the end, having relived some of his experiences, Jordan comes to realize that his didactic message has more practical application in his own life than he had been able to admit. Youthful vigor begins to return to him as the sun rises at dawn: "I taught those little bastards well, didn't I? I taught with a passion. Wrong things or not. Some of them are big shots today, judges. But I was a holy terror in that classroom, boy. . . . I taught them with the love that comes through books and I inspired the fear that would give them confidence."[23] At last, Jordan is at peace with his inner voice. By way of relieving the seriousness of his overt pronouncement, Walcott concludes the play with bittersweet words from Jordan's departed but still-contentious wife: "you was argumentative, stupid, and a stubborn man, but you was a king to me. I tired now, and I going. Turn off the stove. And Albert. . . . Don't bother with the sweepstake ticket, you hear? 'Cause you ent going win it" (84). With that out of the way, Jordan is now ready to begin recording, and the reverie that constitutes the play is at an end.

Another play from this period that recalls the past, in a way slightly different from *Remembrance,* is *Pantomime* (1978). *Pantomime* was first staged in Port-of-Spain, and in January 1979 it was performed over BBC radio in England. It is not retrospective in the sense of looking back at the past, but it revives once more Walcott's familiar Robinson Crusoe theme.

On the surface *Pantomime* appears inconsequential. The plot involves a running argument between Harry, English manager of a second-rate tourist hotel, and his black assistant Jackson, an erstwhile calypsonian. Their ostensible point of contention is the artistic propriety of a nightclub pantomime that Harry, who is a retired actor, wishes to perform for his seasonal patrons. In spite of its limited cast of two and its apparently light plot, however, the play comes close to delivering more than it promises at first. The narrative takes an ironic turn and quickly becomes seriously involved when Jackson suggests that they switch roles in their Crusoe skit, he becoming the master and Harry assuming Friday's place.

Harry makes an attempt to play the servant, but he balks at the extreme reversal of a black man's culture and gods being imposed on a Christian: "I mean . . . he'd have to be taught by this—African . . . that everything was wrong, that what he was doing . . . I mean, for nearly two thousand years . . . was wrong. That his civilization, his culture, his whatever, was . . . *horrible*. Was all . . . wrong."[24] Jackson, who has quickly entered the spirit of just such an inverted order, does not let the opportunity pass. While Harry wishes to keep the mood lightly satirical, Jackson seizes on the fact that what is happening between them is precisely the history of colonialism itself. Whenever the civilized native rises to the level of his master, the master wants to "call the whole thing off, return things to normal" (128).

Act 2, with Harry's awareness heightened somewhat, has the two men discussing in more specific terms the implications of racial and cultural equality. It is Jackson's contention that Robinson Crusoe would necessarily be a practicing realist, not the lonely romanticist Harry imagines. Instead of pining over his lost wife and son, Jackson's Crusoe would take control of his situation and hew a new life out of the raw material of his environment. He sees him as the first true "Creole" because of the practical efficacy of his faith. The immediate conclusion of his argument is that if Harry is to survive on the island he must adapt himself to circumstances as they exist in the present. Jackson presses him into acting out some of the frustrations he suffers over his having failed as an actor and a husband. In the end the two men acquire, through deeper understanding, a more equitable relationship.

It is difficult to judge from a written text how well plays such as *Pantomime* and *Remembrance* will fare on stage. The New York production of *Remembrance* was thought by one critic to grow tedious in later moments; the *New Yorker's* Edith Oliver found the slowing, darkening action to be effective. Reviewing a Trinidad production of *Pantomime,* Christopher Gunness was impressed with the brilliant verbal exchanges in early scenes which gradually gave way to a somber, highly intensified emotional closing.[25] Directors evidently continue to find both plays viable for the stage: *Pantomime* was produced by the Hudson Guild Theatre in Washington, D.C., 11 December 1986–4 January 1987, and by Brenda Hughes in Port-of-Spain, 26 December 1991–25 January 1992; a revival of *Remembrance* was sponsored by the Central Bank of

Trinidad and Tobago in Port-of-Spain, 3–12 November 1989, and the Carib Theatre Company brought it to the Tricycle Theatre in London, July 1990. In print, at least, *Pantomime* appears to rely rather heavily on exposition and it seems too ambivalent in intention. Gunness remarked this same ambivalence in the staging. It is as though Walcott were no more decided than his characters were as to how serious their seriocomic play should be. There is no trace of this uncertainty in his poetry during this period.

Kingdoms of the Mind

The Star-Apple Kingdom has its meditative pauses, but it starts vigorously and moves with hardly a misstep to a positive conclusion. "The Schooner *Flight*" sets a rapid pace initially by beginning in the midst of a narrative. In his natural patois, Shabine the seaman-poet describes himself and his situation, then goes back to his earlier life at sea. He had smuggled Scotch for a while and tried salvage diving, but nothing gave him satisfaction. For one thing, he was torn between love for his wife and children, on the one hand, and his passion for Maria Concepcion, the woman whose beauty had separated him from them, on the other. Religion and liquor offered only temporary respite because his longing runs deeper than sexual and familial needs. In the final movement of the poem he seizes upon his essential theme, the "vain search for one island that heals with its harbor / and a guiltless horizon."[26] Such an ideal, even idle, quest could keep the romantic adrift forever, but Shabine is not chasing a fabulous grail.

Life has focused Shabine's attention on a soberingly real world. History, he says, failed to recognize him: not white enough to be accepted among the wielders of power before the independence movement, he found afterward that he was not dark enough for the blacks who took over. Their revolution in fact strikes him as largely empty gestures and political chicanery. One hallucinatory vision, which has the ships of conquistadors and then slave ships pass by, leaves him with the understanding that no man knows his own grandsire. In a more cynical mood, he concludes that "Progress is history's dirty joke" (14). It was "progress," after all, that led to the annihilation of the Carib Indians, slavery, the decline of great empires, and present colonial neglect.

In spite of his hard opinions about the conditions of life in the Caribbean, Shabine possesses a larger insight. This fact emerges as the result of a storm which fails in all its terrible fury to break the *Flight* and

her crew. In the calm aftermath Shabine muses that whatever the rain
cleanses and the sun irons out is sufficient for him. He has learned, as did
Coleridge's Ancient Mariner, to appreciate the simple, given things.
Arriving at the end of the story, he attests, "I am satisfied / if my hand
gave voice to one people's grief" (19). Without approving the injustice
and the social inequities of the West Indies, Shabine can still accommodate himself there and live fruitfully.

In two poems that follow, "In the Virgins" and "Sabbaths, W.I.," and
in the later poem "The Saddhu of Couva," Walcott slackens his pace
somewhat, perhaps to vary the overall rhythm of the book, counterbalancing the lyric and philosophical intensity of other selections.
"Sabbaths, W.I." and "The Saddhu of Couva" are pleasant evocations of
place, but a singular flaw shows up when he seems to strive too hard for
an effect in the final lines of "In the Virgins":

> Like neon lasers shot across the bars
> discos blast out the music of the spheres,
> and, one by one, science infects the stars.
>
> (22)

Neither the subject nor the mood calls for such metaphorical gesticu-
lation.

"The Sea Is History" and "Egypt, Tobago," two poems at the center
of this small volume, exemplify Walcott's accustomed skill in arranging
words so that they evolve naturally, sufficiently motivated, reining in
their dynamic power. In the first of these poems history is said to have
buried the monuments, martyrs, battles, and tribal memory that should
have survived in the Caribbean. Alluding to key terms from Judeo-
Christian tradition, the poet then tallies his lost heritage: the Genesis of
sailing vessels, the Exodus of slaves, Babylonian exile, Port Royal (their
Gomorrah) swallowed as Jonah was into the sea. There are sufficient
grounds for Lamentations, but as he notes, that is not the whole story.
Emancipation and the New Testament are fused only to show how joy
can degenerate into lost faith. In more recent times the bright expectations of independence had been subverted, but the point is raised once
more that particular facts and disappointed dreams are not "History"
itself.

The latent meaning of the poem and the key to Walcott's understanding of the place of history in the West Indies is reserved for the

final, single-line stanza. There he suggests that history is really just beginning. The implication is that no matter what memory preserves, history is not a sealed book; it remains within the province of man to build with (or in spite of) the present. This very concept is the theme of Walcott's lecture "The Muse of History," delivered at Columbia University in April 1971. He argues the cause of poets who can use tradition without fighting against its sources or being overcome by its force. "Their philosophy, based on a contempt for historic time, is revolutionary, for what they repeat to the New World is its simultaneity with the Old. . . . Their vision of man in the New World is Adamic." Thus freed to transcend time and space, "fact evaporates into myth" for them, and "this is not the jaded cynicism which sees nothing new under the sun, it is an elation which sees everything as renewed."[27]

Judeo-Christian parallels in "The Sea Is History" are followed in "Egypt, Tobago" by a similar transpostion. This time Mark Antony, with Cleopatra asleep beside him, is depicted on a Tobago beach while defeat settles over his ambitious enterprises. The language of description is rife with veiled sexuality, but the emphasis of the poem is on the power of "All-humbling sleep . . . / who swings this globe by a hair's trembling breath" (32). Despite their weight of sin and the crumbling of their world,

> everything else
> is vanity, but this tenderness
> for a woman not his mistress
> but his sleeping child.

(32)

The truth of the sentiment is timeless; the station in life of the participants and their geographical place are irrelevant.

That being the case, it is easier than it might otherwise have been for Walcott to slip two poems into this volume of Caribbean verse that have little to do with the West Indies. "R.T.S.L." is a tribute to Walcott's late friend, the American poet Robert Lowell. The essence of the man is captured in the final lines in words that could be no more spare and appropriate:

> and something that once had a fearful name
> walks from the thing that used to wear its name,

> transparent, exact representative,
> so that we can see through it
> churches, cars, sunlight,
> and the Boston Common,
> not needing any book.

(37)

"Forest of Europe" is dedicated to Joseph Brodsky, filled with the image of Osip Mandelstam, and is aimed at defining the use of poetry. Descending to a tone that is more conversational than anything since "The Schooner *Flight*," the speaker asks,

> what's poetry, if it is worth its salt,
> but a phrase men can pass from hand to mouth?
> From hand to mouth, across the centuries,
> the bread that lasts when systems have decayed.

(40)

The lines and the scene are relaxed. Two men exchange experiences by the light of a winter fire; outside, snow drifts against their cottage.

The contrast between this and the next poem, "Koenig of the River," is striking. Koenig, the narrator, is a Conradian Kurtz, the sole survivor of a shipload of missionaries who had set out to expiate the sins of benighted savages. In his demented condition, he resolves to dominate the jungle river he has found, just as German and English colonists had once established their empires. As he rages with himself, half in and half out of reality, he poles his small craft into the blank obscurity of the river mist and is lost. The unstated theme of the poem is in Koenig himself, his kind of madness, his will to possess.

"Koenig of the River" seems to be a strange selection to place just before the title poem, the crowning achievement of this book; yet Koenig is motivated by a dream, and *The Star-Apple Kingdom* is filled with the type of men who respond imaginatively to their environments. The Jamaican narrator who provides the central focus in "The Star-Apple Kingdom" is at a point in his life where he feels divorced from his heritage and his island home. A sequence of mood changes is triggered by old photographs and other discarded paraphernalia. At first there is nostalgia over the lost pastoral order of plantation life. He had not been admitted to the activities within the Great House, but he remembers a sense of belonging within a meaningful world.

As he looks at the aged photographs of a colonial family, he is struck by the "innocently excluded" servants and menial workers crowded to the background, "their mouths in the locked jaw of a silent scream" (47). The world has changed since that picture was taken, so that he now looks out the window of the former Great House over gardens, fountains, and an old river mill that are no longer functional. Since he has obviously risen in estate, it would seem that he should be more at peace with himself. The problem is that he has never quite fit into the new order.

In a dream that slowly takes over, he drifts back to the period of the emergence of independence. "La Revolución," personified as a militant woman in the dream, is unable to incite him to violence in the cause of blackness. The movement proceeds without him. Then, in one of Walcott's most dispassionate, satirical passages, the poem concentrates on the new exploiters and power brokers who have corrupted the potentials of independence. The islands were parceled and marketed "in ads for the Caribbean Economic Community" (53). The satirical moment yields abruptly to sinister developments. Grenades explode, leading to martial law, shooting, and armed motorcades. With equal abruptness the dark mood ceases as the speaker drops into undisturbed sleep.

> He slept the sleep that wipes out history,
> he slept like the islands on the breast of the sea,
> like a child again in her star-apple kingdom.
>
> (54)

When he awakens at dawn, like Shabine in "The Schooner *Flight,*" he is rejuvenated. There is a residue of healthy anger from the nightmarish elements of his dream, but he is inspired to reaffirm his commitments to his homeland.

Looking at a map, he imagines the archipelagos from Jamaica to Tobago to be a string of turtles, drawn like lemmings by an innate yearning for Africa. He cries out "with the anger of love," the same unvoiced scream of his ancestors in the photograph, warning them of their danger. Tension dissolves with that release of feeling and the final section of the poem settles into a tranquil mood. The speaker's eye falls upon a long-suffering old woman who is cleaning the steps of a cathedral, water dripping from her rag as "vinegar once dropped from a sponge" (57). In one last encircling gesture, the poem closes with the promise of new beginnings:

> and the woman's face, had a smile been decipherable
> in that map of parchment so rivered with wrinkles,
> would have worn the same smile with which he now
> cracked the day open and began his egg.

(58)

It is a fitting conclusion to an energetic and precisely controlled book.

Coming to Terms

Judging by the power and assurance exerted in *The Star-Apple Kingdom,* it seems that poetry was at least temporarily dominant during this phase of Walcott's career. *Remembrance* and *Pantomime* are compact dramas and they ring true to life. They have a sure touch, but they lack the unified force of Walcott's earlier plays—they do not fare well in comparison with *Ti-Jean and His Brothers, Dream on Monkey Mountain,* and *The Joker of Seville.* There is only the faintest hint, given the play within the play of *Pantomime,* that a work as remarkable as *A Branch of the Blue Nile* lay just ahead (1983). An air of stillness, if not complacency, in *Remembrance* and *Pantomime* contributes to a general impression that Walcott was rounding off this phase of his career. It fits the time, in fact (November1976), that he resigned from the Trinidad Theatre Workshop.

His adaptation of Tirso de Molina's masterpiece provided an ideal opportunity to demonstrate the close affinity not only between his personal artistic temperament and that of an older Western model (if that were in doubt), but also between his "provincial" environment and the larger worlds of myth and human psychology. *Sea Grapes* solidifies and extends his already considerable mastery of complex, multidimensional poetic material. In *O Babylon!* and then in *Remembrance* and *Pantomime,* Walcott features two avenues of spiritual reconciliation, one affiliated with an external ideal, the other deriving from greater insight and personal rapprochement. *The Star-Apple Kingdom* is the fruition of a mature poet who has come to terms with a remarkably diversified world.

Chapter 6

American Muse: 1981–1992

Only two years separate *The Star-Apple Kingdom* from Walcott's next collection, *The Fortunate Traveller* (1981), yet in that period Walcott became a "fortunate traveller" himself—leaving the West Indies to accept successive teaching positions at Columbia, Yale, Harvard, and eventually Boston University. The change of scene alters little his fundamental commitments; if anything, residence in the United States has broadened his vision and deepened his appreciation of the Americas as the repository of world cultures. In a 1982 interview with Nancy Schoenberger, he reaffirmed his need to maintain contact with his Caribbean roots, going back regularly for nourishment.[1] Rather than regretting his suspension between tropical and temperate climates, he capitalizes on their dialectical tensions.

"North and South"

Selections in *The Fortunate Traveller* are grouped in three sections entitled "North," "South," and again "North." The most obvious change in Walcott's style for this eighth poetry collection is actually an extension of his propensity to incorporate influences into his repertoire. In keeping with his northern relocation, New England and Robert Lowell come to the fore. Subject matter, imagery, and even language reflect Lowell, particularly in the two "North" portions. The opening poem, "Old New England," conjures up whaling ships, church spires, and broken promises, and mixes the past of Indian battles with fatalities "back from 'Nam."[2] "Upstate" finds the poet "falling in love with America" (6) even while the muse appears to be deserting the country. In "American Muse" he describes her as emaciated, worn, and pitiable. This fin de siècle atmosphere is palpable in "Piano Practice" where he concludes that the muse avoids him because she does not want to be "seen / with someone who has only one climate" (10).

With this reference to his tropical origins, the narrator's geographic and spiritual dichotomy becomes an issue. Though he feels out of place, subtle connections insinuate themselves into his consciousness. He may claim no guilt in the assassination of an archduke in Europe; his East River may lack the cachet of the Seine; nevertheless, understated irony rises from "a steel drum" he hears practicing "something from old Vienna, / the scales skittering like minnows across the sea" (10). The artistic linkage prepares for the closing poem of this section, "North and South," which is itself a bridge over time and space.

In "North and South" the poet accepts his position as a "colonial upstart" witnessing the twilight of yet another empire. Sidon, Tyre, Alexandria, Carthage, and Rome form a catalog that leads through the American Civil War and the smokestacks of Treblinka. Disparate as these names are, in their wake modern victims of the Jewish and African diasporas suffer from prejudice and paranoia. That reality comes home as the poet notices a cashier wince as her hand brushes his dark skin. The "upstart" murmurs to himself, yes,

> I am one of that tribe of frenetic or melancholy
> primates who made your music for many more moons
> than all the silver quarters in the till.
>
> (16)

When he turns his attention southward, Walcott continues to cast a broad net, encompassing Greece, Rome, and Latin America, as well as the islands of the Caribbean. While critical opinion tends to favor certain poems comprising the section entitled "South," a number of reviewers express reservations about mannerisms or turns of phrase that ring false. Alan Jenkins in *Encounter* decries the Lowellian images, terms, narrative progression, tone, dense phraseology, and alliteration of "Old New England."[3] Ben Howard fears that Lowell overwhelms Walcott's own voice in "North and South."[4] Helen Vendler shares the concern of a number of reviewers who find the poet's high Jacobean rhetoric too overwrought for the uncertain American idiom and subject matter. For example, she questions the "psychic coherence" of "Greece" when Cyclopean molars decorate the landscape metaphorically without literal or poetic explanation; and nothing is made of an innocent cave's "maniacal frothing."[5] In a similar vein, Calvin Bedient judges the calypsonian satire of "The Spoiler's Return" to be rambling "razzle-dazzle."[6] More clearly focused poems—"The Liberator," "Wales," and "Jean Rhys" are singled out by Bedient, while "Hurucan," "The Hotel Normandy Pool," and "The Season of Phantasmal Peace" are favored by Vendler—avoid these defects. "The Season of Phantasmal Peace" in fact exemplifies what Vendler deems to be Walcott's strengths: "[T]he Walcott of observant sharpness, brusque speaking, and social passion, voiced in patois. It is the lyric Walcott who silences commentary."[7]

Incongruous as a critic may find certain elements to be, the continuing saga of an imaginative traveler permeates all three parts of the book. A palm-lined coast reminds the speaker in "Beachhead" of Guam and Guadalcanal as depicted in old copies of American magazines. "Map of the New World" projects the disappearance of a sailboat into mist as a blind man's pen undertakes his *Odyssey* on the ashes of Troy (25). "Roman Outposts" transports the reader from an archaeologist's excavation to centers of modern empires, with Whitehall now supplanted by Washington. In "Greece" the observer not only ascends a Grecian hillside (as Helen Vendler describes it), but he adds his work to the chain of classical writers: "I, signed on to follow that gold thread / which linked the spines down a dark library shelf" (36).

The cumulative implication of such junctures becomes more than the simple fact that Walcott's history is cyclical. His timeless outcast takes in details of life through the eyes of a detached artist. Such alienation runs deeper than those of race, of master/slave, or of newly arrived immigrant. Though he may modulate the voice, its "otherness" is unmistakable. In "The Spoiler's Return" the old calypsonian's ghost—claiming the lineage of Rabelais, Juvenal, Martial, Pope, Dryden, Swift, and Byron—unleashes vituperative satire against parasitic governments, faux art, and internecine squabbling among island nations. Lively patois, subversive metaphors, and bitter puns compel the diatribe until Spoiler is forced to side with the region's most outspoken son, "V. S. Nightfall" (54).

Both "The Hotel Normandie Pool" and "Early Pompeian" strike a less strident, much more personal tone. In the first of these, autobiographical details include the names of his ex-wife and children as the divorced poet lounges beside a hotel pool. Thus the split within his daily life becomes a matter for verse. The arrival of a businessman, "toga-slung" in his towel and robe, triggers a reverie with none other than Ovid settling down for a tête-à-tête. The Roman poet sympathizes with the divorcé's self-questioning concerning his roles as father and writer. It is aesthetic rather than marital advice, however, that Ovid offers as cool consolation. Recalling the depression of his own exile, he tells Walcott with a smile that

> Romans . . . will mock your slavish rhyme,
> the slaves your love of roman structures, when,
> from Metamorphoses to Tristia,
> art obeys its own order

(69)

Significantly, the shade of Ovid addresses Walcott's ennui in terms of the demands of art, subtly indicating that the divisions in his life may depend to some extent upon external stimuli, but that they are essentially systemic.

Considerably more personal, "Early Pompeian," dedicated to his third wife, Norline Metivier, captures the alienation a father experiences when his daughter is stillborn on July 22, 1980, in Trinidad (77). In his agony the poet wonders what a father can possibly write for this lost child. By way of answer "Easter," the next poem, provides the unlikely merger of his daughter Anna's pet dog and the miracle of Christ's Resurrection. The dog who follows Anna like a shadow is incorporated into a fable of the shadow of Christ through his final days on earth: the Last Supper, his Crucifixion, his burial in the earth to be raised at the sound of bells on the third day. "Store Bay," the poem ending this "South" section of the book, has the poet-narrator alone in a hotel room bemoaning the severance of familial ties after his second divorce. Comparing himself to a turtle carrying his household possessions in a bag, he envies "the octopus with ink for blood, / his dangling, disconnected wires / adrift, unmarried" (83). Here he echoes J. Alfred Prufrock's plaintive "I should have been a pair of ragged claws / Scuttling across the floors of silent seas." Neither he nor Eliot's lonely protagonist have ink for blood, yet both must bare their souls in song.

The three poems comprising the final "North" section are less intimate than the verse in "South." The title poem introduces a third world envoy in London who is betraying his people's trust. Internal guilt is coupled with clear external threats in "The Fortunate Traveller." An epigraph from Revelation prepares an ominous context and clandestine meetings in isolated places expose the traveler to danger. He receives a warning that two men are asking for him and the closing stanza repeats the biblical refrain *"and have not charity"* while he envisions the leather-helmeted Third Horseman of the Apocalypse. Asked by Nancy Schoenberger how this haunted figure may be called "fortunate," Walcott answered that he originally considered titling his volume the "Unfortunate Traveller" (after Thomas Nashe's 1594 novel), but preferred "fortunate" due to the circumstances that allow his protagonist the luxury of escape from the famine and misery of his people.[8] Given examples within *The Fortunate Traveller,* the advantages of mobility and detachment entail a costly price. "The Season of Phantasmal Peace" uses the pattern of migratory birds flying high above earthly betrayal and seasonal change to capture one transient moment without contention, "between dusk and darkness, between fury and peace" (99).

In response to reviewers who object to Walcott's affinity for other poet's voices in *The Fortunate Traveller,* Richard Dwyer argues that Walcott's borrowings are tributes rather than slavish imitations.[9] On that point, Walcott reiterates to Anthony Milne, in a 1982 interview, his long-standing contention that critics resort to a double standard in evaluating artistic influences. An imperial power is expected to acquire the best from a subject culture. While their "acquisition" is approved, the colonial writer is judged "imitative" when he reciprocates.[10]

Whether he borrows or pays tribute, the most interesting innovations that manifest themselves in *The Fortunate Traveller* are vestiges of self-reflexive intertextuality. Two critics have noticed certain aspects of this addition to Walcott's repertoire. James McCorkle points to the self-revelation of confessional references in "South" and to a series of puns and allusions with historical precedents that reinterpret each other in a world of language: "[I]n so being, it is reiterative, inscriptive, and interminable until silenced . . . [revealing] dialectical tensions descriptive of language."[11] Clement Wyke refers to the "intertextual mingling of literary and oral voices in *The Fortunate Traveller*'s middle section and the Derridean manner by which the conflicting imagery of "The Season of Phantasmal Peace" generates self-negating ambiguity. In this way Walcott's unresolved questions "make up the tormenting world of the colonial; it is an inner and outer world of 'fury and peace,' but this peace is a phantasmal peace, tangible only in a deceptive way, and quite unsubstantial."[12]

An early indication of Walcott's movement toward this postmodern perspective occurs in "The Forest of Europe" from *The Star-Apple Kingdom.* In its first manifestation, Walcott introduces simple synesthesia, musical notes falling as leaves from the branched music-stands of the trees. Then a note of surrealism occurs with direct reference to the lines of poetry on his manuscript page. The opening stanza diverts the reader away from the aural/visual simile and tree/snow metaphor to "lines / ruled on these scattered manuscripts of snow."[13] Similar divertissement occurs at the close of "Piano Practice" in *The Fortunate Traveller* when the sound of a tenor pan (a tempered steel drum tuned in a high register; also called a "ping-pong," the instrument that carries the melody in a steel orchestra) goes "skittering like minnows across the sea" (10). Here the surreal leap has thematic significance as well; the steel drum playing

Viennese music in New York underscores the West Indian listener's multicultural ambivalence.

Intertextual play subtly informs Walcott's "Jean Rhys" by the way it opens up his tribute to this fellow West Indian writer. Against the sepia discoloration of an old photograph of Rhys as a child, the poet imagines her white sigh transformed into an orchid against a log in the Dominican underbrush, then the "V" stroke of a sea gull painted on a Cornwall souvenir, and finally the vacancy separating one sentence from another. Place-names indicate Rhys's two-world heritage; the "white hush between two sentences" evokes a third, her chosen profession. The message resurfaces at the conclusion as Walcott depicts the child's

> right hand married to *Jane Eyre*,
> foreseeing that her own white wedding dress
> will be white paper

(46, 47)

Sea Change

Such subversion of the text's heretofore inviolable surface makes *The Fortunate Traveller* crucial to an understanding of Walcott's evolving technique in the 1980s. Contrary to the conclusions of various critics (Fred D'Aguiar and Patricia Ismond, for example) who stress the "international" bent of *The Fortunate Traveller* and his next collection, *Midsummer* (1984), Walcott's move to the United States has not significantly altered his lifelong concern about the differences between metropolitan center and imperial outpost.[14] D'Aguiar objects to *Midsummer*'s "internationalist, declassed and autobiographical" style which he thinks leaves the collection with no "sense of purpose and resolve."[15] With a similar reaction to Walcott's artistic detachment, Terry Eagleton contends that the book's semiotic metaphors, "tadpoles wriggle like commas, snakes coil like ampersands, boulevards open like novels," undo themselves, "gesturing sardonically to their own incurable literariness."[16] Finally, Steven Ratiner finds that *Midsummer* is "so awash in sparkling language and intricate metaphor, the subject of the poem is all but obscured."[17]

If residence in Boston and a self-reflexive text appear to threaten the focus of *Midsummer* their value must be weighed against whatever cohesive factors remain to link the 54 poems in the book. The thematic function of midsummer as the time of year is self-evident; Walcott states twice (in poems "VIII" and "XXXIV") that the season is the same every-where: past and present, north or south.[18] Thus the scenic movement from Port-of-Spain to Boston, New York, England, Ovid's Rome, and Homer's Troy displays a homogeneity that is imaginatively convincing or merely convenient. The speaking voice is transparently Walcott's own when he refers to his age (in "XIII," "XVII," and "L"), names daughters Lizzie and Anna (in "XXVIII" and "L"), and refers to his efforts in poetry and painting throughout the book. With this constant movement, there is an inevitable undercurrent of transience. In this regard, Ratiner is cor-rect: there is a lack of balance and the poet-tourist is "gliding over but not through settings."[19] Walcott remains the "fortunate traveler," trans-lating experience into the terms of his art.

Ironically, this may be the object lesson of the collection. It is a theme appearing at least as early as the title poem of *The Gulf* (1970). There the speaker looks down from a plane high above Texas, contemplating a landscape through glass and speculating on the fact that gulfs simulta-neously isolate and link individuals in their separate worlds.[20] Just as when he apologized to Anna in *Another Life* for turning their love into poetry, "the noble treachery of art"[21] continues to distance observer from observed. Now in "XLI" he reiterates, "all experience was kindling for the muse." The outer weather of *Midsummer* reflects and is secondary to the uncertain climate within the poet's own soul.

Imagery in the opening poem prepares for the ambiguous settings throughout the collection. The sea and clouds mirrored on its surface immediately become both text and subject matter. Neither cloud nor sea keeps records, but a hole in the cloud's "parchment" opens before the poet's descending plane to reveal "pages of earth, the canefields set in stan-zas." As he lands, it is as though previous visitors to Trinidad, Trollope and Froude, look over his shoulder. Though these predecessors asserted that the island could produce nothing, he notes that light knows no epochs; the sun that lights Rome shines on muddy settlements and rusty harbors like Port-of-Spain. When he looks into his next reflective surface, the mirror in the Queens Park Hotel ("III"), he cannot connect the lines in his aging face with the child he used to be. Contemplating his image, fears arise that he may have failed in everything he has ever written.

This multivalent self-doubt ultimately becomes the radiant center of the book. Prompted by personal misgivings, Walcott begins to invento-ry the disparate elements of his career. The involuted process covers a wide range of geographic locations, yet they are integral to the poet's heritage and to his methods of recording them. As Robert Bensen demonstrates, painters and painting inform certain "poems directly as subject ('Gauguin' XIX and 'Watteau' XX), as a source of imagery, in the handling of qualities of light and color, and in the range of themes."[22] Among his applications Bensen sees the episodic looseness of the book in terms of a painter's sketchbook and the texture of passages varies from impressionist wash to expressionist impasto.[23]

Catalogs of painters point up specific aspects of his interest in the graphic arts. Poem "XVII" exemplifies the metaphysical stretch of his painting lineage. The whirr of cicadas is routinely linked to the sound of his mother's sewing machine and the stitching of his own poetic lines. Then noting the "lemon-rind light in Vermeer," a rust color in van Ruysdael, and the deceptive realism of a Flemish still life, he seizes the occasion to attribute his sensitivity for detail to the Dutch blood running through his veins. As counterweight, he offers "Gauguin/1" (poem "XIX"), where he follows the French painter's lead "to darker nations." Describing himself as a "crumpled colon," he admits to being "Watteau's wild oats, his illegitimate heir." The question of legitimacy, of course, refers to his mixed race as well as his role as a colonial artist.

Significant as the pictorial terminology is, Walcott's primary function as writer receives even more attention. In at least one poem word and picture are concomitant as he aspires to

> a tone colloquial and stiff,
> the brevity of that short syllable, God,
> all synthesis in one heraldic stroke,
> like Li Po or a Chinese laundry mark!

("IX")

At least the Chinese pictograph depicts its own meaning. The poem "IX" closes on the discrepancy between nature and human nature; citing lightning, the sea, wind, and stones, it succinctly enumerates the four basic elements that ultimately defy verbal closure.

Recalling the younger image of himself reflected in an earlier mirror, Walcott turns his attention to drama in "XIII." Plots, actors, imagined characters, and his stagecraft seem too slow in materializing except at rare, luminous moments. Only then can he hope that the young poet staring back from the mirror may smile and accept the man he has become as "an enduring ruin." Personal interrogation concludes part 1, when he asks rhetorically,

What if the lines I cast bulge into a book
that has caught nothing? Wasn't it privilege
to have judged one's work by the glare of greater minds.

("XXIX")

Personal gratification is sometimes his only reward, judging from his assessment of audience response in "XXIII" and later in "XXXVIII." In "XXIII" his attempt to "add some color to the British theatre" is rebuffed with the dictum, "blacks can't do Shakespeare, they have no experience." The pain of that black experience is not wasted on the poet who has devoted his career to integrated drama. He juxtaposes the "whiteness" of his lines and his acceptance into "white fellowships" against riot police confronting skinheads and "Calibans . . . in the alleys of Brixton, burning like Turner's ships." Trying to rationalize what might have gone wrong with some of his earlier plays, in "XXXVIII" he lists the language barrier, his simple characters, the monotony of sets with only one season, overly abundant poetry, and a dissonant age.

Although the tone is not particularly bitter in either of these examples, the voice in the second part of *Midsummer* tends to assume a more critical tone. As Walcott describes such temperate locales as New England, Wales, Warwickshire, and Chicago, he touches on the seasons missing from his tropical birthplace. Western place-names and influences weigh on his musings. In "XXXVI" Warwickshire provided "bastard grandsires" with surnames as familiar as that of his own father, Warwick. The poem "XL" brings up the pronunciation of the letter "R," the shape of "V," and the "O" of a speech that seems to exceed his powers. The act of expression in "the language of white, ponderous clouds" is compared to "lifting nouns like rocks." Significantly, this "white" language and its nouns become the self-reflexive tools with which Walcott formulates his world picture. The poems immediately following, "XLI" and "XLII," provide spiraling smoke columns, goose-stepping pigeons, and trout-bubbling umlauts—recalling Dachau, Auschwitz, and Sachsenhausen. Derelicts huddled under the El in snow-shrouded Chicago conjure up a Warsaw ghetto and an image of some Mongol horde contemplating still another barbaric conquest. Europe's most recent incursion into the New World emerges as the poet journeys to Castro's socialized Cuba in the seven-part sequence of "XLIII," subtitled "Tropic Zone." Observing elderly men sheltering from the sun under a tree, he imagines their nostalgia for some "tradition in these tropical zones." With thoughts extending back 70 years to Sunday promenades, white suits, music, and grace, "Their revolution is that things come in circles. / The socialists do not appreciate that" ("XLIII," part "v").

Walcott brings *Midsummer* itself full circle through reconciliation. Back in St. Lucia in poem "LII," he concludes that the leafy oak of the English language has spread its shade over "a division of dictions, . . . One fought for a queen, the other was chained in her service." History brought both slaves and soldiers to colonial outposts so that as a schoolboy he wore a paper flower on Remembrance Day to celebrate British victory in Flanders. Walcott recognizes that experience is no more neutral than the language in which it is recorded. Thus, he is not romanticizing homely details of the sea, pitch roads, razor grass, shacks, and wood lice in his closing hymn of faith. The last word is spoken to his fellow exile, the Russian poet Joseph Brodsky: "Ah, Joseph, though no man ever dies in his own country, / the grateful grass will grow thick from his heart" ("LIV").

Recurring themes touching on divided loyalties, the mechanics of art, poetry, theater, and personal relationships in both sections of *Midsummer* follow the ebb and flow of a preoccupied mind. Louis James claims that the first section evinces a Caribbean and the second an American perspective.[24] Nevertheless, both are aspects of the same consciousness. The incremental repetition among fluctuating moods, coupled with occasional exposition of the poems' physical grammar account at least in part for the impression of fragmented purposes. In *Midsummer,* after *The Fortunate Traveller,* self-reflexive text becomes as much the object of poetic experience as the poem itself.

Confluences of the Stage

The Last Carnival   What is true of the poetry becomes just as integral to the emerging plays of the 1980s. When Walcott shifts to the dramatic mode, he remains the lyricist with an abiding interest in artistic processes. Although *Three Plays* was published in 1986, the book is comprised of plays dating back as far as 16 years. The unpublished *In a Fine Castle* (from 1970) reappears as *The Last Carnival* which was initially performed under its new title in Trinidad in 1982; *Beef, No Chicken* was staged originally in Trinidad in 1981; and in different versions *A Branch of the Blue Nile* premiered first in Barbados in 1983, then in Trinidad in

1985. Self-reflexive text evolves into its most painterly form in *The Last Carnival.*

In this play the techniques of painting and the quality of light permeate the setting, the characterization, the dialogue, and the imagery so as to become incremental motifs. Amber, saffron, and orange pastels of the setting sun underscore the literal reality of imperial decline. These elements are discernible in *In a Fine Castle* but their role is more sharply defined because Walcott's revisions underscore a new emphasis. The most obvious difference is that the uncommitted black journalist, Brown, is no longer the protagonist, and fraternal squabbles within the Black Power movement disappear from the equation. Instead, Agatha Willett—who was a peripheral housekeeper serving mainly an intercessory role between Brown and members of the aristocratic De La Fontaine family in the earlier version—takes center stage as a catalyst in Trinidad's independence movement.

Rather than heed criticism directed at the number of white actors in the cast of the earlier *In a Fine Castle,*[25] Walcott is obviously intent on dramatizing the overlooked side of Trinidad's political and social revolution: the deposed colonialists. They take precedence over Sydney Waldron, the radical Black Power rebel who is shot by national soldiers; over Brown, the rootless observer who espouses no cause; and over Jean Beauxchamps, the maid who becomes a government official in the prevailing brown meritocracy. Those receiving primary development are the proletarian Englishwoman Agatha Willett (who introduces egalitarian ideas not only to her De La Fontaine charges but also to Sydney, Jean, and other children from the lower classes), the aesthete Victor De La Fontaine (who commits suicide), and his daughter Clodia (whose involvement with the revolutionary Sydney forces her to leave the island she loves).

As is typical of Walcott's works of the 1980s, the context of the action requires as much consideration as the story itself. In this respect, the "wild oats" of Watteau, mentioned in *Midsummer* ("XIX") are ubiquitous in *The Last Carnival.* Watteau's famous *Embarkation for Cythera* is not only prominently displayed in Victor De La Fontaine's life-sized copy, but characters compare themselves and their plight to figures in the painting. Victor begins to describe their debilitated stasis to Agatha:

> . . . those silks and taffetas.
> Those fiery, fading silks, see? He painted

> his whole culture as if it were a sunset,
> because all embarkation is a fantasy. You see
> those pilgrims, in the painting? They can't move.
> It's like some paralyzed moment in a carnival . . .
> . . . what an elegy to the light.[26]

The son, Tony, whom Victor named after Antoine Watteau, completes the comparison years after his father's death:

> Now, with this light like the fire, orange, and silks, the sunset, I see the moment of stillness Victor wanted. Because here we are, we can't move. Just like these people in the painting. (91)

The Last Carnival drops the opening scene from *In a Fine Castle* which had Brown revealed under an amber spotlight, "the hue of memory," discoursing on the play's atmosphere of reverie.[27] However, in the retitled version one of the first things Agatha notices upon her arrival from England is the astonishing tropical light: "So clear! All this. / It's as if the world were making a fresh start" (6). The sights and aromas of the docks are new to her in this early encounter, but 7 of the play's 10 scenes are set during the afternoon, night, or predawn hours. Twilight and glowing pastels enter the dialogue even when they are not being produced by stage lighting. Despite the music and "jumping up" of Carnival that are tied in with Watteau-era costuming, reverie is the tone of this play as much as it is for *Remembrance*.

Walcott goes against popular biases when he dramatizes the ambiguous roles of Eurocentric traditionalists like Albert Jordan or an Englishwoman like Agatha Willett in the convoluted birth throes of a new nation. Ironically, the deaths of Victor and Sydney are not as tragic as the fact that Brown cannot identify with his own people, and that Clodia who advises Brown to "find a cause and love it. Die for it like Sydney" (101) can no longer reside on the island she loves.

Trinidadian novelist and playwright Earl Lovelace argues, in fact, that the main weakness of *The Last Carnival* is Walcott's failure to stress Clodia's claim to Trinidad, not France, as her legitimate home. Lovelace goes on to suggest in his review that Brown should have been stronger and should have been developed more fully. When he complains that Walcott's employment of professional American actors in key roles, "robs us . . . of the opportunity of seeing native talents deal with their own important story," Lovelace raises a point of controversy that suddenly engulfed Walcott when he arrived in Trinidad for the summer of 1982.[28] As Walcott explained the situation in separate interviews—with Anthony Milne of the *Express* and a *Trinidad Guardian* reporter—he had planned to work with new directors of the Trinidad Theatre Workshop to introduce American actors into the local drama. He was promoting what he refers to as a "second phase" of development for West Indian theater. In "Walcott Tells of Local Amateur Actors in Disguise," he contends that after 17 years of training and experience the Workshop had achieved a plateau and that further development required cross-fertilization with foreign, professional talents.[29] Armed with funds from his MacArthur grant, Walcott anticipated an investment over five years of approximately $100,000 to finance this cultural exchange. Unfortunately, due to conflicts over these foreign influences, he was unable to reach agreement with the Workshop. As a result, the summer 1982 revival of *The Joker of Seville* was abruptly canceled,[30] and the Trinidad premiers of *The Last Carnival* (July 1982) and *A Branch of the Blue Nile* (August 1985) were presented by his newly formed Warwick Productions Company.

Beef, No Chicken   Prior to these difficulties the Trinidad Theatre Workshop staged the second of the works published in *Three Plays, Beef, No Chicken,* in April 1981, without Walcott's participation. While *The Last Carnival* focuses on the effects of national liberation on the outgoing regime, *Beef, No Chicken* delineates the neocolonial forces threatening to overwhelm the new order from within. *Beef, No Chicken* is set in Couva, Trinidad, one week before this remote village is to be swept into the modern age by the completion of a broad highway. The central conflict, not unlike that in Wole Soyinka's *The Lion and the Jewel,* pits progressive city people against village conservatives. Almost everyone on the Borough Council looks forward to becoming a mini-Miami, to being McDonaldized and Kentucky Fried. Mayor Cadiz, anxious to outgrow inconsequential rural problems, wants more respectable traffic jams, noise, industrial pollution, "blight, crime, scandal, welfare, all that! Because Couva would be right up there with them, taking its rightful place among the great cities of the world."[31] Mr. Mongroo, whose construction company won the lucrative construction contract, needs the signature of only one man to make his project legal. Blocking the way of "progress" is the recalcitrant Otto Hogan.

Otto stands on principle, insisting that the Americanization of Trinidad is destroying a simple way of life that is worth preserving. To test his resolve, trenches are dug and earth piled around his "Auto Repair and Authentic Roti" shop and the bank refuses to extend his line of credit. In retaliation, by night he disguises himself as a woman and sabotages the road; by day he schemes to starve the construction crews, refusing their orders for roti (a flat bread into which curried meat is folded) and drinks. Minor plots intermingle to bring together a colorful blend of humorous misadventurers. Otto's sister Euphony finally gets to marry the fiancé who took off for Wales 10 years earlier. Euphony also instigates the successful robbery of Mongroo Construction Company's weekly payroll. Although the perpetrators are ultimately caught, so much corruption surrounds the highway contract that no one dares prosecute them. Otto's niece Drusilla, more attuned to soap operas than to the real life around her, escapes to the bright lights of Port-of-Spain with a television announcer. Schoolmaster Eldridge Franco is finally so discouraged with his futile mission to correct the "desers and dosers" of Couva that he relinquishes his guaranteed pension to become a television reporter.

With its loose episodes and light humor, *Beef, No Chicken* can be dismissed as farce; nevertheless, it exhibits facile control and serious implications for third world communities attempting to formulate their aspirations. Reed Dasenbrock prefers it to *The Last Carnival* because the more compressed "farcical mode allows Walcott much greater freedom with language . . . the poetic and comic resources of West Indian English."[32] In a similar assessment, Judy Stone finds it one of Walcott's "most accessible works, genuinely a 'hilarious comedy' . . . but layered with the small personal tragedies that are concomitant with progress."[33] *Beef, No Chicken* unquestionably returns to the lighter kaiso (calypso) influences of some of Walcott's earlier plays. Humor springs nimbly to the surface with jokes and verbal play. As is essential to drama, however, Walcott condenses an amorphous social plight into individually realized characters with specific problems. *Beef, No Chicken* effectively complements the seriocomic weight of *The Last Carnival* and counterbalances the probing intertextuality of *A Branch of the Blue Nile*.

A Branch of the Blue Nile   Anyone aware of the troubled relationship between Walcott and the Trinidad Theatre Workshop since he resigned as its director in 1976 would find it difficult to avoid the autobiographical basis of *A Branch of the Blue Nile*. Lowell Fiet concludes that it depends more heavily on "personal history and experience" than any other of his plays.[34] This correspondence between fact and fiction, however, is but one facet of the multilayered complexity of this third of the *Three Plays.*

An *Express* critic seized upon the second important way in which Walcott manipulates the audience's perception, through the physical properties of the dramatic genre. The 1985 Trinidad premier of *A Branch of the Blue Nile,* under Walcott's direction, brought back an experiment in informal staging that had been employed with *The Joker of Seville* in 1974.[35] What initially strikes the *Express* reviewer is the conviviality of the audience in the friendly atmosphere of a tent theater. Before the opening, he noticed people waving to each other and visiting genially from one side of the clear staging area to the other. More importantly, this communal spirit insinuates itself into the performance. The reviewer observes, "[y]ou really feel you are part of the workings of the theatre in the tent—the bones of it are all around you, not obtrusively, but amicably as though bringing you into the company. The lights are not artfully hidden away, the sound equipment is visible, the workings are shared with the audience, and it is somehow particularly appropriate to the play."[36] It is apropos, essentially, because of the third facet of its complexity: the structure.

Fiet refers to plays within the play, ensuring "that characters play multiple and overlapping roles. Thus, when theatre should be its most "realistic," it portrays—or betrays—itself as more *seamed,* fragmented, and critical than normally assumed."[37] Fascinating as these seams appear to be on the surface, they relate to yet deeper structural relevance, because *A Branch of the Blue Nile* is the most self-reflexive of all Walcott's plays. By offering text as part of the experience of production in the mid-1980s, Walcott has moved beyond the more obvious Brechtian alienation effects that prevail in *Ti-Jean and His Brothers* and *Dream on Monkey Mountain,* effects that were edited out of *In a Fine Castle* when it was reincarnated as *The Last Carnival.*[38]

As Stephen Breslow perceives it, "Intertextual and intercultural references, woven through much of Walcott's poetry and drama, multiply exponentially in *A Branch of the Blue Nile.*"[39] Breslow points out traces of African, French, and English patois; classical Latin; and St. Lucian, Trinidadian, and American linguistic influences in the language of the play. He also accounts for the fact that Walcott is constantly shifting from one plot level to another. These alternating layers of action and meaning in fact motivate the entire narrative development. As the play opens Harvey St. Just, an expatriate British director, is forcing the discipline of method acting upon Sheila Harris as they rehearse a scene from Shakespeare's *Antony and Cleopatra*. When he orders Sheila to pretend that Antony is Chris, the married man with whom she is having an affair, her frustrated outburst results in an amazing theatrical moment. Out of this epiphany grows the multidimensional conflicts of the rest of the play. Sheila fears the "gift" of acting talent that has descended upon a black woman in out-of-the-way Trinidad. Doubting the prospects of using her talents on the local stage and afraid to risk London or New York, she tries passing her gift on to Marylin, a fellow actress who is light-complexioned and ambitious enough to pander to whatever an audience demands. Sheila then abandons the company to join a Seventh-Day Adventist congregation.

Sheila's brush with artistic greatness leads Chris to challenge Harvey's desire to bring classical theater to provincial audiences. An aspiring playwright as well as an actor, Chris has been content to entertain people with lighthearted dialect pieces. Gavin, who has suffered the racist barriers of New York's theatrical world, also wonders why Harvey drives the company so unmercifully beyond what the local audience will accept. Reinforcing Chris and Gavin in the background are the trenchant babblings of Phil, the demented former lead singer of a group called Phil and the Rockets, who broke under the strain of his artistic burden.[40] Harvey admits that he has no finished idea of what can be achieved; nevertheless, he encourages Chris to attempt more challenging work, he defends the value of provincial theater, and he speaks out about their personal and social responsibilities:

> All I can tell you is, even when we're ready, we'll keep trying to purge ourselves of fear, of cowardice, envy, self-contempt, conceit, and you yourselves think who I mean by those. If there's disorder here, in this little world, no trust, no center, no authority, then lunacy is correct, we're wasting time. What is wrong in here is what's wrong with this country. Our country. And if, outside, there's mismanagement and madness, we must not go mad. (223)

Gavin's prediction that such brushes with truth will destroy the company is almost fulfilled. Although he and Marylin stay on, Chris and Sheila are temporarily deterred by the inauspicious prospects for serious art in the provinces.

An example of Chris's peasant burlesque is played out by Marylin and Gavin (act 1, scene 4), when Chris wants Marylin to dramatize her character's social climbing through vocal affectation, inflection, and anomalies of mixed dialect. In frustration, Chris turns on Harvey, complaining that he wants characters and situations applicable to the life he knows, not Racine, Corneille, Shakespeare, and Chekhov, but a reality familiar to lunatics in the street like Phil. Harvey goes so far as to introduce dialect into *Antony and Cleopatra* through the clown who delivers asps for Cleopatra's famous death scene. The success is difficult to assess because of a stagehand's mistake in pushing a banana-tree prop onstage during the critical moment. The stagehand's error not only elicits laughter; it adds fuel to the negative criticism of a narrow-minded newspaper review. Further divisiveness splits the cast when this same review lavishes hyperbolic praise on Marylin.

Each of these separate threads is interdependent, but the most productive outgrowth of dissension among the cast is a new play Chris writes while overseeing a successful business venture in Barbados. It turns out that he has transcribed recordings of the company's chaotic rehearsals and improvisational exercises. Thus the mirror of reflection is held up to both the classical and the peasant theaters as well as to the very real human beings who have brought their pains and dreams into this small theater to project themselves creatively in roles created for other places and other times. From these tapes Chris has derived a play entitled *A Branch of the Blue Nile* that gives artistic form to the chaos of their shared lives. Armed with this manuscript, Chris helps Sheila recognize that her religious fervor is in fact another type of performance, and she returns to the venue that allows the fullest expression of her talents. Marylin takes her career to New York and Harvey dies in England of a disease sounding very much like AIDS, but their legacy lives on in Sheila and in Iris and Wilfred, younger members of the remaining cast. Walcott leaves the final word to a man of the streets. Phil admonishes Sheila:

> Oh, God, a actor is a holy thing. . . . Even in this country. Even here. Show me your palm. Good lines. Good branches. [*He bows*] Press on. It touch me once, that light. It fill me full. A gold brighter than rum. I was His vessel. And it don't matter where it is: here, New York, London. No, miss. . . . Do what you have to do. For all our sakes, I beg you. Please. Continue. Do your work. (312)

Echoes of Walcott's introduction, "What the Twilight Says" in *Dream on Monkey Mountain and Other Plays,* cannot be missed in these words.[41] His years of instilling discipline in the Trinidad Theatre Workshop and fighting provincial criticism are reflected in Harvey's program, and his insistence on the expressive power and flexibility of West Indian dialect is directly voiced by Chris.[42] A discussion of structural self-reflexiveness in *A Branch of the Blue Nile* would be incomplete without reference to some of Walcott's previous plays. The subject of a play within a play appears in *Pantomime*; characters resist the lures of metropolitan life and seek spiritual fulfillment in *O Babylon!*; classics are adapted to the West Indian setting in *The Joker of Seville* and *Pantomime*.

Autobiography, open staging, structural intertextuality: one last facet of self-reflexiveness should be added. The title implicates itself in the script. Not only is Chris's title given to the overall drama, but he also offers Sheila a revealing, if flippant, explanation (in act 2, scene 4): it is a branch "Because it ain't mainstream, okay?"; it is blue "Because white is too obvious"; and he reminds her, Cleopatra's Nile has given her "the blues" (291). During this exchange, when Chris asks Sheila why she has emptied her life, the audience should recall that in an earlier scene Sheila had ritualistically transferred the divine gift from the branched "river in my palm" to Marylin's hand (261). In close proximity to each other, Gavin refers to Chris's business in Barbados as a "branch of the Nile," and Sheila claims to have joined a "branch" of the Adventist church (278, 279). Deconstructive criticism provides one further layer of signification. With modern technology in television and film, by using a blue backdrop it is possible to superimpose foreground subject matter on any background imaginable. Of course, human beings are far more complex than media images; therefore, *A Branch of the Blue Nile* dramatizes the trauma of multicultural transference. Harvey, Chris, and Walcott in their different ways exercise virtually chameleonlike methods to prove that nothing in the background of history and nothing in the foreground of present life obviates creative interchange. There is no text, in other words, only intertext. It is no stretch of the imagination to recognize Walcott's personal imprimatur on the parting lines Chris writes to Sheila,

> I keep adding things that happen. As I hear about them, I add them in. You all once asked me to write about real life. There is no ending in real life. There is just continuity. Even death doesn't stop. So since I'm no artist, and I'm not God, it seems to me that only fiction can make reality real. . . . I'm stuck. It's up to you to help me with the end. . . . Somehow, the mere truth doesn't seem to be enough. (311)

Mere technical proficiency alone would not qualify *A Branch of the Blue Nile* to rank with *Ti-Jean and His Brothers* and *Dream on Monkey*

Mountain, but this play also has delightful humor, sufficient thematic implications, and the philosophical resonance to make it the most significant of Walcott's plays from the 1980s. Like *Dream on Monkey Mountain* it marks the culmination of another phase in Walcott's prolific career as a dramatist. Yet other unpublished dramas from the past decade may eventually see print: *The Isle Is Full of Noises* (1982), *The Rig* (1983), *The Haitian Earth* (1984), *To Die for Grenada* (1986), *The Ghost Dance* (1989), *Viva Detroit* (1990), *Steel* (1991), and *The Odyssey* (1992). The apparent gap here, from 1986 through 1988, is deceptive because during those three years Walcott not only finished *The Arkansas Testament* (1987), he edited *Three Plays* and *Collected Poems 1948–1984,* both published in the fruitful year of 1986.

Collected Poems

Although I have already discussed many of the poems from earlier volumes that were gathered to make up *Collected Poems,* their selected reappearance in one book is not only an important milestone in Walcott's career but an open invitation to critical comparisons. J. D. McClatchy, for example, regards the selections up to *Another Life* as "stiff and unconvincing. . . . deliberately derivative, defiantly literary."[43] In the same vein, Lachlan Mackinnon complains of overwriting and bathos in selections before *The Castaway,*[44] and James Dickey asserts that while Walcott can break through literary influences, "some of his lines can easily take their place among the worst poetry ever written."[45]

The influence of metaphysical poets and such moderns as T. S. Eliot, W. B. Yeats, and Dylan Thomas is commonly acknowledged in the apprenticeship work, but each critic sees a different watershed in Walcott's development. For Katie Jones *The Castaway* and *The Gulf* signal a "new insistence on actuality," detached observations, and plainer style. By the time of *Sea Grapes,* Jones detects an increase in direct social criticism—a side of Walcott she finds not adequately reflected in *Collected Poems.*[46] Echoing Jones's regret at this omission, Rita Dove argues that Walcott's "indignant righteousness and impatience" seem to have diminished as he has spent more and more time in North America.[47] This same note is struck by Bruce King who misses the distinctive tone of the 1970s, when in *Sea Grapes* Walcott becomes "surprisingly taut, angry . . . about local issues . . . coming closer to dialect and pidgin."[48] As a result, King argues, *Collected Poems* "emphasizes universal themes and a myth of Walcott's life, to the neglect of more topical, argumentative poems."[49]

There is a consensus among reviewers that the major influence dominating the later selections—from *The Star-Apple Kingdom, The Fortunate Traveller,* and *Midsummer*—is Robert Lowell.[50] If Walcott's assimilation of successive voices throughout his career gives some critics pause, Irish poet Seamus Heaney sees the end result in a positive light. He considers *Collected Poems* to be the record of a poet finding his own voice in spite of his "highly developed awareness of the literary past."[51] To Heaney's way of thinking, the collection witnesses the rise of a "parochial/Joycean poet" in the best sense of the word: "Walcott's imagination, like Joyce's, works by correspondence and analogy and has a similar joy in sporting itself between languages and cultures, both local and classical. . . . It gave him imaginative and dramatic access to all the categories that might otherwise have stifled and hidebound the play of his intelligence and sympathy."[52] He goes so far as to assert that Walcott's greatest moral and artistic victory is in refusing to be the voice of any particular cause, in remaining true to his own conscience.

In this assessment, Heaney joins such critics as Bruce King, John Lucas, and others who see beyond obvious literary influences to the orchestration of Walcott's personal idiom. According to Lucas, the tracing of older masters "is not pastiche, but an extraordinarily rich, implicated language and rhetorical largess, which seem endlessly capable of creating 'The Word' of Walcott's imagination."[53] King sees evidence of increasing commitment to liberal humanism, an "international, interracial community defined by a mutual concern with literature, especially poetry."[54] In the final analysis, Heaney sees Walcott's language as the cohesive force informing the entire *Collected Poems:* "More important than Walcott's themes or his development or his witness," are "the command and full-bloodedness of his language."[55] The critical reception of this large, diverse work was not, as should be expected, unanimous. On the one hand, J. D. McClatchy is of the opinion that while individual poems are impressive, bulk does not serve Walcott well.[56] Lachlan Mackinnon, on the other hand, insists that *Collected Poems* is a triumph, that Walcott has very few peers, and that "the problem may have been that one must see his work whole to appreciate this fully."[57] Judging from a 1985 interview with Edward Hirsch, Walcott himself seems inclined more to McClatchy's negative evaluation than to Mackinnon's flattering words. With the publication of *Collected Poems* approaching, Walcott expresses misgivings. He feels that with his accumulating fame and publicity, he has somehow failed the ambition, the imagination of the boy who undertook poetry decades ago in St. Lucia. In order to compensate for perceived deficiencies, he hopes to redeem himself with his next book.[58] The volume to which he alludes in this Hirsch interview is *The Arkansas Testament* (1987).

Here / Elsewhere

Given Walcott's reservations about the image conveyed by the gesture of a massive *Collected Poems,* changes of style or new emphases in content take on added significance in *The Arkansas Testament.* Regarding the formal structure, critics have noted both the high incidence of short, rhymed quatrains and the fact that Walcott again subdivides the text according to differences between Caribbean and foreign subject matter. Among the reviewers who have commented on the verse patterns, Paul Jenkins senses that Walcott has ceased to apportion tighter, rhymed meters to "literary and high-brow" material, while using an "unrhymed, expanded pentameter line and verse paragraphs" to treat Caribbean scenes.[59] Consequently, a new aspect of Walcott's style emerges as he switches or combines open and closed forms regardless of subject. Jenkins and others, including Jamaican scholar Edward Baugh, also recognize the fact that although Walcott has been preserving separate categories of poems for tropical and temperate climates, with *The Arkansas Testament* locations and perspectives continually feed into each other.[60] Baugh traces a pattern most pronounced in the "North / South" terminology of *The Fortunate Traveller* which stretches back to *Sea Grapes* (1976), whereby Walcott describes the world from St. Lucia outward— ostensibly the "Here" and "Elsewhere" of *The Arkansas Testament.* As Baugh observes, however, in this book these designations are far more complex. For one thing, the very act of defining his native ground has a distancing effect. Furthermore, Baugh argues, for the much-traveled Walcott "here" is "increasingly a place to which one *returns,* a place one has to reclaim repeatedly in an effort made more and more precarious and compulsive as the gulf of memory widens." At the same time, while "elsewhere" may signify the world outside the Caribbean, as Baugh points out, Walcott is actively engaged in the dialectic interdependency of the two.[61]

Integration of subject and form is at the heart of Walcott's determination to move beyond his *Collected Poems.* After having achieved fame in the larger world, he focuses once again on the colonial St. Lucian milieu that continues to nurture his growth. Vernon Shetley appreciates the advantage Walcott has in his, "genuine, unavoidable subject." Shetley claims that because of his "mixed blood, the great themes of race, colonialism, and exile have pressed themselves upon him with an urgency unlike anything an American poet might feel for what he or she chose to write about. . . . But for Walcott, the very act of writing poetry must inevitably activate a complex of experience in which issues of the utmost contemporary importance lie entangled."[62] Shetley is correct in this assessment and in observing that Walcott continues to work "the personal, reflective vein" of his recent collections.

What remains unaccounted for in *The Arkansas Testament* is the degree of intricacy with which Walcott unifies the disparities of his "personal, reflective" world. A cursory account of thematic references would show that Walcott plies familiar threads of home, the past, memory; love, death, and religion; contrasting cultures, empires, races; prejudice and abandonment. Significantly, however, references to the act of writing, classical allusions, and comparisons between art and life prevail throughout the book. "White Magic" from the "Here" section exemplifies Walcott's method of blending self-reflexive text into a complaint about sociopolitical discrimination. As he catalogs various supernatural creatures of St. Lucian folklore, he suggests that the reader dismiss an unidentified sound as natural "unless our water-mother with dank locks/ is sliding under this page below your pen."[63] Explaining that only simple people, the superstitious, could believe such things, he reminds us that "Dryads and hamadryads were engrained / in the wood's bark, in papyrus, and this paper." The biased difference is that the local "Papa Bois" will be denigrated as "Pan's clone, one more translated satyr" because, "Our myths are ignorance, theirs are literature" (38, 39). The *whiteness* of the title refers simultaneously to the paper on which one myth is enshrined in Western lore and to the white system that subordinates marginal "imitations" of its culture.

This is but a single device for blending craft and theme within one poem. More than in any of his previous collections, Walcott takes measures in *The Arkansas Testament* to interconnect separate poems within the larger design of the book. The first five selections, from "The Lighthouse" through "The Villa Restaurant," reintroduce people and sights from St. Lucia, revive memories, and comment on his vocation as a poet. Since he attempts to impose written form on spoken dialect, trees in "The Lighthouse" protest that he will never get from them what he wants because *"your words is English, | is a different tree"* (10). Since there was no indigenous precedent for poetry, in "Latin Primer" he explains,

> so I shook all the help
> my young right hand could use
> from the sand-crusted kelp
> of distant literatures.
>
> (21)

Near the end of this poem he speaks of metaphors of oars, the scansion of wings, and a horizon at one with the pillars of Hercules. The striking beauty of a waitress deflates those airy gestures in "The Villa Restaurant." Classic statues have taught him "Your sea has its own *Iliads, | Noli me tangere*" (26). The figure of the waitress and the color of her skin lead him to reject marble busts and Greek amphoras in favor of her "living vase."

Local religious observances take primacy in the next two poems: "The Three Musicians," and "Saint Lucia's First Communion." Then other island customs are treated in "Gros-Ilet" and "The Whelk Gatherers," leading up to "White Magic" with its summary pronouncement on condescending evaluations of St. Lucian myths. "A Letter from the Old Guard" seems transitional: a black veteran of the Colonial Service writes on Remembrance Day about the disappointments of independence, recalling the time when "our wars were happier" (43). "Storm Figure" might seem out of place at first; however, as Walcott ponders the atmosphere and a female apparition from a Thomas Hardy novel, he sheds reverie to assert that this is not the nineteenth century, not the Wessex coast. This ghostly figure along with his return to the present lay the groundwork for "Marina Tsvetaeva." Shortly after the narrator retrieves a drink from the Siberian wastes of his refrigerator, he imagines the Russian poetess Tsvetaeva materializing from one of her books (46).

To complement Tsvetaeva's imaginary appearance, "The Light of the World" captures the impression of an actual St. Lucian peasant woman. She reminds Walcott of Delacroix's *Liberty Leading the People,* and the analogy is apropos. Without becoming maudlin, he sees embodied in her the substantial reality of all his countrymen:

> I, who could never solidify my shadow
> to be one of their shadows, had left them their earth,

their white rum quarrels, and their coal bags,
their hatred of corporals, or all authority.

(50)

Riding in this crowded island transport, he senses loss and abandonment, a world available to him only through imagination. He hides his
tears as he steps out at his hotel, knowing "There was nothing they
wanted, nothing I could give them / but this thing I have called 'The
Light of the World' " (51).

A similar cohesiveness prevails in the "Elsewhere" section. The
opening "Eulogy to W. H. Auden" aligns Walcott with another poet
whose calling made his "one mouth to speak for all" (64). The second
poem, which carries the section title, "Elsewhere," catalogs imprison-
ment, torture, and assassination wherever inhumanity occurs around
the world. Successive poems, from "Steam" to "Streams," survey troubled spots of imperial Rome and Nazi-occupied Europe as well as nearby Central America and Castro's Cuba. There are more personal
vignettes as well. In "Winter Lamps" the detritus of a broken marriage
initiates a touchingly personal sequence. Alone in his Brookline apartment, Walcott's faith seems as dead as his marriage and the child he
and his wife had lost. Struggling to regain faith, he delivers the following poem, "For Adrian," from the perspective of a child who has
recently died. Speaking for the child, Walcott comforts grieving family
members, even his estranged wife, Norline, assuring them that their
sad farewell is "a different welcome, / which you will share with me,
and see that it is true" (88). "Safe Conduct" invokes the inspiration of
poets Rilke, Pasternak, and Akhmatova. In "Pentecost" he asserts that
it is preferable to have belief, though uncertain; to have a direction,
even without proof; to have "what, in my childhood gospels, / used to
be called Soul" (90). In describing the sorrow of a friend whose wife
recently died of cancer, Walcott's "The Young Wife" draws the curtain
on one kind of loss, only to clear the way for another in "Summer
Elegies."

"Summer Elegies" is set in the ersatz culture of Los Angeles. It concerns a hedonistic affair with Cynthia, a liaison that has presumably
ended since the past tense predominates. The affair serves as a trigger,
nevertheless, in "A Propertius Quartet" for associations with the Roman
poet Sextus Propertius who wrote of his own Cynthia. When the contemporary Cynthia insists her Propertius must see Italy before he dies,

Walcott repeats the earlier sentiment of "The Villa Restaurant," wondering why he should "scan marble busts after hers." Given a choice, he muses, "The statues themselves would choose life over Art" (98). The poem ends on an autumnal note, with Walcott's modern Propertius contemplating his alien language among strange birch trees, dark trunks standing "in white snow like letters on paper" (100).

That alienation carries over into the title poem that concludes *The Arkansas Testament*. When Walcott finds himself in a cheap motel in Fayetteville, Arkansas, he confronts homesickness for fringed islands and the anxiety of being a lone black in the American South:

> this place for
> disposable shavers
> as well as my disposable people
>
> (107)

Although no overt action is taken against him, he feels vulnerable.

> a neat, evangelical town
> now pointed through decorous oaks
> its calendar comfort—scary
> with its simple, God-fearing folks.
> Evil was as ordinary
> here as good. I kept my word.
> This, after all, was the South,
> whose plough was still the sword.
>
> (112)

In the midst of this depression, Walcott considers the option of taking up American citizenship or remaining "an afterthought of the state" (114). As a man, he admits cowardice; but as an artist, he would have to surmount impossible ethical obstacles:

> Can I swear to uphold my art
> that I share with them too, or worse,
> pretend all is past and curse
> from the picket lines of my verse
> the concept of Apartheid?
>
> (115)

Rather than resolve the dilemma explicitly, Walcott allows the poem to end with the observation that stripes and scars remain to be healed under the stars and stripes of the national flag. The final image is of a televised montage, scenes from the Atlantic to the Pacific coasts, and dawn coming up with *Today*'s news.

[H]omeros

Walcott may have undertaken *The Arkansas Testament* with the idea that he needed to reestablish his attachments in St. Lucia and the Caribbean, but he is wise enough to realize that debts to the past can only be redeemed in the present. When asked in a 1990 interview about his main poetic obsessions, Walcott responded, "The Caribbean people have a dignity, a suppleness and a beauty that I would like to articulate."[64] Both he and the people of the West Indies have grown beyond their origins, yet the past has contributed to what they have achieved together. It is no small challenge to pay tribute to the confluence of riches and suffering in New World history without yielding to the temptations of romantic displacement, without imposing heroic trappings. Yet as soon as Walcott defines his position vis-à-vis St. Lucia and "Elsewhere" in *The Arkansas Testament* he immediately faces just these challenges in writing *Omeros*.

In addressing the epic aspects of Derek Walcott's book-length poem *Omeros*, two obstacles must be overcome at the outset. First is Walcott's insistence that his narrative is not technically an epic. In conversation with a *New York Times* reviewer, Walcott denies epic pretensions when he cites the absence of monumental battles and larger-that-life heroes. He insists he stretches for no classical associations in a book written for "people" rather than academicians.[65] Second is the prevalent opinion that the epic is no longer a viable artistic form. M. M. Bakhtin, for example, pronounced the genre to have been completed and "already antiquated."[66] Nevertheless, most of the critics who review *Omeros* cite Longfellow, Whitman, Joyce, Crane, Eliot, Pound, or others who have experimented more recently with the epic.

In answer to both objections, it may be argued that Walcott has undertaken the rewriting of the epic rather than imitation of an outmoded form. He takes liberties with the epic concept, not the traditional style. Despite Bakhtin's specific caveats, arbitrary definitions of the epic have always been subject to revision. Heretofore, the epic has been viewed as a long, elevated poetic narrative of the supernatural deeds of demigods whose wide-ranging actions shape the destiny of a race or nation. Although the author projects himself into the poem, the narrative voice is objective and set conventional devices complete the established style.

Essential features of *Omeros* correspond with each of these descriptors: national implications, vast scope, remarkable (if not "heroic") protagonists, appropriate prosody, and a sustained authorial presence. Given these parallels, it is natural to wonder how Walcott departs from the expected format. Not the least of his reasons for denying traditional designs is his desire to emphasize the radical intent of *Omeros*. In several places Walcott insists that he has not read Homer or Virgil in their entirety, and that he goes beneath the Western heritage of Homer's work to imagine the unrefined poet himself.[67] Walcott envisions a humble man of the sea, an artist-outcast (remarkably like his ubiquitous Crusoe figure) who records the reality of his own people as they struggle for survival and meaning.[68]

Drawing upon the global infusion of cultures within the Caribbean, Walcott undertakes the creation of a new kind of epic, an epic of the dispossessed. Needless to say, poets have manipulated the epic to their own ends ever since Virgil adapted the Greek folk material of *The Iliad* and the *Odyssey* to manufacture a prototypal Roman Aeneas. Dante revised the format to include himself as emblematic Christian protagonist; and his voice floats from vulgar humor to rhetorical eloquence. Serious as these practitioners are, neither sustains the elevation of tone and subject matter as far as Milton does in presuming to "justify the ways of God to men" in *Paradise Lost*. Walcott breaks with this hallowed tradition because, as he tells D.J.R. Bruckner, he is privileged to be in contact with the earthy Caribbean peasant: "One reason I don't like talking about an epic is that I think it is wrong to try to ennoble people. And just to write history is wrong. History makes similes of people, but these people are their own nouns."[69] To appreciate the significance of that choice, it is necessary to look no farther than Trinidadian V. S. Naipaul's assessment of these same people. In *The Middle Passage* he complains that "[h]istory is built around achievement and creation; and nothing was created in the West Indies."[70] He denounces a "society which denied itself heroes" (41). Noting the genocide and the death tolls among immigrant populations, Naipaul goes on to conclude, "it would seem that simply to have survived in the West Indies is to have triumphed" (204).

Fortunately, Walcott has what he calls in his famous poem "The Schooner *Flight*" his "nation of the imagination" with which to work. He focuses on the perseverance and integrity of oppressed individuals living close to the earth and sea, no matter what their race or origin. His epic of the dispossessed encompasses the peasants of his native St. Lucia, Indians of the western United States, the underprivileged of Ireland and Europe, people from the past and from the present. Therefore, the geographic and chronological dimensions of *Omeros* match the dimensions of previous epics if not their focus on noble subjects.

Because the poem follows several common men and women rather than a central hero, its structure depends on a variety of unifying devices, not the least of which is the prosody. The volume consists of seven books, totaling 64 chapters of three sections each. The basic hexameter tercet stanzas recall the terza rima of *The Divine Comedy,* without the slightest hint of the medieval numerology that informs Dante's trinitarian masterpiece. Despite the limitations of this short stanza pattern, Walcott varies the rhythm and rhyme so often that it soon loses any vestiges of the Italian original. Brad Leithauser's close study of the scansion of the verse leads him to conclude that standard metrics are less relevant than something like the "music of the sea." He also suggests that the poem may be rhyme-driven. Leithauser's catalog of rhyme types yields such an exhaustive list—feminine, masculine, visual, pararhyme, rim rhyme, anagrammatic, apocopated, macaronic, rime riche, and various off-rhymes—that he offers *Omeros* as a "rhyme casebook."[71] He insists that the poem demands oral presentation.

Other cohesive devices include three interlocking narrative strands. An initial group of peasants is comprised of Philoctete, who suffers from a symbolic wound; Ma Kilman, who eventually heals him; and Achille and Hector, two fisherman contending for the attentions of the enigmatic island beauty, Helen. As is the case with her ancient namesake, Helen comes to represent the island of St. Lucia itself—a nation that has yet to be claimed by these transplanted descendants of Africa. Since Helen has lost her job as maid to Major Dennis and Maud Plunkett, she also functions as a link between her peasant group and these two transplanted British colonials. Having no son, and no longer recognizing the United Kingdom as their home, the Plunketts endeavor to confirm their adopted St. Lucian identities. A third plot concerns the peripatetic author (who intervenes self-reflexively to integrate the central themes of dispossession and reconciliation) and his erstwhile guide, the blind "Seven Seas," a contemporary Homeric figure of protean identities, calmly registering the toll of human experience.

Then there are vestiges of familiar epic conventions. The story begins in medias res since Philoctete has already suffered his metaphysical wound, Helen has already been fired, and the Major is already casting about for linkage with the island. For inspiration, Walcott invokes the image of Homer as his muse, though that honor is shared by Helen in her function as the personification of St. Lucia. As to the authorial perspective, Walcott pointedly draws attention to the fictive quality of his narrative "I."[72] An announcement of the theme may be discerned in the scene where the ghost of the poet's father (shades of Anchises admonishing Aeneas on Roman duty) charges his son to give expression to his unsung ancestors:

> . . . and your duty
> from the time you watched them from your grandmother's house
> as a child wounded by their power and beauty
> is the chance you now have, to give those feet a voice.
>
> (76)

One epic battle is recounted: from St. Lucia in 1782 British Admiral Rodney launched his fleet to defeat the French in the Battle of the Saints, off Dominica.

The obligatory visit to the underworld takes two forms. First Walcott has sunstruck Achille journey back in time to tribal Africa; then in his role as narrator he follows the animated statue of Homer into the Dantean Malebolge of St. Lucia's Mt. Soufrière to envision the damned speculators, politicians, entrepreneurs, backbiting poets, and traitors who betrayed their island and their race. Rather than present high-flown speeches declaimed by orators, Walcott has his characters think aloud or carry on dialect-flavored conversations, and he himself addresses the reader in the seasoned imagery of valorized experience. If there is an equivalent to the epic simile, it must be figured in the sea swift that stitches horizons together, adorns Maud Plunkett's quilt, leads Achille to Africa, and finally symbolizes the poet's circular journey overseas and back again to his green island for renewal.

Supernatural intervention is limited to relatively credible manifestations. Ma Kilman communes with creatures of the earth to ferret out the herb powerful enough to cleanse Philoctete of the wound that penetrates his soul. Achille's dazed return to Africa could just as well be a form of Jungian racial memory. The poet's guided tour of the volcanic underworld in book 7 is couched in terms of a nightmare. Side by side in the mixed culture of the islands the Christian deity shares place with Shango, Erzulie, Ogun, and Damballa from Africa.

As I indicated earlier, Walcott's most clear-cut departure from tradition concerns the qualities of his protagonists. Retired British Major Plunkett appears to be an unlikely epic character. He can be excused as Walcott's inclusion of his own white ancestry through his Dutch and English grandfathers. A stronger case can be made by simply recognizing the inevitable European presence in West Indian history. The Major adopts the island just as he confiscates the name of the young Ensign Plunkett, who died in the pivotal Battle of the Saints, to seal his personal ties with local history. At the beginning of the poem he assumes the burden of legitimizing Helen by creating around her a history of the island. Thus he might grant St. Lucia the kind of written narrative that provides Western nations their confirming textuality. Politically correct as this gesture might be, were it to succeed, it would contradict Walcott's determination in *Omeros* to subvert traditional forms of ennobling marginalized peoples.

In the final analysis, the hero of this poem is an overt composite of the poet's imaginings. At one time or another, Walcott the narrator assumes the mask of Major Plunkett or of Catherine Weldon, a pioneering woman in the American Dakotas. He plays with the paradox of his being father to his own father, given the fact that he has not only lived to be older than Warwick Walcott, but that he is the creator of the paternal shade who materializes to offer advice within the poem. Blind St. Omere ("Seven Seas") is equally protean since he is an African griot, a Sioux shaman, and a derelict bargeman driven from the steps of St. Martin-in-the-Fields clutching the manuscript which is eventually identified as Walcott's own *Omeros*. Therefore, Omeros is Walcott as well.

Helen's role is equally complex, in person and personification. St. Lucia has been called the Helen of the Caribbean because of its natural beauty, and because European nations fought numerous wars for its possession. By Walcott's own count, the island has changed flags 13 times.[73] Earlier prototypes of the woman herself may be traced to "Janie, the town's one clear-complexioned whore," who is nicknamed "Helen" in *Another Life*.[74] Her most immediate incarnation, according to Walcott, is the woman he elegizes in "The Light of the World."[75] In later manuscript versions he was calling her "Elena," expressly because he conceives her to be as much an object of contention as were the island of St. Lucia and her classical namesake.[76]

Hector and Achille are at odds over their Helen, but these personal differences afford more extensive social implications as well. Because Hector abandons the sea to become a taxi driver, he reveals the encroachments of urbanization in a tourist-ridden island. Achille's agonized identification with the natural contours of geography and history puts him within the lineage of Walcott's well-known Creole Crusoe figure. Although his Helen is no Penelope waiting faithfully at home, Achille's odyssey reestablishes African roots and affirms their influence in island customs. Achille's new appreciation of local rituals, costumes, stilted dancers, and native instruments is confirmed as he tenderly explains them to Helen in the 55th chapter.

Of course, manifestations of these various characters are only part of the more explicit design. Significant as fictional patterns may be, Walcott's authorial perspective is the deciding factor. His autobiographical interweavings and his personal observations subvert the written text far more critically than Dante's occasional asides in the *Divine Comedy*. In refusing to follow the epic's tendency to ennoble its heroes, Walcott preserves the common clay of his people. They not only have their foibles and self-deprecating consciousness, but the openness of the *Omeros* text permits explicit disclaimers.

Near the end of the book, three instances may be cited. In chapter 56 the shade of Homer advises Walcott that the love of a girl like Helen is merely an excuse for an epic, "but the love of your own people is greater." When Walcott responds that this is the reason he follows in his footsteps, Homer asserts the primacy of raw reality over literature: "A girl smells better than the world's libraries" (284). A second example occurs in Major Plunkett's ultimate recognition of Helen as a human being: no longer his appropriated emblem, "She was not a cause or a cloud, only a name / for a local wonder" (309). The closing example is the most pervasive, beginning with Walcott's initial confession that "every 'I' is a fiction" in chapter 5 (28). This "I" of imagination culminates elaborately in the 57th chapter with Walcott's reference to his own "I" as the mast supporting the sail of his dual odyssey—as a man born in St. Lucia and as an author. The pronouncement is given to Seven Seas:

Your wanderer [Walcott] is a phantom from the boy's shore.

Mark you, *he* does not go; he sends his narrator;
he plays tricks with time because there are two journeys
in every odyssey, one on worried water,

the other crouched and motionless, without noise.
For both, the "I" is a mast; a desk is a raft
for one, foaming with paper, and dipping the beak

of a pen in its foam, while an actual craft
carries the other to cities where people speak
a different language, or look at him differently

(291)

Walcott brings both journeys to closure as he describes Achille cleaning his daily catch of mackerel and snapper. Achille turns homeward as "the sea was still going on" (325).

Omeros is an epic, one that invites its own deconstruction. It is innovative and original in the sense defined by Edward Said in *The World, the Text, and the Critic*: "Originality of contemporary literature in its broad outlines resides in the refusal of originality, or primacy, to its forebears. Rather than look for first instances of a phenomenon—see duplication, parallelism, symmetry, parody, echoes. Rather than seeing something confined to a book, see something released from a book in writing.[77] There are sufficient parallels with classical names, episodes, and structural details to require recognition of epic conventions in *Omeros*. Nevertheless, deviations from classical functions, the liberating detachment of protagonists from heroic paraphernalia, and the author's subversion of the logical categories normally separating living experience from literary expression and fictive masks comprise a new kind of epic: a deconstructive genre that may well be designated the epic of the dispossessed.

Nobel Laureate

The self-reflective intertextuality of *Omeros* and other works in the 1980s erodes artificial barriers between ordinary life and the fictions and myths that give meaning to existence. Walcott bases his literary explorations of the world in St. Lucia, yet he reaches outward to include not only all of the Americas but the Old World influences that continually re-create themselves in modern thought. Back in 1976 a reviewer condemning the ineffectuality of *O Babylon!* wondered whether the play were "An Interlude for Rest or a Prelude to Disaster."[78] The answer is evident both in the number of plays and poetry collections Walcott has written and published since the 1970s as well as in the increasing power and assurance of these works.

Reviewing *Collected Poems,* Peter Balakian not only perceives latent "epic consciousness" but he is struck by the resourcefulness carrying through the *The Star-Apple Kingdom* and beyond. Balakian argues that Walcott's "ability to renew himself, to revitalize his imagination, to rediscover the myth of his life and his culture, places him among the greatest poets of our century—Yeats, Neruda, Rilke, Williams, Elytis, for example—poets who write out of their obsessions without repeating themselves."[79] The future remains promising as well. Walcott still lectures, directs, and writes plays, poetry, and occasional articles. Any number of his unpublished dramas, poems, and uncollected essays could appear at any time.

As Walcott's production continues, recognition has kept pace into the 1990s. The Welsh Arts Council's International Writer's prize (1980) was followed by the lucrative MacArthur Foundation Award (1981), then the W. H. Smith prize for *Omeros* (1990). Remarkable as each of his individual volumes may be, his *Collected Poems* and the epic *Omeros* are undeniably monumental achievements. The crowning acknowledgment of his lifelong devotion to the arts occurred in December 1992 when Walcott was awarded the Nobel Prize for Literature.

Chapter 7
Archipelagoes of Man: The Critic

Derek Walcott is accomplished in many fields. He has been at one time or another poet, playwright, producer, theatrical manager, set designer, director, painter, newspaper columnist, lecturer, critic, and cultural commentator. An overview of his expository writing since the 1950s reveals definitive attitudes and interests as well as maturation. It appears (with the advantage of hindsight) that he has always had a sense of where he stands emotionally and where his healthy, if divided, intellectual gifts are rooted. The evidence is available in personal interviews, speeches, candid articles, and in the numerous columns he once wrote for the *Trinidad Guardian*.

In approaching Walcott's expository as opposed to his creative writing, it is worth noting that he distrusts the sensible confidentiality of prose delivered from a lectern. Addressing a conference on West Indian literature in 1988, he objected to critical and philosophical prose on the grounds that it is too political, too rational. He insists that poetry in contrast is open to "accident as illumination, error as truth, typographical mistakes as revelation."[1] Furthermore he claims—punning ineluctably as he does throughout his poems and plays—that his "life-long sentence" has been served between two flexible margins, not fixed to the left-hand rigidities of prose. With typical verbal legerdemain, he seizes upon the political implications of this "left/right" imagery. "The business of politics is the business of discourse, and the language of discourse is prose, and the language of one margin only, and the one margin, in politics may be called right when it is left and left when it is right" (139). Ironically, he would have been justified in remarking as well that as a West Indian artist he speaks from the perspective of one who began his career as a "marginal" writer, outside the mainstream of Western literature. That perspective is on his mind when he closes by advising aspiring writers to "sneer, to turn away from these linear pronouncements," as he did when he was a boy (142). Regardless of such personal reservations, Walcott's explicit insights into life and art—never pedestrian, never prosaic—continue to reward careful scrutiny.

Theater and Society

Walcott's public voice emerged almost simultaneously with his decision to settle in Trinidad after the period of his Rockefeller Fellowship in New York. As early as January 7, 1959, in the form of a letter to the editor of the *Guardian*, he expressed sadness over hearing that *Bim* might be forced to cease publication.[2] *Bim* did not go under, but Walcott's letter records his concern for writers who choose to live among their people and who need a regional outlet for their work. This was shortly before he became a regular *Guardian* columnist, when he was in the process of founding his Theatre Workshop. During the formative years of the Workshop Walcott frequently used the newspaper to assess the general progress of the arts in the region. On occasion, he was not above promoting his first love: the theater. One of his dominant themes was the need for an adequate theater building in Trinidad.

From the beginning it was obvious that some kind of subsidy would be required. In "Future of Art Promising," he is adamant about his claims for government support: "More than any other art, the theatre can express the national spirit, and it needs intense concentration of purpose. There is enough talent to formulate its direction."[3] Typically, in this 1963 article, Walcott states not only a need, but also a reason. At the same time he is too realistic to await governmental response. Barely two months after he spoke of "concentration of purpose" in another article he spelled out the manner in which the demands of necessity could be turned to advantage. Taking a hint from Off-Broadway productions he had observed, he argued that staging could be adapted to special limitations. The solution to the problem was to be found in concentration on physical details that could give the illusion of width and depth. This solution, unfortunately, only revealed a more serious problem. It awakened him to the fact that space was not the essential difficulty. The real deficiency was lack of equipment and professionally trained technicians.[4]

By August 1964 his call for assistance was opened to include a broader spectrum of talents.[5] Again, in March 1966, he advocated scholarships to train actors, dancers, choreographers, technicians, directors, and writers.[6] Through October 1966 (the official opening of the Basement Theatre's first performances) he continued to publicize needs while extolling the virtues of simplified, reduced, "essentialised" theatrical techniques.[7] Then, in 1967, perhaps sensing that his tone might be too strident and that he could be accused of serving his own personal inter-

ests, Walcott introduced an important qualification into his campaign.
He stressed, in a July interview with Carl Jacobs, that he had never
applied for a governmental subsidy.[8]

That there is more to this qualification than a subtle distinction
between making a public plea and filing an official application becomes
apparent in a more extensive article in 1970. In "Meanings" Walcott
specifies that his request for state assistance is not simply for a subsidy,
but for a shared experience. He contends that just as some form of
socialism is essential for political survival, the only hope for broadening
the base of the arts in the Caribbean is through a shared, "communal
effort."[9] His long struggle on behalf of theater was in part self-serving,
but inasmuch as it was for the sake of the larger society as well, it was
never selfish.

In waging his struggle on behalf of society and of art, Walcott faced
the perennial dilemma of serving two masters. Rather than compromise
his art, he decided from the beginning that he could best serve the community by serving art well. As early as 1960, in "Artists Need Some
Assistance," he argued that individual talents on government pay could
be better utilized than in the glorification of the ruling party.[10] Just as
the state as patron imposes certain expectations, the public also offers to
corrupt the artist's aims. He made clear in "Why Is Our Theatre So
Tame?" that a mindlessly chauvinistic national theater was not his intention. He deplored the obvious shortcuts that some local writers used in
order to curry popular acceptance: dialect humor and shallow stereotypes that elicit a quick laugh or elevate the folk image. He noted, "In
the theatre peasants are no more exciting than clerks."[11] Reviewing a
recently published poetry anthology in 1966, he suggested, "It is time
that we start separating racial or political enthusiasm from good verse,
however noble and instructive our purpose."[12]

Others have since added their voices to Walcott's in calling for government support of independent artists and for facilities adequate to
encourage continued growth. State and corporate money is available
through scholarships and awards to calypso and Carnival contestants,
but as late as 1990 little found its way into the other arts. Articles by
Marylin Jones in 1975 and Keith Smith in 1976 are but two of many
that raise the issue of the need for subsidizing work as significant as that
of the Trinidad Theatre Workshop.[13] Ten years after Smith's complaint
regarding inadequate financing, Walcott surmised that aside from the
popular tourist attractions Trinidad can offer only the house where V. S.

Naipaul grew up, a modest museum, and a theater that remains poorly equipped.[14]

Despite the history of physical deprivations and official neglect, Walcott foresees dynamic possibilities for theater both in the provinces like Trinidad and in metropolitan countries. He sees opportunity where much contemporary drama has abandoned the original poetry, the cathartic sublimity of the stage for static, rhetorical minimalism.[15] While metropolitan arbiters of taste smugly assume that marginal, provincial theater will follow suit, there is exciting exuberance in Wole Soyinka and ghetto theater. As he has for most of his career, Walcott still cites Brecht and the importance of both artificiality and vulgarity in drama, an engaged audience that talks back, not passive eavesdroppers ("Poet," 5).

That artificiality, Walcott insists, is requisite for great art, as it has been traditionally. To his thinking 20th-century poets W. H. Auden, Elizabeth Bishop, E. E. Cummings, Philip Larkin, Ezra Pound, Dylan Thomas, and W. B. Yeats have created a remarkably colloquial, modulated voice that is "as much an advance of the lyric as it is for the possibilities of dramatic poetry in the modern theatre" ("Poet," 6). While he opposes nostalgic revivals of conventional fare, he wants meter, symmetry, the dynamism of music and poetry to "reinvade the theatre, not hang out in the lobby shabbily like a second cousin" ("Poet," 8). At the same time Walcott and Brecht call for artificiality in form, they assume a corresponding degree of intelligence in a responsive audience. Elsewhere, Walcott asserts that art has never been democratic, that it is hierarchical: "It takes all your life to achieve some level where you can be among your peers. But if immediately your peers are made to be the illiterate, or the people who feel education is restricted entirely to self expression without craft, then the society is in danger. It is in more danger than it is from terrorists or revolutionaries."[16] Incongruous as it may seem at first, such insistence on standards reveals the deepest respect for the integrity of the common person in the audience.

Folk Expression

Errol Hill has argued forcefully in his book *The Trinidad Carnival* that a national theater could organize and focus Carnival's rich, dramatic elements to create a more powerful means of human expression.[17] Walcott recognized the potential of certain aspects of Carnival, incorporating them into *Drums and Colours, In a Fine Castle, The Charlatan, The Joker of*

Seville, and *The Last Carnival*; but while it is a necessary part of local setting, it is basically incompatible with the type of drama that he was
writing. His *Guardian* article "Carnival: The Theatre of the Streets"
(1964) points out a central stillness in all serious art, the classics, that is
antithetical to the spirit of Carnival: "The essential law of Carnival is
movement. . . . As a mass art, an idiosyncratic form of popular expression. . . . The artist works in isolation from the crude, popular forms."[18]
He reached the conclusion in "Problems of Exile" (1966) that Carnival
was not adaptable to the stage. "The truth is that West Indian theatre
will continue to be literary, humanistic in its concept just as much as the
West Indian novel is." Carnival is too ephemeral in nature; its impact
depends on unrepetitive pageantry, season after spectacular season.[19]

In spite of his open reservations about its theatrical potentials,
Walcott is not opposed to the rightful place of Carnival. What he does
resent is the way Carnival, steel bands, and calypsos as well are taken
from the people as spontaneous expression and used by the government
to exploit the tourist trade. He made that explicit in his interview with
Selden Rodman and in his introduction to *Dream on Monkey Mountain.* In
his opinion, the state, intellectuals, and a brown meritocracy who court
the masses—glorifying folk forms, calling calypsos poems, pretending to
educate the peasant while leaving him "intellectually unsoiled"—are the
real enemies of cultural growth: "[F]or the colonial artist the enemy was
not the people, or the people's crude aesthetic which he refined and
orchestrated, but the enemy was those who had elected themselves as
protectors of the people, . . . who urged them to acquire pride which
meant abandoning their individual dignity, who cried out that black was
beautiful . . . without explaining what they meant by beauty."[20] Openly
resisting these corrupting influences left Walcott in a position that
appeared to some to indicate an unpopular, elitist attitude.

Criticism of Walcott's position and practice ranges from Raoul
Pantin's passing reference to the expensive ticket prices that exclude all
but well-to-do patrons, to Sule Mombara's unsupported accusation that
parts for whites were hastily written into *O Babylon!* to placate European
members of the Workshop, to Ralph Campbell's long list of abuses: as a
promoter Walcott had not recruited participants from underprivileged
neighborhoods, had not provided a training program and enough
encouragement for young recruits, and had done nothing toward "building our image."[21] One response to such complaints is to observe the
record of attendance at performances and Walcott's own discussion of
the type of audience he hoped to impress.

By the time the Theatre Workshop had been presenting its repertoire for about 18 months, it had played many times before varied audiences. In July 1967 Walcott made the emphatic point that his performance halls were never divided into special seating areas and that the 2,000 patrons who had come to see "Moon on a Rainbow Shawl" at Queen's Hall and Naparima Bowl were tangible evidence of his harboring no biases toward an intellectual elite. Income from recent productions was to help defray expenses for the Toronto opening of *Dream on Monkey Mountain*.[22] When *O Babylon!* was produced in Jamaica in July 1976, free admission was arranged for the Rastafarian community to attend and react to the play based on their life-style. It seems that a necessary ordering of priorities, not prejudice, governed the Workshop's policies. Walcott was certainly not above doing all of the onerous tasks required of a struggling theater promoter. He knew the requirements well enough to advise Astor Johnson in "Mixing the Dance and Drama" that if his Repertory Dance Theatre were to survive, more than effective stage performance would be needed: "There is an equal amount, if not more, of choreography required in advertising, interviewing, and begging as there is in staging his pieces."[23]

From the opening year of the Workshop, Walcott expressed concern in regard to popular, "mob" influences; nevertheless, he insisted in "What the Lower House Demands" that the brutal honesty of the pit must be respected. Their demands for "[b]uoyancy, warmth, even the right vulgarity" are actually the "gifts of entertainer-geniuses from Shakespeare to Fellini."[24] To listen to their expectations, Walcott suggests, may be a difficult task for conscientious artists, but it can be done. His theory, shown in an interview with Raoul Pantin in 1973, was that every member of an audience, including his concrete image of "a fat woman laughing," is capable of reacting even to a sophisticated classic on his or her own terms. The writer's duty is to move the audience without "any lowering of standards or literacy . . . but by an intensity and a clarity of performance that will affect everybody . . . from a Minister of Culture down to . . . somebody's maid."[25]

His audience over the years has covered that broad spectrum. The "folk" for him are not Rousseauistic innocents, but people of all walks of life. Mervyn Morris recalls an amusing anecdote Walcott once used in a seminar. Walcott painted the comic scene of an ecstatic poet rushing with his latest creation to a laborer to exclaim, "Have you heard this one?"[26] Morris subsequently argues for the fact that not everyone has an inclination to undertake the disciplined thinking that subtle poetry demands. Only a year prior to this seminar in the article "Kaiso, Genius of the Folk," Walcott distinguished between the personal impulse of the poem and the collective, public aspect of the calypso: "Where a poem can be beyond the total comprehension of the reader or of a generation, the calypso must succeed immediately. It is assessed by its impact."[27]

Drama labors under similar strictures, and, as Walcott once explained to Edward Hirsch, the thing that makes it more attractive than working on a poem is its communal basis. Not only has he devoted half his artistic career to a theatrical form equally capable of Shakespeare and calypso, but he celebrates a society and unaffected actors for whom highly rhetorical productions come naturally. He told Hirsch, "It's a coarse thing—a great range between a wonderful vulgarity and a great refinement, and we have it here."[28] He also told Hirsch that one of the drawbacks is the petit-bourgeois mentality of the middle class that undervalues serious art and settles for amateurism (219). As long as he was connected with the Trinidad Theatre Workshop, he attempted to inculcate professionalism. Subsequent to his taking up residence in the United States, he undertook an abortive second phase, introducing foreign actors and actresses to elevate performance to an international standard. As he put it in a *Sunday Guardian* interview, the intermingling of local and outside talent could have been beneficial not only in terms of method and technique for his mixed cast, but it might have served as a check against the exaggerated praise too often showered on competent amateurs by provincial critics.[29]

Although differences in objectives have widened the breach between Walcott and current Workshop directors, the Workshop regularly mounts performances of a variety of plays by Walcott and other writers; and individual members occasionally participate in Walcott's ongoing productions. Walcott continues to divide his year between Boston and the West Indies, maintaining ties with the audience he favors, and advocating artistic standards that will bring out the best in him and his society. In recent years, with his more diversified, far-flung public, he has striven to reach out to the "provincial" listener on an international scale. The poet and dramatist may speak at times as if their audience simply overhears their private meditation, but insofar as they communicate with people, they serve the "folk." In reference to V. S. Naipaul, Walcott observes of the area's most scathingly critical native son that he re-creates life, "and this is the first cause of a writer."[30]

The Angel of Influence

Walcott's relationship with the community of writers and critics over the years has been relatively antagonistic at times. The give-and-take was intense enough that Errol Hill was moved to say after the success of *Dream on Monkey Mountain*, "One hopes he [Walcott] has now lost some of the testy impatience and frustration that have distorted his theatre critiques of other people's work. Perhaps it is too much to expect that one so actively involved in his own theatre enterprise can be objective in reviewing the work of others."[31] In most cases the "impatience and frustration" were due not only to his own company's problems, but to the status of poetry and drama in general.

Almost from the outset as a *Guardian* critic, Walcott protested against the amateurism of local theater, calling it "the chronic disease of West Indian life" in his August 1963 article "Future of Art Promising."[32] Earlier, in June of the same year, he had delivered a lecture in which he spoke against the messianism and rhetoric of local writing that too often merely preached deliverance or revenge, and against a prevalent tendency to exaggerate that reduced comedy to burlesque and turned tragic themes into melodrama.[33] On the matter of poetry his evaluation is equally negative. In several places he complains of the scarcity of good verse in the English-speaking Caribbean. "Anthologies" is brutally frank: "[T]he bulk of West Indian verse is bad, only bearable if one forgives its origins and sympathises self-insultingly with its efforts. It has lagged far behind the novel, its structure is either sprawling 'modern,' or embarrassingly imitative. It is weakened into more rhetoric by such themes as national pride and racial peevishness."[34] Walcott is capable of admiring the work of individual writers, but his harshest judgment is against the general mediocrity.

In his opinion, there is a corresponding lack of professional competence on the part of literary critics in the area as well, which aggravates the problem. Local criticism, he charges in "Judging Standards," is colored by envy, unfounded awe, or nationalistic feeling. The extended difficulty he sees in biased, provincial criticism is that it endangers the artist and the public's conception of what is truly well done.[35] They do not always have enough distance to establish a balanced view. It may be interesting to note in passing that the same weakness—overly subjective bias—was precisely Errol Hill's accusation against Walcott seven years after this column appeared. Judging by what Walcott has argued else-

where, it is likely he would be in complete sympathy with Hill's contention: "It remains one of the serious defects in the West Indies, name-
ly, informed, dispassionate yet understanding criticism of efforts to create
a West Indian drama and theatre."[36] As poor as the situation has been in
the past, there has been some improvement. Walcott found that in the
case of critics like Mervyn Morris, Edward Brathwaite, Kenneth
Ramchand, and Gordon Rohlehr, the analytical perception has occasionally been superior to the literature they reviewed.[37] His estimation of the
general function of criticism has not improved over the years. Addressing
a 1988 conference on West Indian literature, Walcott complained about
the literary critic who must explain away the fortuitous accidents of
poetic composition in rational prose. He confesses, "I am one who cannot accept these processes, of games of self-contradiction, of essays on
poetry, any more than I can accept the right-hand margin of History,
which begins, in our language, from the left and proceeds without trim,
without metre, without that closing question of the couplet until it sat-
isfies itself with cause and effect. This ignorance is old. It is the future of
the Caribbean."[38]

Impassioned as Walcott can be concerning some of his favorite topics,
he is an informed, meticulous, well-read observer. The names of literary
figures that he refers to, some of them repeatedly and at length, would
constitute a formidable who's who of world writers. Most prominent
among those of the Caribbean are Naipaul and Brathwaite, but he
touches on Césaire, Harris, Mais, Hearne, Selvon, Lamming, and
Mittelholzer. From South America there are Borges and Neruda; Brecht
from Germany; Soyinka and Senghor from Africa; Genêt, Ionesco, and
Beckett of France; the Russians Chekhov, Pasternak, and Brodsky;
Kurosawa in Japan; from the United States Pound, Inge, Stevens, and
Lowell; from the United Kingdom Hardy, Conrad, Joyce, Thomas, Eliot,
Osborne, Larkin, and Hughes. The list could be extended, but the point
is that the young writer who began dreaming of carrying on the line of
the Elizabethans has reached out in all directions to establish points of
reference throughout the world.

Yet he never once loses sight of his origins. It is appropriate that he
should have turned a considerable amount of his attention on other writers in the Caribbean. In an interview in 1975 he argued that it would be
more difficult to understand the beginnings of West Indian literature
than it would be to grasp the emergence of literature from the American
colonies. In the cases of Naipaul, Lamming, Harris, and others there
were broken islands, and no coherent racial and social experience for the

populace as a whole.[39] Perhaps the most obvious fact concerning the area's literary history is that the novel has far outstripped other literary genres—in quality and in recognition.

Questioning this phenomenon in "Why Is Our Theatre So Tame?" he arrived at the conclusion that it was the result of economic necessity—his own experiences as a theatrical entrepreneur and poet, no doubt, served as basic evidence. What makes this all the more unfortunate, as Walcott observed, is that his people are given to self-dramatization and are highly rhetorical. Yet, due to the costs of production, some of the best writers choose the novel. He then goes on, "Yet how theatrical our novels are: What a finer, more selective instinct for dialogue our novelists have, and how many one-act situations they crowd into their plots. There are subtler comedies in short West Indian fiction than in the U.W.I. Drama library [*sic*], especially in Selvon and in Naipaul" (8). Consequently, Walcott has made frequent references to the potential of adapting fictional scenes for the stage, and to the examples of craftsmanship available in the region's novelists.

Foremost among these is V. S. Naipaul. Even as he took note of the cynical and caustic remarks that were leading up to *The Middle Passage,* Walcott recognized the positive achievement of Naipaul's masterpiece, *A House for Mr Biswas*: "[I]t enhances the ordinary and illuminates the defeat of millions like us."[40] In order to handle Naipaul, Walcott hit upon the expedient of weighing his travel books *The Middle Passage* and *An Area of Darkness* against the fictional works. He found in "Is V. S. Naipaul an Angry Young Man?" that Naipaul's savage indignation and despair were balanced by his "major virtues: his reticence, his refusal and his compassion." In order to reach these underlying qualities, he recommended looking beyond the outward mask of despair. The two levels parallel each other precariously in *The Mimic Men.* As Walcott sees it, a "chronicle of decline towards madness and anonymity" began with Naipaul's first mimic-man hero Ganesh Ramsumair in *The Mystic Masseur* and reached a predictable culmination in Ralph Singh. Ralph records the deterioration of his own life, but there is a fundamental contradiction between the elegant artistry of his writing and the failure to which it is supposed to testify.

The narrator-writer's dilemma, Walcott concluded, was Naipaul's also: "[T]hat he makes art but now distrusts it, that he loves and suffers with and for his people but that love chokes on abhorrence, that there is despair but it lacks resonance, that the writing of novels seems a futile occupation yet no West Indian writer is so prodigious."[41] Stemming from this unresolved contradiction, Walcott felt that the major flaw in *The Mimic Men* was its lack of "the authority of cohesion." Years later, returning to the question, he temporarily reversed that judgment. Talking with Selden Rodman, he confessed that he had come to recognize Naipaul's supposed retreat into total despair as actually a withdrawal into contemplation: the same withdrawal that his own Makak makes at the end of *Dream on Monkey Mountain*.[42] Reading *The Enigma of Arrival* in 1987, however, Walcott was disappointed to find the book "negligible as a novel and crucial as autobiography."[43] He reaches the conclusion that in spite of Naipaul's having profited enormously from his heritage and becoming something of a phenomenon, "a singular, contradictory genius who survived the cane fields and the bush at great cost," he is prejudiced; and worse, in perpetuating his myth he has failed to advance.

As understanding as Walcott has attempted to be in reading Naipaul, he is simply not temperamentally suited to accept the bitter novelist's attitude. Whereas Naipaul asserts that nothing has ever been created in the West Indies and that his society denies itself heroes, Walcott counters by offering the calypso, steel drums, and Carnival costumes as examples of creative activity.[44] It is no weakness in his argument that each of these had precedent in other cultures. Mimicry itself, according to his understanding, is an imaginative act. As he expounded upon this theme during a conference at the University of Miami, he proposed that the alternative to mimicry in its strict sense would be the failure to adapt: cultural and racial suicide.[45] The secret is in taking what is given and turning it to practical and spiritual use.

The second major artist from the West Indies, one who occupies almost as much of Walcott's attention as Naipaul does, is Edward Brathwaite. Like Walcott, who maintained residence in Trinidad until he was almost 50 years old and still returns annually for artistic sustenance, Brathwaite has chosen to remain in the Caribbean. His major writing also has been devoted to examining the predicament of man transplanted in the New World. His most famous work is *The Arrivants: A New World Trilogy* (1972) comprising *Rights of Passage* (1967), *Masks* (1968), and *Islands* (1969). This trilogy is a series of lyrical poems tracing the black man's ancient loss of Africa, his sojourn in various parts of the world, and his struggle to reconcile himself to the conflicts of his heritage and his present environment. Reviewing the first volume of the trilogy in "Tribal Flutes," Walcott indicated that Brathwaite invokes Naipaul in his compassion and goes beyond him in understanding the pattern that can be made from broken artifacts and unshaped memories. He appreciates the flexibly resilient overall design, and certain sequences that evoke the worlds of Mais and Lamming in their style. Other passages, however—those that depart from the central, melancholic, blues tone to rage or exhortation—fall short of the emotion called for by the rhetoric. They suffer in comparison with Césaire and Saint-John Perse.[46] In a later reference to the entire trilogy Walcott expressed admiration for Brathwaite's skill at characterization and his ability to dramatize moments, to capture various dialects and the music of spoken language. Walcott finds little to argue with in Brathwaite's view of life, but in fact the two poets are frequently placed into categories opposite each other. Brathwaite is presented (and he accepts the label) as a "folk" poet. Walcott is viewed (and he finds such designations arbitrary) as a literary humanist.

Such convenient labels aside, several major literary influences have come to occupy Walcott's attention on the northern end of his Caribbean–Boston axis. There have always been Brecht, Yeats, Eliot, and Dylan Thomas. Most recently Walcott has discovered affinities with such poets as Joseph Brodsky, Seamus Heaney, and Robert Lowell. It is not only taste that binds these seemingly disparate writers in friendship. Brodsky, a Russian, and Heaney, an Irishman, share with Walcott the experience of living and writing in America as expatriates. Among Walcott's remarks on Brodsky's *To Urania* (1988), it would be difficult to avoid observations that reflect equally on the reviewer as well as the author under review. Noting that Brodsky has translated Virgil, Ovid, Propertius, Donne, and various modern poets, Walcott finds no derivations, only homage, a tribute to a beloved second language. He respects the fact that as a Russian Jew Brodsky rejects the grounds for anger in his background and has earned the same happiness Walcott finds in exile. Brodsky might well be a citizen of Shabine's "nation of the imagination," a voice "muttering a complicated monologue which does not simplify its references, and whose spirit seems not to lament but to cherish its disinheritance."[47]

In his tribute "On Robert Lowell," Walcott candidly admits that his biographical sketch is a projection of his own creation. Understandably, then, Walcott himself can be discerned in his reading of Lowell. Several favorite parallels stand out. That Walcott admires what he calls Lowell's "unrelenting ordinariness" is not surprising from one who celebrates the earthiness of Makak, Shabine, and the Achilles of St. Lucia. Given Walcott's increasing penchant for self-reflexive text, significant compatibility exists in the idea that all of Lowell's "writing is about writing, all of his poetry is about the pain of making poems." Finally, Walcott stresses the manner in which Lowell draws from literary tradition: "In taking on the voices of the poets he loved and unashamedly envied, he could, in rewriting them, inhabit each statue down the pantheon of the dead and move his hand in theirs."[48]

Walcott might have developed the confessional strain in his verse, or he might have proceeded with the deconstruction of his writing processes without the model of Lowell, but as with the example of Brecht in theater, he has seized upon and made artistic use of precedent. Defending the disparities of his *The Joker of Seville* for a seminar at the College of the Virgin Islands, Walcott typically cited precedents even closer to home: "In the whole West Indian experience, the fact that we can take chunks from anywhere at all is not a matter of diffuseness for us. It is a matter of an experience in which the disparate is the whole."[49] Eclectic "borrowing" is an indelible mark of his brand of "humanism."

On Humanism

Mervyn Morris reports that Brathwaite once indicated that there were three approaches to West Indian literature: the humanist, the personal, and the folk. Morris sees little value in the distinctions since a poet can shift focus from one period and from one poem to another.[50] The implication behind much of the criticism of Walcott's more sophisticated and Western-influenced poems is that he is not thoroughly West Indian. One of the most intemperate examples of this kind of futile exercise is available in an anonymous article that raises the question as part of its rambling title, "How Far Are Derek Walcott and Edward Brathwaite Similar? . . ." The author's findings are that Walcott is elitist, that his reasoning is discursive, and that the Caribbean needs Brathwaite but "has absolutely no place for Derek Walcott."[51] Less-biased comparisons on the part of critics such as Lloyd Brown and Patricia Ismond provide greater insight into both poets and also clarify the grounds upon which legitimate distinctions may be made.[52]

On the difference between a folk and a humanist writer, Walcott's contention is that there is too much access in a mobile society for the term "folk" to be restricted to peasants and menial laborers. When asked whether the labels "regional" and "provincial" were not dangerously confining, he answered that on the contrary, "The more particular you get, the more universal you become."[53] For Selden Rodman he spelled out the essential qualities of a "colonial" as opposed to a "revolutionary" writer. The colonial writer is more mature. His subtle method is to assimilate the ageless features of his ancestors in the arts. The overt attack of the revolutionary serves to galvanize the very tradition he opposes and thereby perpetuate it.[54] From this it should not be concluded that Walcott is reactionary. He wants change, but is practical enough to be concerned about the kind of change. Nationalization of resources and the enforcement of some kind of national service would be advantageous if they contributed to people's self-respect and improved their productivity and their sense of personal responsibility.[55]

Walcott's program for change centers primarily on the individual, but it is broad in scope and concerned with the result of revolution. It might have been better had he used the term "extreme radical" rather than "revolutionary" when he defined his position for Rodman. It becomes clear in his interview with Raoul Pantin that he considers himself (and any colonial writer who speaks to the issue of social problems and values) to be revolutionary in the larger sense of the word. As a humanist and as an artist, he denounces younger, extremist poets who for the sake of immediate relevance project themselves into the thinking of the masses. He states, "It's a complete contradiction of what the poet does because the poet does not listen to anything but his 'inner ear.' . . . The feeling that they have of relevance increases because of the rush. They want to say something now and it has to be said without any decoration and so on. This leaves out the most exciting part of poetry, which is its craft."[56] Pursuing the question of whether the poet's calling might prevent necessary exchange between the writer and his audience, Walcott explained that his craft required working with a living language and that activities of the Workshop involved him deeply in the ordinary chores of daily life.[57]

Over his career Walcott has maintained a remarkable balance between his public and his private commitments. Within his work is a fine blend of that which is traditional and that which is most intimately his own. His form of revolution, stressing the quality of existence, obviously requires mature patience. His regionalism, since it implies the universal dimensions of particulars, must be broadly expansive. His humanism, concerning itself with man first rather than races and creeds, seems all-embracing.

In an age of uncertainty and disillusionment, Walcott is a realist with his feet planted solidly in experience, yet his appreciation of the power of imagination and his dedication to the artist's role in society are refreshing, even ennobling. He has said: "I am not mystifying the process of composition which is often downright hard work, as magic, but I believe that poetry originates in magic, in the sense that one accepts the possibility of God. What is true is that the good poet is the proprietor of the experience of the race, that he is and has always been the vessel, vates, rainmaker, the conscience of the king and embodiment of society, even when society is unable to contain him."[58] In keeping with that sentiment, Walcott told Edward Hirsch that his lifelong ambition had been "to articulate not my own experience, but what I saw around me."[59] It is this comprehensive vision that provides the rich, contradictory variety of Walcott's oeuvre. Thus when the Nobel Prize Selection Committee examined Walcott in 1992, they found a repository of the best of New World culture, a writer who by birth, by environment, and by personal commitment had lived multiculturalism long before the bête noire of political correctness made this term a cause célèbre.

Perhaps fellow West Indian V. S. Naipaul offers the surest formula by which any artist may best serve his country and humanity: "In the end it is the writer and the writing that matter. The attempt to perfect Indian English or achieve Canadian-ness is the private endeavour of an irrelevant nationalism. . . . a country is ennobled by its writers only if these writers are good."[60] The artist is confronted with many distracting temptations. As an artist, however, his commitment demands that he see through appearances to the underlying foundations. His twofold task is not only to observe and pass along knowledge as a philosopher might, but also to re-create the substance of his vision so that it comes to life in the experience of mankind. Derek Walcott has already added invaluable living treasure to the world's store of experience that is literature.

Notes and References

Chapter One

1. V. S. Naipaul, *The Middle Passage* (London: André Deutsch, 1962), 29.
2. Louis James, ed., *The Islands in Between* (London: Oxford University Press, 1968), 10.
3. Edward Brathwaite, "Themes from the Caribbean," *Times Educational Supplement,* 6 September 1968, 396.
4. Edward Baugh, "Towards a West Indian Criticism," *Caribbean Quarterly* 14 (March–June 1968): 141.
5. Arthur Drayton, "West Indian Fiction and West Indian Society," *Kenyon Review* 25 (Winter 1963): 129.
6. William Walsh, *Commonwealth Literature* (London: Oxford University Press, 1973), 60.
7. James, "Caribbean Poetry in English—Some Problems," *Savacou* 2 (1970): 78–79, 83.
8. "Meanings," *Savacou* 2 (1970): 50.
9. "A Far Cry from Africa," in *In a Green Night* (London: Jonathan Cape, 1962), 18.
10. "Meanings," 49.
11. Henry Swanzy, "Prolegomena to a West Indian Culture," *Caribbean Quarterly* 1 (July–September 1949): 21.
12. "Meanings," 51.
13. "What the Twilight Says," in *Dream on Monkey Mountain* (New York: Farrar, Straus & Giroux, 1970), 4.
14. John Dryden, "An Essay of Dramatic Poesy," in *Essays of John Dryden,* 2 vols., ed. W. P. Ker (New York: Russell and Russell, 1961), 1: 82.
15. Michel Fabre, " 'Adam's Task of Giving Things Their Name': The Poetry of Derek Walcott," *New Letters* 41, no. 1 (Fall 1974): 92–93.
16. "Twilight," 31.
17. "Some West Indian Poets," *London Magazine* 5 (September 1965): 15.
18. "Twilight," 9.
19. "West Indian Poets," 15.
20. "Poetry—Enormously Complicated Art," *Trinidad Guardian,* 18 June 1962, 3.
21. "Twilight," 8, 10.
22. "Twilight," 12–13.
23. "Meanings," 48.

24. "Meanings," 47.

25. T. S. Eliot, *The Use of Poetry* (London: Faber and Faber, 1933), 153.

26. Kenneth Ramchand, "The West Indies," in *The Literature of the World in English,* ed. Bruce King (London: Routledge and Kegan Paul, 1974), 203.

27. Cameron King and Louis James, "In Solitude for Company," in *The Islands in Between,* ed. Louis James (London: Oxford University Press, 1968), 90.

28. "The Kabuki . . . Something to Give to Our Theatre," *Sunday Guardian* (Trinidad), 16 February 1964, p. 14.

29. "Meanings," 51.

30. Patricia Ismond, "Walcott versus Brathwaite," *Caribbean Quarterly* 17, nos. 3–4 (December 1971): 58–59.

31. Lloyd King, "Derek Walcott: The Literary Humanist in the Caribbean," *Caribbean Quarterly* 16, no. 4 (December 1970): 40.

32. "Young Trinidadian Poets," review of *The Flaming Circle,* by Jagdip Maraj, *Sunday Guardian* (Trinidad), 19 June 1966, p. 5.

33. "Twilight," 18.

34. Ralph Campbell, "The Birth of Professional Theatre in Trinidad," *Sunday Guardian* (Trinidad), 22 July 1973, p. 4.

35. "Walcott's New Play," *Caribbean Contact* 5 (April 1977): 14.

36. *Collected Poems 1948–1984* (New York: Farrar, Straus & Giroux, 1986), 504.

37. Denis Solomon, "Beginning or End," *Tapia,* 22 April 1973, 3.

38. "Young Trinidadian Poets," 5.

Chapter Two

1. Frank Collymore, "An Introduction to the Poetry of Derek Walcott," *Bim* 3, no. 10 (1949): 125.

2. "Leaving School," *London Magazine* 5, no. 6 (1965): 12.

3. "Twilight," 31.

4. "Elegies," in *25 Poems* (Bridgetown: Advocate Company, 1949), 11.

5. "The Yellow Cemetery," in *25 Poems,* 20–23.

6. *Epitaph for the Young* (Bridgetown: Advocate Company, 1949). Subsequent references to this work appear in the text.

7. Robert D. Hamner, "Conversation with Derek Walcott," *World Literature Written in English* 16, no. 2 (November 1977): 411.

8. Keith Alleyne, review of *Epitaph for the Young, Bim* 3, no. 11 (1949): 267.

9. Hamner, "Conversation," 411.

10. "Montego Bay—Travelogue II," in *Poems* (Kingston: Kingston City Printery, [1951]), 6–7. Subsequent references to poems in this work appear in the text.

11. Gordon Rohlehr, "Withering into Truth: A Review of Derek Walcott's *The Gulf and Other Poems," Trinidad Guardian,* 10 December 1969, p. 18.

12. Robert Graves, quoted from dust jacket of Walcott's *Selected Poems* (New York: Farrar, Straus & Giroux, 1964).

13. A. N. Forde, review of *In a Green Night, Bim* 9, no. 36 (1963): 288.

14. P. N. Furbank, "New Poetry," review of *In a Green Night, Listener* 68 (5 July 1962): 33.

15. "Prelude," in *In a Green Night* (London: Jonathan Cape, 1962), 11. Subsequent references to poems in this work appear in the text.

16. "Margaret Verlieu Dies," in *Poems,* 32.

17. See John Figueroa's detailed analysis in "Some Subtleties of the Isle," *World Literature Written in English* 15, no. 1 (April 1976): 190–228.

18. Mervyn Morris, "Walcott and the Audience for Poetry," *Caribbean Quarterly* 14, nos. 1–2 (1968): 21.

19. John Figueroa, review of *In a Green Night, Caribbean Quarterly* 8, no. 4 (1962): 67.

20. Morris, "Walcott," 11.

21. Errol Hill, "The Emergence of a National Drama in the West Indies," *Caribbean Quarterly* 18, no. 4 (1972): 32.

22. "Meanings," 45.

23. Walcott's plays predating 1950 include *Another World for the Lost, A Simple Cornada,* and *The Matadors* (all c. 1947); *The Price of Mercy* (1948); *Flight and Sanctuary* and *Cry for a Leader* (both c. 1949). Dates unconfirmed.

24. "Twilight," 11.

25. "Twilight," 13.

26. *Henri Christophe* (Bridgetown: Advocate Company, 1950), 2. Subsequent references to this work appear in the text.

27. G. A. Holder, "B.B.C.'s Broadcast of Henri Christophe," *Bim* 4, no. 14 (January–June 1951): 142.

28. *Harry Dernier* (Bridgetown: Advocate Company, [1951]), 9. Subsequent references to this work appear in the text.

29. In Hamner, "Conversation," 411.

30. J. M. Synge, *The Complete Works of John M. Synge* (New York: Random House, 1935), 3–4.

31. *The Sea at Dauphin,* in *Dream on Monkey Mountain,* 61. Subsequent references to this play appear in the text.

32. Slade Hopkinson, "So the Sun Went Down," *Sunday Gleaner* (Kingston, Jamaica), 15 April 1956, n.p.

33. *Ione,* Caribbean Plays, no. 8 (Kingston, [1957]), 55.

34. *Drums and Colours, Caribbean Quarterly* (Special Issue) 7, nos. 1–2 (1961): 11. Subsequent references to this work appear in the text.

35. "Leaving School," 13.

Chapter Three

1. Carl Jacobs, "Bajans Are Still Very Insular and Prejudiced," *Sunday Guardian* (Trinidad), 23 July 1967, p. 5. The company performed *Dream on Monkey Mountain* in Toronto.

2. "Meanings," 46.

3. "Meanings," 46.

4. "Meanings," 50.

5. "Carnival Spirit a Contempt for Material Treasures," *Sunday Guardian* (Trinidad), 24 February 1963, p. 10.

6. Errol Hill, *The Trinidad Carnival* (Austin: University of Texas Press, 1972), 4.

7. Hill, *Trinidad Carnival,* 21, 49.

8. "Meanings," 48, 51.

9. "Meanings," 47, 49, 51.

10. "The Kabuki," 14.

11. "Meanings," 48.

12. "Kabuki," 14.

13. "Meanings," 49.

14. "National Theatre Is the Answer," *Trinidad Guardian,* 12 August 1964, p. 5.

15. "Kabuki," 14.

16. "Patterns to Forget," *Trinidad Guardian,* 22 June 1966, p. 5.

17. Lloyd Coke, "Walcott's Mad Innocents: Theatre Review," *Savacou* 5 (1971): 121.

18. *Ti-Jean and His Brothers,* in *Dream on Monkey Mountain* (New York: Farrar, Straus & Giroux, 1970), 85. Subsequent references to this play appear in the text.

19. Theodore Colson, "Derek Walcott's Play: Outrage and Compassion," *World Literature Written in English* 12, no. 1 (April 1973): 83.

20. Albert Ashaolu, "Allegory in *Ti-Jean and His Brothers,*" *World Literature Written in English* 16, no. 1 (1977): 203.

21. "Meanings," 48.

22. Hill, "Emergence of a National Drama," 33.

23. "Meanings," 48.

24. *Malcochon,* in *Dream on Monkey Mountain* (New York: Farrar, Straus & Giroux, 1970), 167. Subsequent references to this play appear in the text.

25. "Bronze," in *Selected Poems* (New York: Farrar, Straus & Giroux, 1964), 48. Subsequent references to poems in this work appear in the text.

26. Morris, "Walcott," 10–11.

27. Morris, "Walcott," 11.

28. Robert Mazzocco, "Three Poets," review of *Selected Poems, New York Review of Books* 3 (31 December 1964): 18.

29. Winston Hackett, "Identity in the Poetry of Walcott," *Moko* 8 (14 February 1969): 2.

30. Hackett, "Identity," 2.

31. Morris, "Walcott," 21.

32. King and James, "In Solitude for Comfort," 93–94.

33. "The Figure of Crusoe; on the Theme of Isolation in West Indian Writing" (Typescript of lecture, University of the West Indies, St. Augustine, [1965]; publication forthcoming in Robert Hamner, *Critical Perspectives on Derek Walcott* [Washington, D.C.: Three Continents Press, 1993]) Subsequent references to this lecture appear in the text.

34. "Veranda," in *The Castaway* (London: Jonathan Cape, 1965), 39. Subsequent references to poems in this work appear in the text.

35. James, "Caribbean Poetry in English," 83–84.

36. James Livingston, "Derek Walcott: Poet of the New World" (Paper delivered at the annual conference of the National Council of Teachers of English, Las Vegas, Nevada, 26 November 1971), 6.

37. Therese Mills, "No 'Stardust' Just the Polish of Hard Work," *Sunday Guardian* (Trinidad), 23 July 1967, p. 6.

38. *Jourmard.* Unpublished typescript of play produced in Trinidad, 1967.

Chapter Four

1. Raoul Pantin, quoting Walcott in "Any Revolution Based on Race Is Suicidal," *Caribbean Contact* 1, no. 8 (August 1973): 14.

2. Hill, "Emergence of a National Drama," 33.

3. "A Note on Production," in *Dream on Monkey Mountain* (New York: Farrar, Straus & Giroux, 1970), 208. Subsequent references to this play appear in the text.

4. Theodore Colson, "Derek Walcott's Plays," *World Literature Written in English* 12, no. 1 (April 1973): 90–91.

5. Victor Questel, "Dream on Monkey Mountain," *Tapia,* 8 September 1974, p. 6.

6. Denis Solomon, "Ape and Essence," review of *Dream on Monkey Mountain, Tapia,* 19 April 1970, p. 6.

7. Selden Rodman, "Derek Walcott," in *Tongues of Fallen Angels* (New York: New Directions, 1974), 241.

8. Lloyd Brown, "Dreamers and Slaves," *Caribbean Quarterly* 17, nos. 3–4 (September–December 1971): 39.

9. Rodman, "Derek Walcott," 242.

10. Gordon Rohlehr, "Withering into Truth," review of *The Gulf, Trinidad Guardian,* 10 December 1969, p. 18.

11. "Nearing Forty," in *The Gulf* (New York: Farrar, Straus &

Giroux, 1970), 106. Subsequent references to poems in this work appear in the text.

12. "Islands," in *In a Green Night* (London: Jonathan Cape, 1962), 77.

13. Dennis Scott, "Walcott on Walcott," *Caribbean Quarterly* 14, nos. 1–2 (March–June 1968): 78.

14. Scott, "Walcott on Walcott," 82.

15. Scott, "Walcott on Walcott," 79.

16. Roy Fuller, review of *The Gulf, London Magazine* 9, no. 8 (November 1969): 89.

17. Denis Donoghue, "Waiting for the End," review of *The Gulf, New York Review of Books,* 6 May 1971, p. 27.

18. Edward Baugh, "Metaphor and Plainness in the Poetry of Derek Walcott," *Literary Half-Yearly* 11, no. 2 (1970): 50–51.

19. Baugh, "Metaphor and Plainness," 51.

20. Baugh, "Exiles, Guerrillas and Visions of Eden," *Queen's Quarterly* 84, no. 2 (Summer 1977): 283.

21. Lloyd King, "Derek Walcott: The Literary Humanist in the Caribbean," *Caribbean Quarterly* 11, no. 4 (December 1970): 40.

22. Rohlehr, "Making Love Look More Like Despair," review of *The Gulf, Trinidad Guardian,* 13 December 1969, p. 8.

23. "Twilight," 18.

24. Pantin, "Any Revolution," 14, 16.

25. Therese Mills, "This Is an Experiment in Courage," *Sunday Guardian* (Trinidad), 15 April 1973, p. 8.

26. See Eric Roach, "Experiment in Establishing the West Indian Theatre," review of *Franklin, Trinidad Guardian,* 18 April 1973, p. 4; John Figueroa, review of *Another Life, Bim* 15, no. 58 (June 1975): 160; and Denis Solomon, "Beginning or End?" review of *Franklin, Tapia* 3, no. 16 (22 April 1973): 3. A good example of the type of reaction they note is in Ralph Campbell, "The Birth of Professional Theatre in Trinidad," *Sunday Guardian,* 22 July 1973, p. 4.

27. Rodman, "Derek Walcott," 255.

28. *In a Fine Castle* (unpublished typescript of play produced in 1970). Extensively revised and under the new title *The Last Carnival,* it was later published in *Three Plays* (New York: Farrar, Straus & Giroux, 1986).

29. Pantin, "Any Revolution," 14.

30. *Franklin* (unpublished typescript of play produced in 1973), p. 2.

31. *Franklin,* 40.

32. *The Charlatan,* Caribbean Plays Series, mimeograph (Kingston, [1973]), 5.

33. Henry Goodman, "Charlatan Scores in Los Angeles," review of *The Charlatan, Sunday Guardian* (Trinidad), 16 June 1974, p. 6. Reprints "Carnival with a Calypso Beat," *Wall Street Journal,* 4 June 1974, p. 20.

34. John Melser, "We Haven't Developed Our Own Idiom in Theatre," *Trinidad Guardian,* 20 May 1969, p. 4.

35. Hamner, "Conversation," 411.

36. *Another Life* (New York: Farrar, Straus & Giroux, 1973), 1. Subsequent references to this work appear in the text.

37. Lloyd Brown, *West Indian Poetry* (Boston: Twayne, 1978), 137.

38. Carl Jacobs, quoting Walcott in "There's No Bitterness in Our Literature," *Sunday Guardian* (Trinidad), 22 May 1966, p. 9.

39. "Leaving School," 4–5.

40. Hamner, "Conversation," 411.

41. Rodman, "Derek Walcott," 257. Walcott delivered these statements in an address at Columbia University, 13 April 1971. The speech was subsequently published as "The Muse of History," in *Is Massa Day Dead?,* ed. Orde Coombs (Garden City, N.Y.: Doubleday, 1974), 1–28.

42. "The Caribbean," *Journal of Interamerican Studies and World Affairs* 16, no. 1 (February 1974): 13.

43. "The Caribbean," 12.

Chapter Five

1. "The Caribbean," 12.

2. "Walcott's New Play," *Caribbean Contact* 5, no. 1 (April 1977): 14.

3. Tirso de Molina, *Tirso de Molina,* ed. Raymond R. MacCurdy (New York: Dell Publishing Company, 1965), 135.

4. MacCurdy, "Introduction," in *Tirso,* 21.

5. "Soul Brother to 'The Joker of Seville,'" *Trinidad Guardian,* 6 November 1974, p. 4.

6. Patricia Ismond, "Breaking Myths and Maidenheads," review of *The Joker of Seville, Tapia,* 1 June 1975, p. 7.

7. *The Joker of Seville,* in *The Joker of Seville and O Babylon!* (New York: Farrar, Straus & Giroux, 1978), 138. Subsequent references to this play appear in the text.

8. *The Joker of Seville* (unpublished typescript, fol. I–38).

9. Hamner, "Conversation," 412.

10. "Man of the Theatre," *New Yorker,* 26 June 1971, p. 30.

11. Rodman, "Derek Walcott," 240.

12. Keith Smith, "*O Babylon* an Adventure in Reggae," review of *O Babylon!, People* 1, no. 9 (April 1976): 36.

13. Naseem Khan, "Fringe in Performance," review of *O Babylon!, Drama* 168 (1988): 33–34.

14. Victor Questel, "Interlude for Rest or Prelude to Disaster?," *Tapia,* 28 March 1976, p. 4.

15. Sule Mombara, "'O Babylon!'—Where It Went Wrong," review of *O Babylon!, Caribbean Contact* 4, no. 2 (April 1976): 15.

16. Raoul Pantin, "O Babylon!," review of *O Babylon!, Caribbean Contact* 4, no. 1 (April 1976): 17.

17. *O Babylon!* (unpublished typescript, fol. I–1).

18. *O Babylon!* in *The Joker,* 254.

19. Richard Pevear, "Caribbean Images," review of *Sea Grapes, Nation,* 12 February 1977, p. 186.

20. "Sea Grapes," in *Sea Grapes* (London: Jonathan Cape, 1976), 9. Subsequent references to poems in this work appear in the text.

21. Edward Baugh, "Ripening with Walcott," *Caribbean Quarterly* 23, nos. 2–3 (June–September 1977): 89.

22. Valerie Trueblood, "On Derek Walcott," *American Poetry Review* 7, no. 3 (May–June 1978): 8.

23. *Remembrance,* in *Remembrance & Pantomime* (New York: Farrar, Straus & Giroux, 1980), 86. Subsequent references to this work appear in the text.

24. *Pantomime,* in *Remembrance & Pantomime,* 126. Subsequent references to this work appear in the text.

25. Richard Eder, "Stage: Walcott's 'Remembrance,' Tale of Trinidad," review of *Remembrance, New York Times,* 10 May 1979, sec. C, p. 18; Edith Oliver, "Displaced Person," review of *Remembrance, New Yorker,* (21 May 1979), pp. 105–6; Christopher Gunness, "White Man, Black Man," review of *Pantomine, People* 3, no. 26 (June 1978): 52.

26. "The Schooner *Flight,*" in *The Star-Apple Kingdom* (New York: Farrar, Straus & Giroux, 1979), 19. Subsequent references to poems in this work appear in the text.

27. "The Muse of History," 2–3.

Chapter Six

1. Nancy Schoenberger, "An Interview with Nancy Schoenberger," *Threepenny Review* (Fall 1983): 16.

2. *The Fortunate Traveller* (New York: Farrar, Straus & Giroux, 1981), 3. Subsequent references to this work appear in the text.

3. Alan Jenkins, review of *The Fortunate Traveller, Encounter* 59, no. 5 (November 1982): 62.

4. Ben Howard, "Trailways Fantasist," review of *The Fortunate Traveller, Prairie Schooner* 51, no. 1 (Spring 1983): 94.

5. Helen Vendler, "Poet of Two Worlds," *New York Review of Books* 129 (4 March 1982): 23, 26.

6. Calvin Bedient, "Derek Walcott: Contemporary," *Parnassus* 9, no. 2 (Fall–Winter 1981): 38.

7. Vendler, "Poet of Two Worlds," 26.

8. Schoenberger, "Interview," 16.

9. Richard Dwyer, "One Walcott, and He Would Be Master," *Caribbean Review* 11, no. 4 (1982): 37.

10. Anthony Milne, "Derek Walcott," *Express,* 14 March 1982, p. 18.

11. James McCorkle, "Re-Mapping the New World," *Ariel* 17 (April 1986): 6–7.

12. Clement H. Wyke, "Divided to the Vein: Patterns of Tormented Ambivalence in Walcott's 'The Fortunate Traveller,' " *Ariel* 20, no. 3 (1989): 66, 69.

13. *The Star-Apple Kingdom* (New York: Farrar, Straus & Giroux, 1979), 38.

14. Fred D'Aguiar, " 'Lines with Their Knots Left In,' *Third World Poems* by Edward Kamau Brathwaite and *Midsummer* by Derek Walcott," *Wasafiri* 1, no. 2 (Spring 1985): 37; Patricia Ismond, "North and South—A Look at Walcott's *Midsummer,*" *World Literature Written in English* 27, no. 1 (Spring 1987): 86.

15. D'Aguiar, "Lines with Their Knots," 38.

16. Terry Eagleton, "Plenty of Life," review of *Midsummer, Times Literary Supplement,* 9 November 1984, p. 1290.

17. Steven Ratiner, "In His Own Way," review of *Midsummer, Christian Science Monitor,* 6 April 1984, B9.

18. *Midsummer* (New York: Farrar, Straus & Giroux, 1984). Subsequent references to this work appear in the text; poems are cited by Roman numeral.

19. Ratiner, "In His Own Way," B9.

20. "The Gulf," in *The Gulf* (New York: Farrar, Straus & Giroux, 1970), 58–62.

21. *Another Life* (New York: Farrar, Straus & Giroux, 1973), 94.

22. Robert Bensen, "The Painter as Poet: Derek Walcott's *Midsummer,*" *Literary Review* 29, no. 3 (Spring 1986), 259.

23. Bensen, "Painter as Poet," 259, 263.

24. Louis James, "Midsummer," in *The Art of Derek Walcott,* ed. Stewart Brown (Bridgend, Mid Glamorgan, Wales: Dufour, 1991), 118.

25. For references to the criticism over racial balance in Walcott's plays, see chapter 4, note 26.

26. *The Last Carnival,* in *Three Plays* (New York: Farrar, Straus & Giroux, 1986), 17. Subsequent references to this work appear in the text.

27. *In a Fine Castle,* (unpublished typescript of play produced in 1970).

28. Earl Lovelace, "The Last Carnival," *Express* (Trinidad) 25 July 1982, pp. 15, 18.

29. Milne, "Derek Walcott," 18; "Walcott Tells of Local Amateur Actors in Disguise," *Sunday Guardian* (Trinidad), 11 July 1982, p. 5.

30. Anonymous, "What Ever Happened to Walcott's Second Phase?" *Express* (Trinidad), 25 July 1982, pp. 24–25.

31. *Beef, No Chicken,* in *Three Plays* (New York: Farrar, Straus & Giroux, 1986), 167.

32.   Reed Way Dasenbrock, review of *Three Plays, World Literature Today* 61, no. 1 (Winter 1987): 147.

33.   Judy Stone, "Warner's *Beef, No Chicken* an Inspired Production," *Caribbean Contact* 13, no. 1 (June 1985): 14.

34.   Lowell Fiet, "Mapping a New Nile: Derek Walcott's *Later Plays*," in *The Art of Derek Walcott,* ed. Brown, 150.

35.   Anonymous, " 'Joker of Seville' to Be Staged Gayelle-Style," *Sunday Guardian* (Trinidad), 17 November 1974, p. 7.

36.   Anonymous, "Walcott's 'Blue Nile' at Home in Tent Theatre," *Express* (Trinidad), 18 August 1985, p. 8.

37.   Fiet, "Mapping a New Nile," 150, italics added.

38.   Three articles supply insights into Walcott's understanding of Brecht: "The Kabuki . . . Something to Give to Our Theatre," *Sunday Guardian,* 16 February 1964, p. 14; "National Theatre Is the Answer," *Trinidad Guardian,* 12 August 1964, p. 5; "Meanings," *Savacou* 2 (1970): 48.

39.   Stephen P. Breslow, "Trinidadian Heteroglossia: A Bakhtinian View of Derek Walcott's Play *A Branch of the Blue Nile,*" *World Literature Today* 63, no. 1 (Winter 1989): 36.

40.   See *A Branch of the Blue Nile,* in *Three Plays* (New York: Farrar, Straus & Giroux, 1986), 299, for Phil's confession. Subsequent references to this work appear in the text.

41.   "What the Twilight Says: An Overture," in *Dream on Monkey Mountain and Other Plays* (New York: Farrar, Straus & Giroux, 1970), 39–40.

42.   Milne, "Derek Walcott," 18.

43.   J. D. McClatchy, "Divided Child," *New Republic,* 24 March 1986, p. 36.

44.   Lachlan Mackinnon, "Nobody or a Nation," review of *Collected Poems, Times Literary Supplement,* 24 October 1986, p. 1185.

45.   James Dickey, "The Worlds of a Cosmic Castaway," review of *Collected Poems, New York Times Book Review* 91 (2 February 1986): 8.

46.   Katie Jones, "The Mulatto of Style: Derek Walcott's *Collected Poems 1948–1984,*" *Planet* 62 (April–May 1987): 98.

47.   Rita Dove, "Either I'm Nobody or I'm a Nation," *Parnassus* 14, no. 1 (1987): 73.

48.   Bruce King, "The Collected Poems and Three New Plays of Derek Walcott," *Southern Review* 23, no. 1 (January 1987), 744.

49.   King, "Collected Poems," 741.

50.   Mackinnon, "Nobody or a Nation," 1186; McClatchy, "Divided Child," 37.

51.   Seamus Heaney, "An Authentic Poetic Voice that Bridges Time, Cultures," *Boston Globe,* 9 February 1986, p. A27.

52.   Heaney, "An Authentic Poetic Voice," A28.

53.   John Lucas, "In Multitudinous Dialects," *New Statesman and Nation* 3 (2 February 1990): 33.

54. King, "Collected Poems," 745–46.

55. Heaney, "An Authentic Poetic Voice," A28.

56. McClatchy, "Divided Child," 38.

57. Mackinnon, "Nobody or a Nation," 1186.

58. Edward Hirsch, "The Art of Poetry," *Paris Review* 28 (Winter 1986): 230.

59. Paul Jenkins, review of *The Arkansas Testament, Massachussetts Review* 29, no. 1 (Spring 1988): 128.

60. Jenkins, review, 130.

61. Edward Baugh, *"The Arkansas Testament,"* in *The Art of Derek Walcott,* ed. Brown, 126.

62. Vernon Shetley, review of *The Arkansas Testament, Poetry* 152, no. 2 (May 1988): 106.

63. *The Arkansas Testament* (New York: Farrar, Straus & Giroux, 1987), 38. Subsequent references to this work appear in the text.

64. J. P. White, "An Interview with Derek Walcott," *Green Mountain Review,* ns, 4, no. 1 (Spring–Summer 1990): 27.

65. D.J.R. Bruckner, "A Poem in Homage to an Unwanted Man," *New York Times,* 9 October 1990, pp. 13, 17.

66. M. M. Bakhtin, *The Dialogic Imagination,* ed. Michael Holquist, trans. Caryl Emerson and Michael Holquist (Austin: University of Texas Press, 1981), 3.

67. See Bruckner, "A Poem," 13; White, "Interview," 35; and Mary Lefkowitz, "Bringing Him Back Alive," *New York Times Book Review,* 7 October 1990, p. 1.

68. *The Castaway* (London: Jonathan Cape, 1965), 51–57.

69. Bruckner, "A Poem," 13.

70. V. S. Naipaul, *The Middle Passage* (London: André Deutsch, 1962), 29.

71. Brad Leithauser, "Ancestral Rhyme," *New Yorker,* 11 February 1991, pp. 93–94.

72. *Omeros* (New York: Farrar, Straus & Giroux, 1990), 28; subsequent references to this work appear in the text.

73. "Native Women under Sea Almond Trees," *House and Garden* 156, no. 8 (August 1984): 115.

74. *Another Life* (New York: Farrar, Straus & Giroux, 1972), 19.

75. *The Arkansas Testament,* 48–55.

76. White, "Interview," 35.

77. Edward Said, *The World, The Text, and the Critic* (Cambridge: Harvard University Press, 1983), 135.

78. Victor Questel, "Interlude for Rest or Prelude to Disaster?," *Tapia,* 28 March 1976, p. 4.

79. Peter Balakian, "The Poetry of Derek Walcott," *Poetry* 148, no. 3 (June 1986): 170, 174.

Chapter Seven

1. "Caligula's Horse," *Kunapipi* 11, no. 1 (1989): 138; subsequent references to this article appear in the text.

2. "Bim Will Cease Publication," *Trinidad Guardian,* 7 January 1959, p. 7.

3. "Future of Art Promising," *Sunday Guardian* (Trinidad), 31 August 1963, p. 26.

4. "Derek Walcott Looks at Off-Broadway Theatre," *Sunday Guardian* (Trinidad), 20 October 1963, p. 15.

5. "National Theatre Is the Answer," *Trinidad Guardian,* 12 August 1964, p. 5.

6. "The Prospect of a National Theatre," *Sunday Guardian* (Trinidad), 6 March 1966, p. 6.

7. "More Appeals," *Trinidad Guardian,* 22 October 1966, p. 6; "Opening the Road," *Sunday Guardian* (Trinidad), 23 October 1966, p. 6.

8. Carl Jacobs, "Bajans Are Still Very Insular and Prejudiced," *Sunday Guardian* (Trinidad), 23 July 1967, p. 5.

9. "Meanings," *Savacou* 2 (1970): 50–51.

10. "Artists Need Some Assistance," *Sunday Guardian* (Trinidad), 3 April 1960, p. 7.

11. "Why Is Our Theatre So Tame?," *Sunday Guardian* (Trinidad), 30 April 1967, p. 8.

12. "Time to Separate Politics from Good Verse," review of *Caribbean Literature,* by G. R. Coulthard, *Trinidad Guardian,* 17 March 1966, p. 5.

13. Marylin Jones, "A Home for Our Artists Please!", *Trinidad Guardian,* 9 April 1975, p. 4; Keith Smith, "*O Babylon!* an Adventure in Reggae," *People* 1, no. 9 (April 1976): 39.

14. "On the Beat in Trinidad," *New York Times Magazine,* 5 October 1986, p. 41.

15. "The Poet in the Theatre," *Poetry Review* 80, no. 4 (Winter 1990–1991): 4. Subsequent references to this article appear in the text.

16. Anthony Milne, quoting Walcott in "Derek Walcott," *Express* (Trinidad), 14 March 1982, p. 18.

17. Errol Hill, *The Trinidad Carnival: Mandate for a National Theatre* (Austin: University of Texas Press, 1972), 119.

18. "Carnival: The Theatre of the Streets," *Sunday Guardian* (Trinidad), 9 February 1964, p. 4.

19. "Problems of Exile," *Trinidad Guardian,* 13 July 1966, p. 5.

20. "What the Twilight Says," in *Dream on Monkey Mountain* (New York: Farrar, Straus & Giroux, 1970), 34–35.

21. Raoul Pantin, "Back to Africa Theme," review of *O Babylon!, Tapia,* 28 March 1976, p. 9; Sule Mombara, " 'O Babylon'—Where It Went Wrong," *Caribbean Contact* 4, no. 2 (April 1976): 15; Ralph Campbell, "The Birth of Professional Theatre in Trinidad," *Sunday Guardian* (Trinidad), 22 July 1973, p. 4.

22. Jacobs, "Bajans," 5.

23. "Mixing the Dance and Drama," *Trinidad Guardian,* 6 December 1972, p. 5.

24. "What the Lower House Demands," *Trinidad Guardian,* 6 July 1966, p. 5.

25. Raoul Pantin, quoting Walcott in "We Are Still Being Betrayed," *Caribbean Contact* 1, no. 7 (July 1973): 14, 16.

26. Mervyn Morris, "Walcott and the Audience for Poetry," *Caribbean Quarterly* 14, nos. 1–2 (March–June 1968): 10.

27. "Kaiso, Genius of the Folk," *Sunday Guardian* (Trinidad), 9 February 1964, p. 13.

28. Edward Hirsch, quoting Walcott in "The Art of Poetry," *Paris Review* 28 (Winter 1986): 216. Subsequent references to this article appear in the text.

29. Anonymous, "Walcott Tells of Local Amateur Actors in Disguise," *Sunday Guardian* (Trinidad), 11 July 1982, p. 5.

30. "The Achievement of V. S. Naipaul," *Sunday Guardian* (Trinidad), 12 April 1964, p. 15.

31. Errol Hill, "The Emergence of a National Drama in the West Indies," *Caribbean Quarterly* 18, no. 4 (December 1972): 37.

32. "Future of Art," 26.

33. "W. I. Writers Must Risk Talent," *Trinidad Guardian,* 6 June 1963, p. 8.

34. "Anthologies," *Sunday Guardian* (Trinidad), 3 July 1966, p. 6; see also "Young Trinidadian Poets," *Sunday Guardian* (Trinidad), 19 June 1966, p. 5; and Dennis Scott, "Walcott on Walcott," *Caribbean Quarterly* 14, nos. 1–2 (March–June 1968): 80.

35. "Judging Standards," *Trinidad Guardian,* 20 October 1965, p. 5.

36. Hill, "Emergence," 37.

37. "Bim: Putting on the Style," *Sunday Guardian* (Trinidad), 18 September 1966, p. 6; see also Robert Hamner, "Conversation with Derek Walcott," *World Literature Written in English* 16, no. 2 (November 1977): 414.

38. "Caligula's Horse," 141.

39. Hamner, "Conversation," 415.

40. "The Man Who Was Born Unlucky," review of *A House for Mr. Biswas,* by V. S. Naipaul, *Sunday Guardian* (Trinidad), 5 November 1961, p. 17.

41. "Is V. S. Naipaul an Angry Young Man?," *Trinidad Guardian,* 6 August 1967, [n.p.].

42. Rodman, "Derek Walcott," 253–54.

43. "The Garden Path," review of *The Enigma of Arrival,* by V. S. Naipaul, *New Republic,* 13 April 1987, p. 28.

44. "The Caribbean: Culture or Mimicry?," *Journal of Interamerican Studies and World Affairs* 16, no. 1 (February 1974): 9; also see "The Garden Path," 30.

45. "The Caribbean," 10–11.

46.   "Tribal Flutes," review of *Rights of Passage*, by Edward Brathwaite, *Sunday Guardian* (Trinidad), 19 March 1967, p. 2.

47.   "Magic Industry," review of *To Urania*, by Joseph Brodsky, *New York Review of Books* 35, no. 18 (24 November 1988): 36–37.

48.   "On Robert Lowell," *New York Review of Books* 31, no. 3 (1 March 1984): 25, 28.

49.   "Derek Walcott Talks about *The Joker of Seville*," *Carib* 4 (1986): 12.

50.   Morris, "Walcott and the Audience," 11.

51.   Anonymous, "How Far Are Derek Walcott and Edward Brathwaite Similar? . . . " *Busara* 6, no. 1 (1974): 98, 100.

52.   Lloyd Brown, *West Indian Poetry* (Twayne: Boston, 1978), 139–40; Patricia Ismond, "Walcott versus Brathwaite," *Caribbean Quarterly* 17, nos. 3–4 (December 1971): 54–71.

53.   Hamner, "Conversation," 412.

54.   Rodman, "Derek Walcott," 251.

55.   Rodman, "Derek Walcott," 243.

56.   Raoul Pantin, "Any Revolution Based on Race Is Suicidal," *Caribbean Quarterly* 1, no. 8 (August 1973): 14.

57.   Pantin, "Any Revolution," 14.

58.   "Poetry Enormously Complicated Art," *Trinidad Guardian*, 18 June 1962, p. 3.

59.   Hirsch, "The Art of Poetry," 210.

60.   V. S. Naipaul, "Images," review of *Commonwealth Literature*, by John Press, *New Statesman*, 24 September 1965, p. 453.

Selected Bibliography

Primary Sources
Books and Plays

Another Life. New York: Farrar, Straus & Giroux, 1973.

The Arkansas Testament. New York: Farrar, Straus & Giroux, 1987.

Beef, No Chicken (1981). In *Three Plays.*

A Branch of the Blue Nile (1983). In *Three Plays.*

The Castaway. London: Jonathan Cape, 1965.

The Charlatan. Caribbean Plays Series, mimeograph. Kingston: Extra-Mural Department, University of the West Indies, [1973].

Collected Poems 1948–1984. New York: Farrar, Straus & Giroux, 1986.

Dream on Monkey Mountain and Other Plays. New York: Farrar, Straus & Giroux, 1970.

Drums and Colours: An Epic Drama. Commissioned for the opening of the First Federal Parliament of the West Indies, 23 April 1958. *Caribbean Quarterly,* Special Issue, 7, nos. 1–2 (March–June 1961): 1–104.

Epitaph for the Young: A Poem in XII Cantos. Bridgetown, Barbados: Advocate Company, 1949.

The Fortunate Traveller. New York: Farrar, Straus & Giroux, 1981.

Franklin, a Tale of the Islands. Unpublished [c. 1961, revised 1973].

The Gulf. New York: Farrar, Straus & Giroux, 1970.

Harry Dernier: A Play for Radio Production. Bridgetown, Barbados: Advocate Company, [1951].

Henri Christophe: A Chronicle in Seven Scenes. Bridgetown, Barbados: Advocate Company, [1950].

In a Fine Castle. Unpublished [1970]. (Later published as *The Last Carnival.*)

In a Green Night: Poems 1948–1960. London: Jonathan Cape, 1962.

Ione. Caribbean Plays Series, no. 8. Kingston: Extra-Mural Department, University of the West Indies, [1957].

The Joker of Seville and O Babylon! New York: Farrar, Straus & Giroux, 1978.

Jourmard. Unpublished [c. 1958; produced 1967].

The Last Carnival (1982). In *Three Plays.*

Malcochon (1959). In *Dream on Monkey Mountain and Other Plays.*

Midsummer. New York: Farrar, Straus & Giroux, 1984.

O Babylon! (1976). In *The Joker of Seville and O Babylon!*

Omeros. New York: Farrar, Straus & Giroux, 1990.

Pantomime (1978). In *Remembrance and Pantomime.*

Poems. Kingston: Kingston City Printery, [1951].

Remembrance (1977). In *Remembrance and Pantomime.*

Remembrance and Pantomime. New York: Farrar, Straus & Giroux, 1980.
The Sea at Dauphin (1954). In *Dream on Monkey Mountain and Other Plays.*
Sea Grapes. London: Jonathan Cape, 1976.
Selected Poems. New York: Farrar, Straus & Giroux, 1964.
The Star-Apple Kingdom. New York: Farrar, Straus & Giroux, 1979.
Three Plays. New York: Farrar, Straus & Giroux, 1986.
Ti-Jean and His Brothers (1958). In *Dream on Monkey Mountain and Other Plays.*
25 Poems. Bridgetown, Barbados: Advocate Company, 1949; 1st ed., Port-of-
    Spain, Trinidad, privately printed, 1948.

Essays and Periodical Publications

"The Achievement of V. S. Naipaul." *Sunday Guardian* (Trinidad), 12 April
    1964, p. 15.
"Anthologies." *Sunday Guardian* (Trinidad), 3 July 1966, p. 6.
"Artists Need Some Assistance." *Sunday Guardian* (Trinidad), 3 April 1960,
    p. 7.
"Bim: Putting on the Style." *Trinidad Guardian,* 18 September 1966, p. 6.
"Bim Will Cease Publication." *Trinidad Guardian,* 7 January 1959, p. 7.
"Caligula's Horse." *Kunapipi* 11, no. 1 (1989): 138–42.
"The Caribbean: Culture or Mimicry?" *Journal of Interamerican Studies and World
    Affairs* 16, no. 1 (February 1974): 3–13.
"Carnival Spirit a Contempt for Material Treasures." *Sunday Guardian*
    (Trinidad), 24 February 1963, p. 10.
"Carnival: The Theatre of the Streets." *Sunday Guardian* (Trinidad), 9 February
    1964, p. 4.
√ "A Colonial's-Eye View of the Empire." *Tri-Quarterly* 65 (Winter 1986): 73–84.
"Derek Walcott Looks at Off-Broadway Theatre." *Sunday Guardian* (Trinidad),
    20 October 1963, p. 15.
"Derek Walcott Talks about *The Joker of Seville.*" Edited by Jeannette B. Allis
    and Gilbert A. Sprauve. *Carib* 4 (1986): 1–15.
"Eulogy to W. H. Auden." *New Republic,* November 1983, p. 39.
"The Figure of Crusoe: On the Theme of Isolation in West Indian Writing."
    Lecture given at the University of the West Indies, St. Augustine, 1965.
    Publication forthcoming in Robert Hamner, *Critical Perspective on Derek
    Walcott.* Washington, D.C.: Three Continents Press, 1993.
"Future of Art Promising." *Sunday Guardian* (Trinidad), Independence Progress
    Supplement, 31 August 1963, pp. 26–27.
√ "The Garden Path." Review of *The Enigma of Arrival,* by V. S. Naipaul. *New
    Republic,* 13 April 1987, pp. 27–31.
"History and Picong . . . in *The Middle Passage.*" Review of *The Middle Passage,*
    by V. S. Naipaul. *Sunday Guardian* (Trinidad), 30 September 1962, p. 9.
"Is V. S. Naipaul an Angry Young Man?" *Trinidad Guardian,* 6 August 1967,
    [n.p.].

"Judging Standards." *Trinidad Guardian,* 20 October 1965, p. 5.

"The Kabuki . . . Something to Give to Our Theatre." *Sunday Guardian* (Trinidad), 16 February 1964, p. 14.

"Kaiso, Genius of the Folk." *Sunday Guardian* (Trinidad), 9 February 1964, p. 13.

"Leaving School." *London Magazine* 5, no. 6 (1965): 4–14.

"Magic Industry." Review of *To Urania,* by Joseph Brodsky. *New York Review of Books,* 24 November 1988, pp. 35–39.

"The Man Who Was Born Unlucky." Review of *A House for Mr Biswas,* by V. S. Naipaul. *Sunday Guardian* (Trinidad), 5 November 1961, p. 17.

"Meanings." *Savacou* 2 (1970): 45–51.

"Mixing the Dance and Drama." *Trinidad Guardian,* 6 December 1972, p. 5.

"More Appeals." *Trinidad Guardian,* 22 October 1966, p. 6.

"The Muse of History: An Essay." In *Is Massa Day Dead?,* edited by Orde Coombs, 1–28. Garden City, N. Y.: Doubleday, 1974.

"National Theatre Is the Answer." *Trinidad Guardian,* 12 August 1964, p. 5.

"Native Women under Sea Almond Trees: Musings on Art, Life, and the Island of St. Lucia." *House and Garden* 156, no. 8 (August 1984): 114–15, 161–63.

"On Robert Lowell." *New York Review of Books,* 31, no. 3 (1 March 1984): pp. 25, 28–31.

"On the Beat in Trinidad." *New York Times Magazine,* 5 October 1986, pp. 38, 40–41, 43–44.

"Opening the Road." *Sunday Guardian* (Trinidad), 23 October 1966, p. 5.

"Patterns to Forget." *Trinidad Guardian,* 22 June 1966, p. 5.

"The Poet in the Theatre." *Poetry Review* 80, no. 4 (Winter 1990–1991): 4–8.

"Poetry—Enormously Complicated Art." *Trinidad Guardian,* 18 June 1962, p. 3.

"Problems of Exile." *Trinidad Guardian,* 13 July 1966, p. 5.

"The Prospect of National Theatre." *Sunday Guardian* (Trinidad), 6 March 1966, p. 6.

"Some West Indian Poets." *London Magazine* 5 (September 1965): 15–30.

"Soul Brother to *The Joker of Seville.*" *Trinidad Guardian,* 6 November 1974, p. 4.

"Time to Separate Politics from Good Verse." Review of *Caribbean Literature,* by G. R. Coulthard. *Trinidad Guardian,* 17 March 1966, p. 5.

"Tribal Flutes." Review of *Rights of Passage,* by Edward Brathwaite. *Sunday Guardian Magazine* (Trinidad), 19 March 1967, p. 2.

"W. I. Writers Must Risk Talent." *Trinidad Guardian,* 6 June 1963, p. 8.

"What the Lower House Demands." *Trinidad Guardian,* 6 July 1966, p. 5.

"What the Twilight Says: An Overture." In *Dream on Monkey Mountain and Other Plays,* 1–40. New York: Farrar, Straus & Giroux, 1970.

"Why Is Our Theatre So Tame?" *Sunday Guardian* (Trinidad), 30 April 1967, p. 8.

"Why This Astigmatism toward the Workshop's White Actors?" *Trinidad Guardian,* 19 April 1973, p. 5.

"Young Trinidadian Poets." Review of *The Flaming Circle,* by Jagdip Maraj. *Sunday Guardian* (Trinidad), 19 June 1966, p. 5.

Secondary Sources
Bibliographies

Goldstraw, Irma E. *Derek Walcott: A Bibliography of Published Poems with Dates of Publication and Variant Versions, 1944–1979.* St. Augustine, Trinidad: University of the West Indies Research and Publication Committee, 1979.

————. *Derek Walcott: An Annotated Bibliography of His Works.* New York: Garland, 1984. A thorough listing of primary publications to 1984.

Hamner, Robert, ed. *Critical Perspectives on Derek Walcott.* Washington, D. C.: Three Continents Press, 1993. Contains extensive bibliography of primary and secondary publications into the 1990s.

Articles and Books

Alleyne, Keith. Review of *Epitaph for the Young. Bim* 3, no. 11 (1949): 267–72. Argues that the poem is allegorical, full of traditional influences.

Ashaolu, Albert Olu. "Allegory in *Ti-Jean and His Brothers." World Literature Written in English* 16, no. 1 (April 1977): 203–11. Examines six levels of allegory: artistic, historical, political, moral, Christian, and social.

Bakhtin, M. M. *The Dialogic Imagination.* Edited by Michael Holquist. Translated by Caryl Emerson and Michael Holquist. Austin: University of Texas Press, 1981.

Balakian, Peter. "The Poetry of Derek Walcott." *Poetry* 148, no. 3 (June 1986): 169–77.

Baugh, Edward. "*The Arkansas Testament.*" In *The Art of Derek Walcott,* edited by Stewart Brown, 123–36. Bridgend, Mid Glamorgan, Wales: Dufour, 1991.

————. "Exiles, Guerrillas and Visions of Eden." *Queen's Quarterly* 84, no. 2 (Summer 1977): 273–86. Suggests that balanced, affirmative spirit grows in Walcott.

————. "Metaphor and Plainness in the Poetry of Derek Walcott." *Literary Half-Yearly* 11, no. 2 (1970): 47–58. Claims that expressive tension created by metaphors is a concentrating force in poetry through *The Gulf.*

————. "Ripening with Walcott." *Caribbean Quarterly* 23, nos. 2–3 (June–September 1977): 84–90. Argues that breadth of vision in *Sea Grapes* is rooted in personal experience.

————. "Towards a West Indian Criticism." *Caribbean Quarterly* 14 (March–June 1968): 140–44. Presents background of criticism.

Bedient, Calvin. "Derek Walcott: Contemporary." *Parnassus* 9, no. 2 (Fall–Winter 1981): 31–44.

Bensen, Robert. "The Painter as Poet: Derek Walcott's *Midsummer*." *Literary Review* 29, no. 3 (Spring 1986): 257–68.

Bowen, W. Errol. "Rastafarism and the New Society." *Savacou* 5 (June 1971): 41–50. Offers resume of Rastafarian concepts.

Brathwaite, Edward. "Themes from the Caribbean." *Times Educational Supplement,* 6 September 1968, p. 396. Defines problems of writing in the West Indies.

Breslow, Stephen P. "Trinidadian Heteroglossia: A Bakhtinian View of Derek Walcott's Play *A Branch of the Blue Nile*." *World Literature Today* 63, no. 1 (Winter 1989): 36–39.

Brown, Lloyd. "Dreamers and Slaves—The Ethos of Revolution in Walcott and Leroi Jones." *Caribbean Quarterly* 17, nos. 3–4 (September–December 1971): 36–44. Points to parallel between works by Jones and Walcott that reveal pan-African links.

————. *West Indian Poetry.* Boston: Twayne, 1978. Argues for elements of available West Indian tradition; Walcott's private self becomes metaphor for Caribbean and universal implications.

Brown, Stewart, ed. *The Art of Derek Walcott.* Bridgend, Mid Glamorgan, Wales: Dufour, 1991. This collection of 12 essays covers individual works and phases of Walcott's career from the apprenticeship years through the publication of *Omeros.*

Bruckner, D.J.R. "A Poem in Homage to an Unwanted Man." Review of *Omeros. New York Times,* 9 October 1990, pp. 13, 17.

Campbell, Ralph. "The Birth of Professional Theatre in Trinidad." *Sunday Guardian* (Trinidad), 22 July 1973, p. 4. Points out inadequacies of amateur theater in Trinidad.

Coke, Lloyd. "Walcott's Mad Innocents: Theatre Review." *Savacou* 5 (June 1971): 121–24. Claims that Walcott is a "fusionist." Offers production details for *Ti-Jean* and *Dream.*

Collymore, Frank A. "An Introduction to the Poetry of Derek Walcott." *Bim* 3, no. 10 (June 1949): 125–32. Argues that *25 Poems* is the work of an accomplished poet.

Colson, Theodore. "Derek Walcott's Plays: Outrage and Compassion." *World Literature Written in English* 12, no. 1 (April 1973): 80–96. Claims that Walcott is a voice for Anglo, Negro, and mixed races. Analyzes *Ti-Jean, Malcochon,* and *Dream.*

D'Aguiar, Fred. " 'Lines with Their Knots Left In': *Third World Poems* by Edward Kamau Brathwaite and *Midsummer* by Derek Walcott." *Wasafiri* 1, no. 2 (Spring 1985): 37–38.

Dasenbrock, Reed Way. Review of *Three Plays. World Literature Today* 61, no. 1 (Winter 1987): 147.

De Mott, Benjamin. "Poems of Caribbean Wounds." Review of *The Star-Apple Kingdom. New York Times Book Review,* 13 May 1979, pp. 11, 30.

Dickey, James. "The Worlds of a Cosmic Castaway." *New York Times Book Review* 91 (2 February 1986): 8.

Donoghue, Denis. "Waiting for the End." Review of *The Gulf. New York Review of Books,* 6 May 1971, p. 27.

Dove, Rita. "Either I'm Nobody or I'm a Nation." *Parnassus* 14, no. 1 (1987): 49–76. Offers extended overview of Walcott's career through review of *Collected Poems.* Regrets apparently diminished power in later works.

Drayton, Arthur. "West Indian Fiction and West Indian Society." *Kenyon Review* 25 (Winter 1963): 129–41. Discusses social mixture, the conflict and synthesis within literature.

Dryden, John. "An Essay of Dramatic Poesy." In *Essays of John Dryden,* edited by W. P. Ker, 28–108. New York: Russell and Russell, 1961.

Dwyer, Richard. "One Walcott, and He Would Be Master." *Caribbean Review* 11, no. 4 (1982): 36–37. Discusses *The Fortunate Traveller* and Walcott's growing reputation.

Eagleton, Terry. "Plenty of Life." Review of *Midsummer. Times Literary Supplement,* 9 November 1984, p. 1290.

Eder, Richard. "Stage: Walcott's *Remembrance,* Tale of Trinidad." Review of *Remembrance. New York Times,* 10 May 1979, sec. C, p. 18.

Eliot, T. S. *The Use of Poetry.* London: Faber and Faber, 1933.

Fabre, Michel. " 'Adam's Task of Giving Things Their Name': The Poetry of Derek Walcott." *New Letters* 41, no. 1 (Fall 1974): 91–107. Focuses on the dialectical development of folk and traditional elements in Walcott's poetry.

Fiet, Lowell. "Mapping a New Nile: Derek Walcott's *Later Plays.*" In *The Art of Derek Walcott,* edited by Stewart Brown, 139–153. Bridgend, Mid Glamorgan, Wales: Dufour, 1991. Distinguishes between earlier St. Lucian, poetic plays and later Trinidadian, social plays.

Figueroa, John. Review of *Another Life. Bim* 15, no. 58 (June 1975): 160–70. Examines mythological and linguistic aspects of Walcott's style.

———. Review of *In a Green Night. Caribbean Quarterly* 8, no. 4 (December 1962): 67–69. Argues that the strands of Walcott's heritage converge advantageously.

———. "Some Subtleties of the Isle: A Commentary on Certain Aspects of Derek Walcott's Sonnet Sequence, *Tales of the Islands.*" *World Literature Written in English* 15, no. 1 (April 1976): 190–228. A thematic and structural study of difficulties turned to strength.

Forde, A. N. Review of *In a Green Night. Bim* 9, no. 36 (January–June 1963): 288–90.

Fox, Robert Elliot. "Big Night Music: Derek Walcott's *Dream on Monkey Mountain* and the 'Splendours of Imagination.' " *Journal of Commonwealth Literature* 17, no. 1 (1982): 16–27. Argues that Makak is mythological:

his dream, the work, and the world merge at the crossroads of imagination.

————. "Derek Walcott: History as Dis-ease." *Literary Half-Yearly* 26, no. 1 (January 1985): 105–17. Discusses history as the informing image in Walcott's work.

Fuller, Roy. Review of *The Gulf. London Magazine* 9 (November 1969): 89–90.

Furbank, P. N. "New Poetry." Review of *In a Green Night. Listener* 68, no. 1736 (5 July 1962): 33.

Goodman, Henry. "Carnival with a Calypso Beat." Review of *The Charlatan. Wall Street Journal,* 4 June 1974, p. 20.

————. "Charlatan Scores in Los Angeles." Review of *The Charlatan. Sunday Guardian* (Trinidad), 16 June 1974, p. 6.

Gunness, Christopher. "White Man, Black Man." Review of *Pantomime. People* 3, no. 26 (June 1978): 14, 51–52.

Hackett, Winston. "Identity in the Poetry of Walcott." *Moko* 8 (14 February 1969): 2. Claims that unresolved ambiguities persist in *Green Night* and *Castaway*.

Hamner, Robert D. "The Art of Chiaroscuro—Caliban Confronts the White World." In *International Literature in English,* edited by Robert Ross, 703–16. New York: Garland Press, 1991. Discusses the use of light and shadow for three-dimensional effects in Walcott's poetry and plays.

————. "Aspects of National Character in V. S. Naipaul and Derek Walcott." In *Language and Literature: ACLALS Proceedings,* edited by Satendra Nandan, 179–88. Suva, Fiji: University of the South Pacific, 1983.

————. "Caliban Agonistes: Stages of Cultural Development in Plays of Derek Walcott." *Literary Half-Yearly* 26, no. 1 (January 1985): 120–31. Discusses the means by which Walcott's West Indian background yields artistic and social themes.

————. "Conversation with Derek Walcott." *World Literature Written in English* 16, no. 2 (November 1977): 409–20. Focuses on theater, the nature of poetry, and criticism in Trinidad.

————, ed. *Critical Perspectives on Derek Walcott.* Washington, D. C.: Three Continents Press, 1993. A collection of essays by and about Walcott from the 1940s to the 1990s.

————. "Derek A. Walcott." In *Magill's Critical Survey of Drama: English Language Series,* edited by Frank N. Magill, 1997–2005. Englewood Cliffs, N.J.: Salem Press, 1985.

————. "Derek A. Walcott." In *Magill's Critical Survey of Poetry,* edited by Frank N. Magill, 3001–7. Englewood Cliffs, N.J.: Salem Press, 1982.

————. *Derek Walcott.* Boston: Twayne, 1981. Assesses Walcott's career to 1980.

————. "Derek Walcott's Theater of Assimilation." *West Virginia University Philological Papers* 25 (February 1979): 86–93. Discusses the synthesis of cultural and artistic elements in Walcott's plays.

————. "Exorcising the Planter Devil in the Plays of Derek Walcott." *Commonwealth* 7, no. 2 (Spring 1985): 95–102.

————. "Mythological Aspects of Derek Walcott's Drama." *Ariel* 8, no. 3 (July 1977): 35–58. Claims that archetypal figures, themes, and images speak to condition of modern life.

Heaney, Seamus. "An Authentic Poetic Voice that Bridges Time, Cultures." *Boston Globe,* 9 February 1986, pp. 27–28.

Hill, Errol. "The Emergence of a National Drama in the West Indies." *Caribbean Quarterly* 18, no. 4 (December 1972): 9–40. Examines historical growth and experiments in utilizing indigenous forms.

————. *The Trinidad Carnival: Mandate for a National Theatre.* Austin: University of Texas Press, 1972. Traces the development of Carnival and discusses its theatrical characteristics.

Hirsch, Edward. "The Art of Poetry." *Paris Review* 28 (Winter 1986): 197–230.

Holder, G. A. "B.B.C.'s Broadcast of Henri Christophe." *Bim* 4, no. 14 (January–June 1951): 141–42.

Hopkinson, Slade. "So the Sun Went Down." *Sunday Gleaner* (Kingston, Jamaica), 15 April 1956, n.p. Reports on a production of *Sea at Dauphin.*

"How Far Are Derek Walcott and Edward Brathwaite Similar? Is It Impossible for the Caribbean to Choose Between the Two? If So, Which Way Should They Choose and Why?" *Busara* 6, no. 1 (1974): 90–100. An illogical and biased misreading of Walcott and Brathwaite.

Howard, Ben. "Trailways Fantasist." Review of *The Fortunate Traveller. Prairie Schooner* 15, no. 1 (Spring 1983): 93–98.

Ismond, Patricia. "Breaking Myths and Maidenheads." Review of *The Joker of Seville. Tapia,* 1 June 1975, p. 7. Discusses the liberating impact of Don Juan's exploits.

————. "North and South—A Look at Walcott's *Midsummer.*" *World Literature Written in English* 27, no. 1 (Spring 1987): 86–93. Examines heightened awareness of third world relations to superpowers since Walcott moved to United States.

————. "Walcott versus Brathwaite." *Caribbean Quarterly* 17, nos. 3–4 (December 1971): 54–71. An exposition of relative positions: Brathwaite is a folk poet, Walcott is a Eurocentric traditionalist. Concludes that Walcott is the superior artisan.

Jacobs, Carl. "Bajans Are Still Very Insular and Prejudiced." *Sunday Guardian* (Trinidad), 23 July 1967, p. 5. An interview about the Workshop repertoire and its financing.

————. "There's No Bitterness in Our Literature." *Sunday Guardian* (Trinidad), 22 May 1966, p. 9. An interview that discusses positive aspects of writing in the Caribbean and the sources of poetic ideas.

James, Louis. "Caribbean Poetry in English—Some Problems." *Savacou* 2 (1970): 78–86. Examines problems of writing in the West Indies, with emphasis on Brathwaite's and Walcott's contributions.

————, ed. *The Islands in Between: Essays on West Indian Literature.* London: Oxford University Press, 1968. Consists of a valuable introduction and studies on major writers in the region.

————. "Midsummer." In *The Art of Derek Walcott,* edited by Stewart Brown, 115–20. Bridgend, Mid Glamorgan, Wales: Dufour, 1991.

Jenkins, Alan. Review of *The Fortunate Traveller. Encounter* 59, no. 5 (November 1982): 62–63.

Jenkins, Paul. Review of *The Arkansas Testament. Massachusetts Review* 29 (Spring 1988): 128–32.

"*Joker of Seville* to Be Staged Gayelle-Style." *Sunday Guardian* (Trinidad), 17 November 1974, p. 7.

Jones, Katie. "The Mulatto of Style; Derek Walcott's *Collected Poems 1948–1984.*" *Planet* 62 (April–May 1987): 97–99.

Jones, Marylin. "A Home for Our Artists Please!" *Trinidad Guardian,* 9 April 1975, p. 4. Recounts hardships of productions in inadequate facilities.

Khan, Naseem. "Fringe in Performance." *Drama* 168 (1988): 33–34. Review of a performance of *O Babylon!* in London.

King, Bruce. "The Collected Poems and Three New Plays of Derek Walcott." *Southern Review* 23, no. 1 (January 1987): 741–49.

King, Cameron, and Louis James. "In Solitude for Company: The Poetry of Derek Walcott." In *The Islands in Between,* edited by Louis James, 86–99. London: Oxford University Press, 1968. Asserts that Walcott is as much a dramatist as a poet. Discusses the conflict between public and private roles.

King, Lloyd. "Derek Walcott: The Literary Humanist in the Caribbean." *Caribbean Quarterly* 16, no. 4 (December 1970): 36–42. Claims that Walcott's fundamental theme is the destiny of the artist in the West Indies.

Lefkowitz, Mary. "Bringing Him Back Alive." *New York Times Book Review,* 7 October 1990, pp. 1, 34–35. Comments on influences of Homer, Dante, Conrad, Hemingway, the people of the Caribbean, and film techniques.

Leithauser, Brad. "Ancestral Rhyme." *New Yorker,* 11 February 1991, pp. 91–95.

Livingston, James T. "Derek Walcott: Poet of the New World." Paper presented at the Conference of the National Council of Teachers of English, Las Vegas, Nevada, 26 November 1971. Argues that Walcott learned his craft and developed an individual voice. Examines particularity of setting and universality of theme in his work.

Lovelace, Earl. "The Last Carnival." *Express* (Trinidad), 25 July 1982, pp. 15, 18.

Lucas, John. "In Multitudinous Dialects." *New Statesman and Nation* 3 (2 February 1990): 33–34.

Mackinnon, Lachlan. "Nobody or a Nation." *Times Literary Supplement,* 24 October 1986, pp. 1185–86.

"Man of the Theatre." *New Yorker,* 26 June 1971, pp. 30–31. An interview in which Walcott notes that *Dream* rises above racial theme and *Fine Castle* contrasts Carnival and revolution.

Mazzocco, Robert. "Three Poets." Review of *Selected Poems. New York Review of Books* 3, no. 10 (31 December 1964): 18–19.

McClatchy, J. D. "Divided Child." *New Republic,* 24 March 1986, pp. 36–38. Argues that Walcott's "style now has a range and a grave radiance that transfigure the smallest detail."

McCorkle, James. "Re-Mapping the New World." *Ariel* 17 (April 1986): 3–14. Claims that Walcott's vision is temporal and durational in *The Fortunate Traveller* and *Midsummer.* Discusses how maps define, as New World is inscribed by Old World.

Melser, John. "We Haven't Developed Our Own Idiom in Theatre." *Trinidad Guardian,* 20 May 1969, p. 4. Claims that the Trinidad theater needs to adapt both foreign and indigenous forms.

Mills, Therese. "No 'Stardust' Just the Polish of Hard Work." *Sunday Guardian* (Trinidad), 23 July 1967, p. 6. Discusses improvements in local theater productions.

———. "This Is an Experiment in Courage." *Sunday Guardian* (Trinidad), 15 April 1973, p. 8. Offers some statistics on financing and attendance for Workshop productions.

Milne, Anthony. "Derek Walcott." *Express* (Trinidad), 14 March 1982, p. 18. An interview that focuses on Walcott's career divided between North America and the Caribbean, and the problems of theater in Trinidad.

Mombara, Sule. " 'O Babylon'—Where It Went Wrong." Review of *O Babylon!. Caribbean Contact* 4, no. 2 (April 1976): 15.

Morris, Mervyn. "Walcott and the Audience for Poetry." *Caribbean Quarterly* 14, nos. 1–2 (March–June 1968): 7–24. Argues that in spite of artistic sophistication, Walcott communicates with people: he is skilled through range of linguistic levels.

Naipaul, V. S. "Images." Review of *Commonwealth Literature,* by John Press. *New Statesman,* 24 September 1965, 452.

———. *The Middle Passage.* London: Andre Deutsch, 1962. A personal, often scathing, travelogue about the West Indies.

Oliver, Edith. "Displaced Person." Review of *Remembrance. New Yorker,* 21 May 1979, pp. 105–6.

Pantin, Raoul. "Any Revolution Based on Race Is Suicidal." *Caribbean Contact* 1, no. 8 (August 1973): 14, 16. An interview with Walcott: discusses the poet and his public, the revolutionary nature of the Workshop, and the value of craftsmanship.

———. "Back to Africa Theme: Walcott at It Again." Review of *O Babylon! Tapia,* 28 March 1976, pp. 9, 11.

———. "O Babylon!" Review of *O Babylon! Caribbean Contact* 4, no. 1 (April 1976): 17.

————. "We are Still Being Betrayed." *Caribbean Contact* 1, no. 7 (July 1973): 14, 16. An interview with Walcott that discusses his audience, maintaining standards, and the advantages of writing in the Caribbean.

Pevear, Richard. "Caribbean Images." Review of *Sea Grapes. Nation,* 12 February 1977, pp. 185–86.

Questel, Victor. "Dream on Monkey Mountain." *Tapia,* 8 September 1974, pp. 6–7, 10. Second in four-part analysis: 1, 8, 15, 29 September 1974. Discusses Brechtian influences and the racial symbolism of characters.

————. "Interlude for Rest or Prelude to Disaster?" *Tapia,* 28 March 1976, pp. 4, 11. Claims that *O Babylon!* is insufficiently motivated.

Ramchand, Kenneth. "The West Indies." In *Literature of the World in English,* edited by Bruce Alvin King, 192–211, 224–25. London: Routledge and Kegan Paul, 1974. Walcott uses dialect, reaches the folk, and advances regional drama.

Ratiner, Steven. "In His Own Way." Review of *Midsummer. Christian Science Monitor,* 6 April 1984, B9.

Roach, Eric. "Experiment in Establishing the West Indian Theatre." Review of *Franklin. Trinidad Guardian,* 18 April 1973, p. 4.

Rodman, Selden. "Derek Walcott." In his *Tongues of Fallen Angels,* 232–59. New York: New Directions, 1974. An interview with extended personal insights that includes discussion of *Dream,* spiritual revolution, and third world literature.

Rohlehr, Gordon. "Making Love Look More Like Despair." Review of *The Gulf. Trinidad Guardian,* 13 December 1969, p. 8."

————. "Withering into Truth." Review of *The Gulf. Trinidad Guardian,* 10 December 1969, p. 18.

Said, Edward. *The World, the Text, and the Critic.* Cambridge: Harvard University Press, 1983.

Schoenberger, Nancy. "An Interview with Nancy Schoenberger." *Threepenny Review* (Fall 1983): 16–17. In this interview conducted after publication of *Fortunate Traveller,* Walcott speaks of exile, the immediacy of Jacobean construction in Barbadian speech, his predecessors, and myth in his culture.

Scott, Dennis. "Walcott on Walcott." *Caribbean Quarterly* 14, nos. 1–2 (March–June 1968): 77–82. An interview in which Walcott discusses the influences of West Indian prose and the relationship between poetry and drama.

Shetley, Vernon. Review of *The Arkansas Testament. Poetry* 152, no. 2 (May 1988): 106–7. Examines the paradox of Walcott's status as a representative of Western cultural affluence when he entered the English tradition from a colonial origin.

Smith, Keith. "*O Babylon* an Adventure in Reggae." *People* 1, no. 9 (April 1976): 34–39.

Solomon, Denis. "Ape and Essence: Derek Walcott's *Dream on Monkey Mountain.*" *Tapia,* 19 April 1970, p. 6. Argues that the play synthesizes public and private suffering.

———. "Beginning or End?" Review of *Franklin. Tapia,* 22 April 1973, pp. 2–3.

Stone, Judy. "Warner's *Beef, No Chicken* an Inspired Production." *Caribbean Contact* 13, no. 1 (June 1985): 14. This review compares separate productions of the play and credits the director, technicians, performers, and the dramatist for making the work succeed.

Swanzy, Henry. "Prolegomena to a West Indian Culture." *Caribbean Quarterly* 1 (July–September 1949): 21–28. This essay provides a general background study of life and issues in Caribbean society.

Synge, J. M. *The Complete Works of John M. Synge.* New York: Random House, 1935.

✓ Thomas, Jo. "For a Caribbean Poet, Inner Tension and Foreign Support." *New York Times,* 21 August 1979, p. 2. Notes that Walcott lives on foreign money; discusses the banality and indifference of the wealthy in Trinidad.

Tirso de Molina [pseud. Gabriel Tellez]. *Tirso de Molina.* Edited by Raymond R. MacCurdy. New York: Dell Publishing Company, 1965.

Trueblood, Valerie. "On Walcott." *American Poetry Review* 7, no. 3 (May–June 1978): 7–10. Argues that Walcott is a balanced, meditative poet who seeks resolutions and blames angrily.

✓ Vendler, Helen. "Poet of Two Worlds." *New York Review of Books,* 4 March 1982, pp. 23, 26–27.

"Walcott Tells of Local Amateur Actors in Disguise." *Sunday Guardian,* (Trinidad) 11 July 1982, pp. 5, 10.

"Walcott's 'Blue Nile' at Home in Tent Theatre." *Express* (Trinidad), 18 August 1985, p. 8. Notes that a tent is appropriate for a drama about a struggling West Indian theater troupe.

"Walcott's New Play." *Caribbean Contact* 5, no. 1 (April 1977): 14. Announces *Remembrance* and Walcott's resignation from the Workshop.

Walsh, William. *Commonwealth Literature.* London: Oxford University Press, 1973. Contains a useful section on the West Indies and other third world countries.

"What Ever Happened to Walcott's Second Phase?" *Express* (Trinidad), 25 July 1982, pp. 24–25. Discusses conflict in Trinidad Theatre Workshop over Walcott's desire to develop on an international scale.

✓ White, J. P. "An Interview with Derek Walcott." *Green Mountain Review* ns., 4, no. 1 (Spring–Summer 1990): 14–37. Discusses schizophrenia, the excitement of emerging from a slave to a free mentality, Caribbean people, and mistreatment of minorities in the American theater. Walcott claims that *Omeros* is not a rewrite of *The Iliad* or *The Odyssey,* but combines "Homeric line and Dantesque design."

Wyke, Clement H. "Divided to the Vein: Patterns of Tormented Ambivalence
      in Walcott's 'The Fortunate Traveller.' " *Ariel* 20, no. 3 (1989): 66, 69.
      Argues that the persona uses image clusters and patterns of withdrawing
      and advancing to form an apocalyptic vision; claims that an ambiguous
      and paradoxical personality emerges.

Index

The Author

Robert D. Hamner is professor of English and humanities at Hardin-Simmons University. He has written books on V. S. Naipaul (Twayne, 1973) and Derek Walcott (Twayne, 1981) and edited collections of essays on V. S. Naipaul (1977), Joseph Conrad (1990) and Derek Walcott (1993), all from Three Continents Press. Between 1975 and 1976 he was a Fulbright professor of American Literature at the University of Guyana. He has traveled in and done extensive research throughout the West Indies.